The Social Life of Unsustainable Mass Consumption

Environment and Society

Series Editor
Douglas Vakoch

As scholars examine the environmental challenges facing humanity, they increasingly recognize that solutions require a focus on the human causes and consequences of these threats, and not merely a focus on the scientific and technical issues. To meet this need, the Environment and Society series explores a broad range of topics in environmental studies from the perspectives of the social sciences and humanities. Books in this series help the reader understand contemporary environmental concerns, while offering concrete steps to address these problems.

Books in this series include both monographs and edited volumes that are grounded in the realities of ecological issues identified by the natural sciences. Our authors and contributors come from disciplines including but not limited to anthropology, architecture, area studies, communication studies, economics, ethics, gender studies, geography, history, law, pedagogy, philosophy, political science, psychology, religious studies, sociology, and theology. To foster a constructive dialogue between these researchers and environmental scientists, the Environment and Society series publishes work that is relevant to those engaged in environmental studies, while also being of interest to scholars from the author's primary discipline.

Recent Titles in the Series

The Social Life of Unsustainable Mass Consumption, by Magnus Boström
Everyday Life Ecologies: Sustainability, Crisis, Resistance, by Alice Dal Gobbo
Environmental Legacies of the Copernican Universe, by Jean-Marie Kauth
Anticipatory Environmental (Hi)Stories from Antiquity to the Anthropocene, edited by Christopher Schliephake and Evi Zemanek
Mapping the Environmental Humanities: The Emerging Role of GIS in Ecocriticism, edited by Mark Terry and Michael G. Hewson
The Bangladesh Environmental Humanities Reader: Environmental Justice, Developmental Victimhood, and Resistance, by Samina Luthfa, Mohammad Tanzimuddin Khan, and Munasir Kamal
Loren Eiseley's Writing across the Nature and Culture Divide, by Qianqian Cheng
The Saving Grace of America's Green Jeremiad, by John Gatta
Art and Nuclear Power: The Role of Culture in the Environmental Debate, by Anna Volkmar
Contesting Extinctions: Decolonial and Regenerative Futures, edited by Luis I. Prádanos, Ilaria Tabusso Marcyan, Suzanne McCullagh, and Catherine Wagner
Embodied Memories, Embedded Healing: New Ecological Perspectives from East Asia, edited by Xinmin Liu and Peter I-min Huang
Ecomobilities: Driving the Anthropocene in Popular Cinema, by Michael W. Pesses

The Social Life of Unsustainable Mass Consumption

Magnus Boström

LEXINGTON BOOKS
Lanham • Boulder • New York • London

Published by Lexington Books
An imprint of The Rowman & Littlefield Publishing Group, Inc.
4501 Forbes Boulevard, Suite 200, Lanham, Maryland 20706
www.rowman.com

86-90 Paul Street, London EC2A 4NE

British Library Cataloguing in Publication Information Available

Library of Congress Cataloging-in-Publication Data

Names: Boström, Magnus, author.
Title: The social life of unsustainable mass consumption / Magnus Boström.
Description: Lanham : Lexington Books, [2024] | Series: Environment and society | Includes bibliographical references and index.
Identifiers: LCCN 2023028607 (print) | LCCN 2023028608 (ebook) | ISBN 9781666902440 (cloth) | ISBN 9781666902457 (ebook)
Subjects: LCSH: Consumption (Economics)
Classification: LCC HC79.C6 B678 2024 (print) | LCC HC79.C6 (ebook) | DDC 339.4/7–dc23/eng/20230801
LC record available at https://lccn.loc.gov/2023028607
LC ebook record available at https://lccn.loc.gov/2023028608

To Ivar

Contents

List of Figures ix

Introduction: The Social Roots of Ecologically Destructive Consumerism xi

Chapter 1: Social Relations, Everyday Rituals, and Consumerism 1

Chapter 2: Social Comparison and Consumerism in Stratified Social Life 29

Chapter 3: The Temporalities of Mass Consumption in Social Life: A Lost Future 61

Chapter 4: Sites of Consumption: The Home, the Mall, the Internet 95

Chapter 5: The Social Stock of (Not) Knowing: Normalization and Ignorance of Unsustainable Mass Consumption 127

Conclusion: A Collective Detox from Consumerism 151

Afterword 179

References 181

Index 201

About the Author 213

List of Figures

Figure 1.1. Interaction Ritual Chain 4

Figure 1.2. Rituals of Consumption 7

Figure 2.1. Identity Deficits and Consumerism 36

Figure 2.2. Inequality, Relative Poverty, and Consumerism 55

Figure 3.1. The Cycle of Desire 79

Figure 3.2. Increased Abundance, Fear of Missing Out, and the Cycle of Desire 81

Figure 3.3. Time Pressure and Consumerism 90

Figure 4.1. Demand for Space and Stuff 109

Figure C.1. Collective Detox from Consumerism 165

Introduction

The Social Roots of Ecologically Destructive Consumerism

Ours is a time of mounting crisis on planet Earth.[1] Carbon emissions have increased by a factor of almost seven since World War II. More than half of all emissions since 1751 were emitted after 1990, a period when the problem of climate change was well known and documented. The CO_2 concentration in the atmosphere (around 420 ppm in 2023) is 50 percent above its preindustrial level (280 ppm). Species are becoming extinct 1,000 times faster than they would without human impacts. One million species are threatened with extinction. Ninety-six percent of the biomass of mammals are humans or livestock, and the land available for wild animals is shrinking. Over 300 million tons of plastic are produced every year, at least 14 million of which end up in the ocean, causing serious damage to marine ecosystems and species. Plastic pollution threatens food safety, food quality, and human health, causes biodiversity loss, and contributes to climate change. In cities and rural areas, air pollution causes strokes, heart disease, lung cancer, and numerous other diseases. The combined effects of ambient and household air pollution are associated with seven million premature deaths annually. A new geological epoch, the Anthropocene, has arrived. Human-made materials are now equal to the mass of all life on Earth. Human activity is the prime driver of change in the Earth system. This is facilitated by the Great Acceleration, the exponential growth of any good or service that you can imagine, from paper products to global transport. Leaving aside the ecological threats, the broad outsourcing of production to developing countries in the last thirty to forty years has caused alarming sweatshop conditions for workers.[2]

We know the effects: droughts, flooding, hurricanes, and forest fires. And worse: conflict, war, starvation, and massive migration flows. We also know the cause: society! In the article "Scientists' Warning on Affluence," published in *Nature Communications*, a group of sustainability scientists led by Thomas Wiedmann write: “Consumption of affluent households worldwide is by far the strongest determinant and the strongest accelerator of increases of global environmental and social impacts” (Wiedmann et al. 2020, 1).

The data is available for everyone, at least for those on the lucky side of the digital divide. People may worry, but social life goes on as usual. Patterns of everyday life remain the same, as if nothing was at stake. Consumer culture thrives and thrills, while Earth Overshoot Day arrives a few days earlier each year. This is the day when humanity is estimated to have used all the biological resources that Earth regenerates during the year. In 2022, Earth Overshoot Days was July 28. This date appears sooner or later depending on country and its consumption patterns: For Qatar it was February 10, the USA March 13, Sweden April 3, Japan May 6, Spain May 12, Vietnam September 12, and Ecuador December 6. Globally, on average, humans use as much ecological resources as if we lived on 1.75 Earths. In rich countries like Sweden, Austria, and New Zealand, four Earths would be needed to sustain current average lifestyles.[3]

Overconsuming lifestyles, particularly in wealthy countries, are destroying the conditions for human life—and the lives of millions of other species—on Earth. On one hand, there is increasing awareness that contemporary lifestyles are fundamentally unsustainable, both from an ecological and a social perspective. On the other hand, people around the world continue to overconsume as if everything is fine, and nothing has happened. In a rich country like Sweden, total consumption, measured in fixed prices, increased by 55 percent between 2001 and 2021, despite a dip during the first year of the COVID-19 pandemic (Holmberg 2023, 12). The United States now has more cars than licensed drivers, and since 1973, US homes have increased in size by 65 percent (Stuart et al. 2020, 208). The demand for air travel has exploded in recent decades. Between 1990 and 2017, emissions from international aviation more than doubled in the United States, the UK, Sweden, Italy, Germany, and Czechia, more than tripled in Spain and Australia, and increased even more in Luxembourg, Turkey, and Iceland (Gössling and Humpe 2020).

The message is clear, even if we only look at one of the global risks: climate change. Akenji et al. (2021) have calculated that the climate footprints in high-income countries need to be reduced by 91–95 percent by 2050, and this drastic reduction needs to begin immediately. The most important areas where efforts need to be made to reduce or eliminate consumption are food (meat, dairy products), housing (in terms of both space and the energy required to maintain a high living standard), transport (car travel, flights) and consumer goods such as electronic appliances, clothing, shoes, and furniture (see also Moore 2015, Dubois et al. 2019). If we add the other crises—species extinction, pollution, etc.—the message is even more compelling.

Look around you wherever you are: at home, at work, on the road, in a city center, among people. What do you see? How much of what you see is needed to live a decent, practical, and respectable life in the country where you live? Perhaps most of the things you see make sense. There is a reason why the thing is there. If you purchased a product, there was a reason why you did it. Everything you see may appear normal, standard, constructed for you because you deserve it, are worthy of it, really need it. Look at the photos in your album or mobile phone. What do these photos say about you and your habits of consumption, your way of life, your daydreams and aspirations, your hurriedness and demand for convenience, your social relationships and status, your fear of being ugly, different, and socially excluded?

It seems obvious that the average lifestyle in many countries is one of gross abundance and ecological overconsumption. Overconsuming is what society and history have taught us to do. There is a paradox involved: overconsumption is both visible, known through graphs, statistics, scientists' warnings, overshoot days, and other concepts, and invisible, being both ubiquitous and normalized at the same time.

Excessive consumption is certainly not a new phenomenon. Elite classes throughout history have indulged in excesses of food, drink, drugs, sex, luxury, and jewelry, and larger segments of middle classes have found their own ways of enjoying pleasures. Frank Trentmann (2016), in his remarkable volume *The Empire of Things,* traces the roots of modern consumer culture five hundred years back in time. This is a story of colonialism, imperialism, capitalism, industrialism, and urbanization. But it is more than that. His analysis reveals the importance of consumer culture as a historical force. It is not just an effect of other economic, political, and technological factors, but itself is an independent factor in shaping societies and production. Even if mass consumption seems to be connected to the exponential growth that has taken place since World War II and especially in recent decades, the construction of the macro institutional and infrastructural setting of our consumer society has developed from a much longer process.

This book focuses on our contemporary period, which is a paradoxical time because unsustainable mass/excess consumption continues despite awareness of and warnings about global climate change and ecological catastrophe on a planetary scale. The now living generations have been born into this extremely troublesome situation. Some are rich, and their excess completely penetrates their social and everyday lives. Others are poor, and their perception of poverty is accentuated precisely by the knowledge of other people's material welfare. The distribution of wealth—and ecological/climate footprint—is extremely unequal, and the gap is widening (Hylland Eriksen

2015; Sayer 2016; Oxfam 2020; Akenji et al. 2021). The wealth of the rich is connected to exploitation of the poor through an "imperial mode of living" (Brand and Wissen 2021). Approximately 20 percent of the world's population consume about 80 percent of the world's wealth. Most of the growth of CO_2 emissions between 1990 and 2015 is due to the richest 10 percent of the population (Akenji et al. 2021), and these people are mostly found in North America, Europe, and increasingly China and the Middle East. The richest 1 percent emit twice as much as the poorest half (Oxfam 2020; Stoddard et al. 2021). According to the UN's World Food Program, 828 million people are going to bed hungry every night in 2022,[4] while a much larger share of the world population suffer from obesity/overweight (in 2016, 39 percent, Ritchie and Roser 2017).

What can anyone do about this? Do capitalism, industrialism, the growth system, and spending culture have any brake? Are we destined to experience total collapse, or can we develop pathways to sustainable ways of living and producing things? While the institutions and infrastructures of mass consumption may appear overwhelming, there is a need to understand how consumption drivers operate on all levels: societal, interpersonal, personal, emotional, and physiological. This book undertakes to do this from a sociological and sociopsychological perspective, emphasizing the level of social life.

The broad message of this book is that we need to better understand why the patterns and drivers of unsustainable mass consumption are reproduced despite growing awareness of mounting crisis. This book primarily targets the wealthy part of the world. It focuses on the consumption side, even if production and consumption are interrelated. Mass consumption involves both material and cultural factors on the macro level that shape what, why, when, where, how, how much, and how often people consume. Through market exchanges, we access the majority of goods and services required to satisfy our needs, wants, desires, aspirations, and identities. The book focuses on the micro- and meso-levels of social life dynamics, while the macro-institutional and infrastructural factors are present in the background. Even if consumerist goals and motivations often have a materialist frame, these goals and motivations are fundamentally social in nature. We consume not just because we physically need the commodities, but because we are social. These social goals of consumption do not make it less pervasive in everyday life; they make it more so. This is why it is so important to learn about these social goals, motivations, and dynamics.

This book assumes that achieving a sustainable society, which necessarily is a radically transformed society, will require that the drivers of mass consumption are exposed and counteracted. My message is also that we need to understand the social role of consumption, how consumption is embedded in social life, in order to have a better chance to guide society onto a more sustainable trajectory. This emphasis on the *social embeddedness* of consumption (Warde 2022) implies that we need to avoid and critique an over-individualization of responsibility, while at the same time not neglecting people's potential for action. Moreover, the intention is not to blame consumers,[5] or cause paralyzing anxiety,[6] but rather to encourage (joint) reflection, transformative learning, action, and politicization of consumption (see conclusion), particularly among the segments of populations that certainly could live well (and better) with less. You may have noticed that I often use the word "we." I do this because as an author I am a part of what I am studying, and as an author from a wealthy country I am part of an overconsuming society and a social life in which overconsumption is normalized.

The following sections in this introduction are conceptual and theoretical. I introduce key concepts used in the book, give an overview of the key macro-institutional and infrastructural factors reproducing patterns of mass consumption, introduce the concept of social life, and introduce the key themes of the chapters in this book.

APPROACHING THE STUDY OBJECT: KEY CONCEPTS

This book is inspired by a pluralistic view of theories within sociology and social psychology in general, and the sociology of consumption and environmental sociology in particular.[7] I draw on a wide range of historical and contemporary research within interdisciplinary fields. I argue that there is a need to combine theories on different scales, while acknowledging that certain theories also contradict each other. I view consumption, including its causes and effects, as involving several layers of factors. Accordingly, I seek to avoid the traps of reductionism, determinism, and mono-causal types of theorizing (see Boström and Davidson 2018). I aim to show the relevance of a broad range of theories and empirical research to understanding the complex, heterogeneous, fleeting, and omnipresent nature of consumerism. I prefer to lean in the direction of eclecticism rather than reductionism. I select theories and present research that I consider relevant and illustrative of the various themes. In the book I illustrate with examples from different parts of the world.

In this section I briefly introduce and define a few key concepts used in this book: needs/wants/desires, consumption, consumerism, commoditization, mass consumption, excess, sufficiency, rebound effects, and drivers.

Everyone obviously depends on consuming in order to survive. In modern society, humans must purchase a variety of goods and services to satisfy their basic needs. Our human needs are not just physical; they are also emotional, cognitive, personal, social, and so on. Psychologist Tim Kasser (2009), who is critical of consumer culture's narrow focus on consumerism and materialism, summarizes four basic needs that require satisfaction for a person to experience well-being. These are (1) feeling safe and secure, (2) feeling competent, (3) feeling relatedness or connection with other people, and (4) feeling free and autonomous.[8] These do not necessarily need to be satisfied by consumption in the form of buying goods and services. Satisfying some needs may require "having," but other strategies could be "being," "doing," or "interacting" (Smith and Max Neef 2011; Rauschmayer and Omann 2015). To satisfy our needs and wants, we could just "be" (like breathing, walking, reflecting), or interact with others (sharing things), or create things and services (make clothes, help each other), or acquire objects (goods and services) for immediate use or for ownership and investment. We use all these strategies every day, but consumer society gives priority to purchasing goods and services. Some even speak of "false needs" to address how consumer capitalism and the advertisement industry manipulate people into adopting overconsuming lifestyles (Marcuse 1963; Stuart et al. 2020).

Consumer researchers Russell Belk, Guliz Ger, and Søren Askergaard (2003) criticize the concept of "needs" for being too naturalistic. They also criticize "wants" for being too dry and rational. According to them, the hotter word "desire" is better able to capture important features of our consumer culture, including the understanding of what consumers are longing for and daydreaming about. I agree that in a study of mass/excess consumption it is necessary to take into account more emotionally engaged consumption. Desire denotes something of a mixed feeling; it is a state of "enjoyable discomfort," according to consumer-culture theorist Colin Campbell (2018 [1987]). Also, "desire is a notion directly addressing the social character of motivation," Belk and colleagues (2003, 328) write. My take on it is that it makes sense—theoretically, empirically, and intuitively—to make use of all these terms: needs, wants, and desires. In a study of contemporary mass/excess consumption, we need a plurality of concepts to understand the complexity of motivators and drivers behind this behavior.

"Consumption" is used in this book to refer to an actor, individual or collective, acquiring goods and services for immediate, durable, or later use. Accordingly, I see consumption as comprising both buying and using (see Warde 2022). In modern consumer capitalism, these goods and services are normally obtained through exchange in the marketplace, whether purchased new or secondhand. Exchange of a particular item could be done through other means such as redistribution of goods (via institutions like the state) or reciprocity (give-and-take within families, among friends or within communities) (Swedberg 2003). Market exchange is thus not necessary to be able obtain goods and services for consumption. But it has become the standard way in contemporary societies.

Consumption is often, if not always, both material and immaterial. Even if we can distinguish between physical objects and less tangible services, services too always have a material dimension. Also, consumption often has symbolic meaning. It is communicative. Consumer objects may symbolize group membership, belonging, identity, friendship, masculinity, status, reward for achievement, creativity, freedom, values, and many other things. This is a core reason why consumption is social.

"Consumerism" is another term that frequently occurs in the sociology of consumption literature and serves as a core concept in this book. Consumerism is associated with a culture and/or society in which consumption and possessions more or less permeate everyday social life. For example, Zygmunt Bauman (2007) makes a distinction between consumption and consumerism. While the former is banal—everyone must consume food, clothes and energy to survive and satisfy basic needs—consumerism concerns situations where the wishes and desires underpin the economy and become the very condition of existence and human togetherness. In this book, I employ consumerism as an umbrella term for various drivers behind our propensity to buy (much, more, better, newer, bigger, etc.). Consumerism applies when consumption of commoditized goods and services is the default tool for solving all sorts of problems and for the aspiration to satisfy needs, wants and desires. These drivers include both mundane and extravagant goods. When consumerism is hegemonic in a society, we can speak of a culture of consumerism.

"Mass consumption" is viewed in this book as both the context and a consequence of this culture of consumerism. As an outcome (historical result) it consists of a growing range of commoditized goods and services, a process also referred to as "commoditization" (Sassatelli 2007). Commoditization (or commodification[9]) and consumerism overlap. In a mass-consumption society, inhabitants try to satisfy their needs/wants/desires with "commodities." Consumption is the default tool/solution whenever a problem or need/want/desire pops up. There are few things and services today that cannot be sold under any circumstances. In a mass-consumption society with far-reaching commoditization, we are firmly socialized and trained to be "consumers" within more and more areas of social life. As consumer culture sociologist Roberta Sassatelli notes:

> we are accustomed to being addressed as "consumers" by a plethora of scientific disciplines, mundane discourses and social institutions which contribute to circumscribing and delineating what "consumption" means and what kind of people we are when we act as "consumers." (2007, 2)

Mass consumption takes many forms, and does not just involve mass-produced, standardized goods like Ford automobiles, McDonald's hamburgers, or Ikea's bookshelf Billy. Very differentiated and personalized products also increasingly make up part of the volume of consumption on Earth (Southerton 2020). This development of the global mass consumption society has accelerated since World War II. The term "mass consumption" refers to the entirety of consumption, including a culture of consumerism, supporting institutions and infrastructure on the macro level, and a social life deeply shaped by and shaping it. The far-reaching commoditization makes it increasingly difficult—and often basically impossible—to avoid being a consumer and making choices in the market.

Given that there will soon be eight billion people on planet earth, even "sufficient" consumption, if this is possible to define, will require production and consumption on truly massive scales, though not necessarily using the institutions and infrastructures of mass consumption as defined in this book, and not necessarily in a culture of consumerism. Scholars and critical movements employ a variety of terms to describe the unsustainability of mass consumption: excess, overconsumption, abundance, hyperconsumption, opulence, climate and ecological footprints, and more. The word "sufficiency" and similar terms apply to the search for more sustainable levels. The acquisition, use, and disposal of goods and services ought to be more in line with reasonable needs. Goods ought to be taken care of. Wants and desires ought to be constrained or redirected to other sources of well-being and happiness.

How can we define shortage, sufficiency, and excess? On the most formalistic and abstract level, excess is what exceeds that which is sufficient, and shortage is its opposite. Translating these definitions into concrete matters and measures will however require contextual understanding. Excess, sufficiency, and shortage can relate to aesthetic, scientific, ecological, humanitarian, social, and economic bases of valuation. Excess in some areas might imply shortages in others. A society/community/person overly focused on one need may neglect others. For example, an excess of material welfare may lead to other forms of poverty: personal, cognitive, emotional, and social (Briceno and Stagl 2006; Smith and Max-Neef 2011). To speak of sufficiency is to speak about limits, "about limiting our wants and curbing our insatiability" (Callmer 2019, 29). For the individual, sufficiency can make intuitive sense, and represents the idea that there can be enough and there can be too much (Princen 2005; Jungell-Michelsson and Heikkurinen 2022). These words can provide means for description and analysis, but also for reflection and critique.[10] Yet, consumerism continues to dominate. I will return to the prospect of critique and formulation of an alternative particularly in the last chapter, after reviewing the important forces and drivers in the other chapters but will also provide questions for reflections on possibilities in the conclusion of each chapter.

The concept of "rebound" is important in studies of (un)sustainable consumption levels because it addresses the risk of failure in efforts to reduce volumes of consumption. The term "rebound effect" refers to the net effect when resource use increases despite improved resource efficiencies. Growth in demand outstrips the effect of efficiency gain, via direct or indirect rebound effects. A "direct rebound effect" is when efficiency associated with an object increases consumption of that object. Lower costs for producing/using an item increase the demand for it (think of email in contrast with postal mail). An "indirect rebound effect" is when savings due to efficiency gains free up resources for increasing demand for other items. In studies of (un)sustainable consumption, failures of "green consumerism" or "climate-friendly consumerism" are often attributed to such rebound effects. Consumers may engage in low carbon consumption in some areas of their everyday lives, while their total carbon footprint may remain constant or even increase, because they have difficulty assessing the totality (Peattie 2010; Akenji 2014; Boström and Klintman 2019a). This explains why technological solutions are always insufficient in themselves. The macro factors discussed in the next section and the drivers connected to the sphere of social life discussed in the rest of the book contribute to understanding the important role of rebound effects.

In the book I use the word "drivers" (of consumerism).[11] Consumerism itself is considered a driver—an umbrella term—which reproduces patterns of unsustainable mass consumption. However, this broad concept must be divided into parts. Drivers can relate to agency (e.g., intention, desire) or they can be contained in structural phenomena (e.g., market competition). We may say that social objects (including human beings, social groups, societal structures) have "causal powers"; they can potentially produce (or be produced by) another phenomenon/outcome. I use the word "driver" in that sense to denote ways in which a social object/phenomenon may lead to a particular outcome. A driver can exist even if it is not activated. A bomb may or may not explode, but it always has the potential to do so. Whether or not a driver is activated may depend on certain conditions and contextual/situational circumstances, including competing drivers. We may think of men (object) tending to buy sports cars (outcome) because masculine identities serve as a driver, a tendency that is activated in communities with traditional gender relations. This outcome may be blocked in another community because of the mobilization (as a competing driver) of alternative gender norms and role models (imagine a soccer star using a bicycle). This book tries to reveal and discuss the most important drivers on the level of social life that are linked with consumerism and reproduce unsustainable mass consumption.

Analytically I focus, on one hand, on drivers at the level of macro-institutions and infrastructures and, on the other, drivers on the level of social life. The book is primarily oriented toward the latter, though it recognizes the fundamental importance of macro-institutions and infrastructures in both constraining and facilitating various activities in social life. The next section discusses these macro-level drivers.

THE MACRO-INSTITUTIONS AND INFRASTRUCTURES OF MASS CONSUMPTION

The concept of institutions is apt for understanding how social action is stabilized and structured. Institutions constrain and facilitate action. Some institutional theories focus on norms, rules, and values. Others focus more on concrete organizational arrangements and institutionalized practices. Both meanings are needed. Institutions provide stability and predictability in social life; common terms in institutional theory are "path dependency" and "inertia." Institutions are containers of power. They shape dominant ways of thinking, feeling, and doing; they are not just external forces outside of us, but are internalized.[12] The concept of institutions can be combined with that of infrastructure to direct attention to the physically constructed and technologically shaped environment surrounding social life, including cities, roads, buildings, provision of energy, internet, and so forth—in sum, the Anthropocene.

What are the core institutional and infrastructural conditions for the development and reproduction of mass consumption? A comprehensive answer to this question would require a book of its own. For the present purpose, it is enough to give a brief overview of six general factors: global capitalism, industrial/technological revolutions, division of labor and social stratification, economic geography, pro-growth dogma, and consumer culture.[13]

The first factor, global capitalism, is an economic system that is forcefully driving consumerism in several direct and indirect ways. To begin with, capitalism is an inherently dynamic economic system (Rostow 1959; Swedberg 2003; Wallerstein 2004; Wiedmann et al. 2020; Brand and Wissen 2021), as opposed to a steady-state economic system. Capitalism is oriented toward continuous growth and capital accumulation, and is characterized by several inner contradictions. Change is the only constant. This drive for capital accumulation relates partly to the profit motive among capitalists, which they can exploit through their structural privileges (private property) and economic power. However, it is also important to consider the situation of market competition. The threat of being run out of business by competing firms taking market shares creates anxious pressure among business owners to reinvest considerable parts of their profits into production. The capitalist economy is accordingly wired toward seeking profit, in contrast with a steady-state economic system oriented toward "sufficiency" or the mere satisfaction of needs. A key condition is the institution of private property, including the legal protections it affords. Capitalism can only exist if private actors have a legal right to exclude others from using their property. Therefore, capitalism is also a structural source of accumulation of (enormous) economic power, a power which feeds into other types of power resources (political, cultural, social capital). Finally, capitalism is characterized by the distribution of produced goods through market exchange, and thus it is a source of far-reaching commoditization. Seeing these features together—being a source of continuous expansion, generating growth of private poverty and economic power, being reliant on market exchange and source of commoditization—it is evident that global capitalism is a fundamental creative/productive and destructive force on this planet (Urry 2010). Capitalism is accordingly an economic foundation for the expansion of needs/wants/desires, that is, of consumerism.

Nevertheless, despite the critical role of global capitalism, we should avoid mono-causal explanations. Even if we hypothetically were able to abolish capitalism overnight—admittedly not a realistic scenario—people would not suddenly forget consumer culture. As anthropologist of material culture Daniel Miller reminds us: "Capitalism plays its role in the construction of desire but it is by no means the sole determinant of where and when values and relationships become subject to commodification" (Miller 1998, 139).

A second major factor is the industrial/technological revolutions. Since at least the invention of the spinning jenny in 1764 and the steam engine during the same century, there has been a constant development of industry/technology, backed up by scientific progress and capital. The key factor is an enormous increase in efficiency and productivity (Princen 2005). For any given input of energy or work, we can achieve tremendously much more now than we could 250 years ago. This increase in productivity has not mainly been used to cut the number of working hours, but to produce more products and services. Capitalism, industrial/technological revolutions, and scientific progress collaborate in creating constantly new needs/wants/desires, which in turn become important engines for the economy. The age of mass markets and mass consumption is characterized by mobility, energy production, housing and durable consumer goods and services becoming leading economic sectors. This industrial/technological revolution is also administrative in kind; it relates to new ways of organizing production, like Fordism, scientific management, new public management, lean management, and the like.

Efficiency/productivity is associated with division of labor, specialization, economics of scale, intensification, and more (Princen 2005). The acceleration of efficiency/productivity is not just about the ability to produce more goods and services. It is also directly related to consumption, in that socio-technical systems of mobility, energy, and communication enable people to achieve more in all areas of everyday life, and not least to become dependent on fast structures and patterns of excessive demand (Shove and Warde 2002; Shove 2003; Rinkinen et al. 2021).

Thirdly, alongside the division of labor associated with economic growth, there is a further social stratification in terms of social classes, status groups and other social divisions. There is a social structure of vertical and horizontal distinctions and separateness between groups, and not least escalating inequalities around the world (Sayer 2016; Oxfam 2020).[14] How the social infrastructure on the macrolevel shapes consumerism is a key topic of chapter 2 in this book.

Fourthly, there is a gigantic economic geography, which facilitates the production, distribution, and inexpensive consumption of items for the masses. This massive infrastructure, which resulted in the Anthropocene, was a significant achievement of the previous century, and it has established a "powerful high-carbon path-dependent system . . . locked in through various economic and social institutions" (Urry 2010, 198). A physical infrastructure is accordingly in place for the mass markets.[15] This economic geography is highly urbanized, and during the earlier parts of industrialization it enabled the concentration and organizing of labor into large systems of production (factories), facilitating mass production via economies of scale, a system previously known as Fordism. It also enabled standardized mass consumption with systems of distribution and provision through, for example, department stores, shopping centers, malls, systems of transportation (heavily reliant on cars) and ample space for parking. The ideal of affordability for the masses has become an important part of the agenda in both politics and business and is built into this geographic infrastructure. Businessmen such as Henry Ford, Ingvar Kamprad, and others established ways of manufacturing and retailing predicated upon high volume and low price. Business success relied on effective merchandising techniques, seductive pricing methods, efficient delivery systems, discount stores, and outlet malls. Everything is available at a fairly close distance everywhere (yet not too close, because a car is needed). Global capitalism supported the outsourcing of production to low-cost countries (with low salaries and poor environmental and social legislation), which supply stuff to wealthy consumers via extremely complex and opaque supply chains. The internet has created a new revolution of this economic geography. The products are only a couple of clicks away.

Fifthly, politics and political ideologies support all these developments with a pro-growth dogma. This growth dogma is internal to the functions of capitalism because capitalism requires an ideology that legitimizes it. Economic growth became more important as a policy goal beginning in the 1950s (Kallis et al. 2018). The idea evolved into a growth dogma which transcends ideological divisions of right and left, including light green ideologies such as those promoting "eco-modernization" or "green growth." If this growth ideology is labeled neoliberalism (see, e.g., Urry 2010), it cannot be forgotten that its content shapes the entire spectrum of political ideologies in wealthy societies. Economic growth is perceived as a political necessity for pacifying political conflicts. Industrialized societies rely on growth to maintain social stability (Jackson 2017). Liberal welfare democracies have become dependent on economic growth for the pacification of class conflicts and other social tensions. Growth has become instrumental for securing employment, tax revenue, and investments in large-scale infrastructure projects. The pro-growth dogma claims that (increased) consumption is necessary to keep the economy spinning. Aggressive consumer spending is even considered patriotic (Schor 1998, 152). This ideology of overconsumption conceals the irrationality and contradictions of capitalism (Stuart et al. 2020). Consumer critique is pacified by related discourses of "corporate social responsibility" and "corporate sustainability."

Last but not least, history has created a culture of consumerism—a broad public propensity to consume—which is supported by a variety of institutions (capitalism, politics, media, education, etc.) and shaped by surrounding physical infrastructure. This culture is not just an effect of the other factors reviewed above. It is better to view consumer culture as both a cause and an effect in relation to capitalism, industrialism, and politics. Consumer culture's partly independent role as a factor of development is shown in important works in the history and sociology of consumption (Campbell 2018 [1987]; Trentmann 2016). Moreover, consumer culture is directly promoted by advertising, entertainment, and fashion industries. A variety of forms of mass media—magazines, television, social media—contribute to disseminating the values and ideals of consumer life.

The concept of culture is often ambiguous in scholarly writings. I understand culture as relating to such concepts as values, belief systems, language and communication systems, rituals, artifacts, and various symbols, like brands. In relation to consumerism, culture has to do with cognitive dispositions in the general public to seek pleasure, happiness, and meaningfulness, as well as to solve everyday problems, via consumption (Marcuse 1964; Campbell 2018 [1987]; Holt 2002; Bauman 2007; Sassatelli 2007; Firat et al. 2013; Jackson 2017). Consumer culture shapes our thoughts, feelings and behaviors; it "frames consumers' horizons of conceivable action, feeling, and thought" (Dittmar 2008, 8). Culture offers a set of symbolic resources that individuals can draw on when defining their personal and social identities and ambitions.

A core feature of consumer culture is the institutional construction of one particular role: the sovereign consumer. In a variety of discourses and institutions, people are being addressed as "consumers" (Sassatelli 2007). This implies that the social category of "consumer" has been developed and cultivated over centuries. Consumers have abilities, rights, roles, and responsibilities.

Culture is also shaped by its material surroundings, as is stressed by material culture theorists (see Miller 1998, 2010). For example, the physical infrastructures of mass production, mass markets, and mass consumption—the Anthropocene—shape our thinking and value systems. They may even shape who we are. Daniel Miller says: " . . . cars, once they exist, become part of what we are. The humanity that existed before roads and traffic jams is not the same as that which exists afterwards" (Miller 2010, 59). For the word "cars" we can substitute railways, radio, television, mobile phones, e-mail, and so on. The invasion and growth of material things like these not only change our possibilities to act, but also change us as human beings.

Consumer culture in general, and neoliberal ideologies in particular, celebrate the free, sovereign individual who makes independent choices. Even if ideologies emphasize that individuals should consume wisely and avoid harming others with their choices and behaviors, the right to consume generally trumps the obligation to consume responsibly. Further, even if "free choice" is celebrated in consumer culture and ideologies, when it comes to actual market exchange, these supposedly free choices are restricted in many ways. Choices are limited by the choice infrastructures put in place by policies and supplies. Also, in many spheres of everyday life, consumers cannot opt out from being a consumer and still fulfill their basic needs. Being an anti-consumer is difficult in consumer society.

The sovereign consumer ideal, says Princen (2005), distorts people's sense of place in nature and society. It fosters a view that the purpose of an economy is to serve consumers. American society, he argues (and we can generalize to much of global society), is preoccupied with consumption, with comfort, luxury, spending, and acquisition. Sovereign consumers are entitled to have their desires satisfied, to have more goods at low prices. Thus, the consumer is free. Unlimited. The only limit is one's wallet and some very specific legislation (e.g., prohibiting consumption of drugs, prostitution, etc.). The personal is unpolitical.

Taken together the institutions and infrastructures of mass consumption are clearly not limited to the wealthy part of the world, but are truly global phenomena, even if there are many places where large populations experience absolute poverty rather than excess. To be sure, there is considerable variation in how mass consumption is locally shaped. A critically important assumption in this book is that these institutional and infrastructural factors –although they are extremely strong forces—cannot alone explain the reproduction and expansion of unsustainable mass consumption. The macro-factors are powerful, but cannot alone explain why mass consumption and mass production continue. We have to add the factor of agency to fully understand the reproduction of structures and cultures (including the possibility to transform them).

THE SOCIAL LIFE OF MASS CONSUMPTION

The external, institutional and infrastructural conditions for humanity's unsustainable mass consumption are at the same time internal; that is, part of our inner lives. Any external institution must also be internalized to become operative (Berger and Luckmann 1991 [1966]). Institutional structures often constrain or facilitate individual action forcefully, but not deterministically. Moreover, the internalized world is not merely individual; it is intersubjective. Even the most apparently individual action has a social dimension. The inner world is a social world. We are individual people, but are not individuals in a social vacuum. We are part of the "machinery." "Shoppers are not zombies. They think about what they do. They strategize. They compare. They work at it. If there is a cabal to induce people to consume wastefully, shoppers are, at the very least, coconspirators" (Hine 2002, 90).

My conception of *social life* is based on sociological and sociopsychological theories that emphasize how agency and meaning are activated through social relations in one's lifeworld (see also Boström 2020). In using this concept, I emphasize the role of the intersubjective agency dimension in reproducing patterns of mass/excess consumption, and eventually also the critique and counteracting of such patterns. Through my perspective on *social life*, I emphasize the essential role of social relations and practices.

By emphasizing the social dimension of consumption, I do not intend to downplay either our inner physiological propensity to overconsume[16] or the psychological/individual level with aspects such as subjectivity, emotions, personality, needs/wants/desires, reflexivity, rationality, and hedonism. On the contrary, these are important, but they have to be related to the social life dimension, as well as to the institutions and infrastructures discussed above. It is of fundamental importance to stress that consumption provides *meaning* for the consumer; it is personally meaningful because it is tied to social life. You consume not just because something feels, smells, tastes, looks, or sounds good. You consume because it brings you social rewards. Consumption fulfills social goals and tasks. Desires come alive in the social context (Belk et al. 2003). Consumption is symbolic; that is, it is part of a communicative act (Wilk 2002). Hence, consumption expresses things. The personal and social dimensions are therefore always entangled. In the coming chapters, I include people's thinking and feeling. Regarding the emotions, it will be clear that individual drivers of consumerism are linked to both negative emotions (e.g., disappointments, fear of failing to care for one's relationships, unfavorable judgment, the breaking of cultural norms, becoming lonely and socially excluded) and positive (e.g., joy, pleasure, convenience, curiosity, social belonging and connection, as well as pride).

This book emphasizes a variety of features of consumption/consumerism, and it is important to consider this heterogeneity to gain a comprehensive understanding of the drivers behind unsustainable mass consumption. Therefore, I will address both mundane and extravagant aspects of consumption, both conscious and unconscious dynamics, planned and impulsive, conspicuous and inconspicuous, chosen and habitual, intentional and unintentional, and consumption that is the focus of attention versus consumption that is part of the scenery of another focused activity, that is, front stage and back stage. Indeed, consumption is multifaceted precisely because it is social.

Theories of social life emphasize the importance of socialization—how children are born into social life, naturalize their lifeworlds, and develop roles and identities. If consumerism is a constant and all-encompassing part of the social life surrounding kids (and structure/culture in the background context) they will firmly internalize consumerism as normal and natural. As the symbolic interactionists stressed long ago (Mead 1962 [1934]; Blumer 1986 [1969]), we all gain our understandings of the world and possible roles we can play in it through interaction with significant others early in life: parents, siblings, friends. The self is fundamentally social, being reflected in interaction with the most important social relations. Reflective capacities are developed later, through secondary socialization, when the older child or adult gradually increases their understanding that their own lifeworld is not the only possible one. Macro and micro factors jointly contribute to socializing the child into mass-consumption habits (Richins 1994; Schor 2004; Sassatelli 2007). Children internalize the sociocultural meanings of commodities and transform these meanings into something private and personal. Gradually, they also become trained consumers by practicing the act of consuming and by following their self-interest, as people are encouraged to do. They are socialized into considering consumption as a default tool for solving problems, and to look for rewards and pleasure in toys, candies, presents, games, clothes, movies, hamburgers, soft drinks, mobile phones, and more—all of which habitualize children into a material landscape of excess. By the time children enter adult life, mass consumption patterns are already deeply internalized, integrated, and habitualized. Such patterns pervade everyday social life.

The social practice perspective is a source of inspiration, in that it emphasizes the social embeddedness of consumption.[17] Consumer research has traditionally been characterized by reductionist assumptions about consumers and their choices. Social practice theory directs attention to the habitual nature of agency (Warde 2005; Shove et al. 2012) and shows how the macro and micro are entangled in the meso. It accordingly entails that we understand actors—their thinking, feeling and doing—as thoroughly embedded in socio-material infrastructures, cultural norms, social relations and, not least, time and space. It pays attention to the sometimes very forceful socio-material and cultural lock-ins that actors face, which can be extremely hard even to comprehend. Material infrastructures (e.g., systems for physical transport, food provision, and heating and cooling buildings and homes), cultural norms (legitimate means of transportation, proper kinds of food, standard temperatures in the home), and tacit knowledge (how to travel; how to purchase, store, and prepare food; how to use energy) together interact to create stable ways of living (Shove et al. 2012; Southerton 2020).

Based on this broad understanding of social life, the chapters of the book elaborate on different aspects. I begin by considering the most important social relations that people have in life. We consume to a considerable extent because we feel a need to establish and confirm our social relationships. In chapter 1, I emphasize this understanding by drawing on theories of everyday rituals connected to consumption research. I draw on the theory of interaction ritual chains formulated by sociologist Randall Collins, who stressed the importance of rituals in fostering social solidarity. Tied to the topic of consumption and consumerism, such rituals include family dinners, holiday vacations, gift-giving, birthday parties, rituals of collecting, shopping, and the role of many consumer symbols like branded goods, cars, and fashion. In the chapter, I focus primarily on intimate relations, including the roles played by love, care, family life, and friendship. I also demonstrate how fear of social exclusion and loneliness are important drivers of consumption.

The next chapter looks at social relations from another angle, namely the role of *social comparisons* in stratified social life. Social relations also involve more distant relations. The chapter explores the various ways in which *social stratification* can be a factor in increasing volumes of consumption, through the human tendency of social comparison. Social stratification implies that society is (increasingly) differentiated, vertically and horizontally, in terms of occupations, classes, genders, status groups, income differences, and other divisions. First, I explore the role of social comparison in stratified social life through three case themes: *luxury*, *brands*, and *social media*. I then proceed to explain how the needs to fit in (belonging, identity) and desires to stand out (distinction, competition for social status) both drive consumerism. Another key theme concerns how increasing income gaps spur consumerism, for example through the drivers of relative deprivation/poverty. I introduce several classical sociological concepts like extended self, identity (deficit), conspicuous consumption, cultural capital, and relative poverty, combined with a broad range of empirical research covering different parts of the world, to demonstrate various ways in which social comparison, appearance anxiety, stratification, peer pressure, and increasing inequalities drive consumerism.

The next chapter focuses on the temporalities of consumption in social life, in particular the sense of hurriedness and speed experienced in contemporary social life. The chapter is divided into two main sections. The first starts from a key structural feature of modern society: the separation between work time and leisure time. The analysis shows how the historically growing role of leisure, as well as contemporary experiences of a work–life imbalance, drive consumerism. This is seen in buying for convenience (timesaving and time-shifting goods and services), buying for instant reward, and buying for future leisure. The other main section deals with a key (temporal) feature of consumer culture: the celebration of novelty. This theme is investigated in terms of concepts and phenomena such as the cycle of desire, fashion, fashion anxiety, rapid obsolescence, and impulse buying. The chapter draws on various theories about time and tempo, such as the social acceleration theory formulated by Hartmut Rosa. It concludes that the future is discounted in favor of present-day consumerism.

Chapter 4 deals with different sites of consumption, and I discuss consumption in terms of both buying and using an object. The social and spatial contexts surrounding one's consumption are segmented—home, work, school, transport, shopping site, holiday destination—and need to be understood as such, because each different site is tied to a different range of consumerist drivers. The chapter delimits the focus to three sites: the home, the mall, and the internet. The home has always been an important site of consumption but has recently become even more so due to digitalization and the COVID-19 pandemic, which have resulted in more stay-at-home lifestyles. A broad range of meanings are associated with home and homeliness, and these involve multiple drivers of consumerism connected to private/family life, social status, and leisure time. The section on the mall—as the key symbol of shopping—shows how shopping has been socially and historically constructed as a site of entertainment and social interaction, and thus contributes to consumerism. Finally, the chapter discusses the abstract site of the internet and social media, which expand the "buyosphere" and peer interactivity into 24/7 phenomena.

Even if insight about unsustainable ecological and climate footprints is increasing in society, the public is still only superficially aware of how deeply reliant we all are on unsustainable mass-consumption structures and habits. Chapter 5 addresses a cognitive dimension of this: our taken-for-granted knowledge and ignorance about matters related to our consumption, and how they derive from the society and culture in which we live. I discuss these issues by referring to two general phenomena: normalization and ignorance. Normalization is about processes that make us inclined to see phenomena as normal, such as the voluminous, omnipresent and historically increasing levels of consumption. A situation of mass ignorance and systemic "anti-reflexivity" facilitates the reproduction of problematic patterns. Ignorance is related to the very complex structure of global commodity chains and the historically unprecedented division of labor and specialization in societies; this explains a couple of the infrastructural factors mentioned in the previous section. This structure disconnects and distances all of us from the present and future consequences of our consumer choices and practices. The forces of normalization and ignorance make us unable to imagine the possibility of radical alternatives.

The concluding chapter of the book begins by exploring the battery of cognitive strategies (arguments) people use to justify their current habits of overconsumption, despite having some level of awareness about its negative consequence for the planet. I present nine such defensive arguments/strategies. The conclusion also includes a section that questions our consumer culture's promise that higher volumes of consumed products and services will contribute to greater well-being, happiness, and quality of life. The arguments in chapters 1–5 emphasize that consumption has a multitude of personal and social meanings. A core message of the book is that consumption is highly meaningful in relation to social life as it confirms social relations, identity, belonging, status, and so on. It is important, however, to address not just its negative effects for wider sustainability, but also the fact that it involves personal and social costs and fails to deliver on its promises. Hence, I conclude that consumerism is not only a socio-ecologically destructive force; it appears, ironically, even unable to genuinely enrich social and inner lives. In this sense, consumerism appears meaningless. This observation can serve as a strong platform for thoroughly critiquing our mass-consumption society, both from an ecological and a social life perspective. Hence, while this book may appear pessimistic it is not meant to be fatalistic. I argue that something can be done about it, and that much of what can be done is already being done by a variety of people and social movements. There are counterforces. The last section of the book is devoted to the question of what we might be able to do to wean ourselves off consumerism and achieve transformative change. I refer to some of my own empirical research as well as others' research on voluntary and involuntary reduction of consumption. I argue that the enterprise of transforming lifestyles must involve all levels of society from the global down to the inner lives of individuals. Macro-institutional structures must be transformed. Societies need to be rebuilt. This is obviously not something that can be done overnight. A key assumption of this book is that such transformation requires empowerment and mobilization from the bottom up as well progressive responses from "above." Structures and cultures do not change by themselves. And the social life aspects discussed in this book must all be well understood.

NOTES

1. I am grateful to Linda Soneryd and Kjell Vowles for constructive comments on an earlier version of the introduction, as well as to an anonymous reviewer.

2. All these figures stem from international expert organizations such as the Intergovernmental Panel on Climate Change (IPCC), the UN Environment Programme (UNEP), Intergovernmental Science-Policy Platform on Biodiversity and Ecosystem Services (IPBES), the International Union for Conservation of Nature (IUCN), the World Health Organization (WHO), and more. For CO_2 emissions, see https://www.c2es.org/content/international-emissions/ 2002-06-02 https://ieep.eu/news/more-than-half-of-all-co2-emissions-since-1751-emitted-in-the-last-30-years 2022-10-15; for mass extinction, see https://www.unep.org/news-and-stories/story/warning-sixth-mass-species-extinction-cards 2022-10-15; for plastic pollution, see https://www.iucn.org/our-work/topic/plastic-and-other-pollution, 2022-11-15; for air pollution, see https://www.who.int/health-topics/air-pollution#tab=tab_2 2022-10-15; for the weight of human-made materials, see https://www.nationalgeographic.com/environment/article/human-made-materials-now-equal-weight-of-all-life-on-earth 2022-10-15; for the mammals biomass, see https://www.ecowatch.com/biomass-humans-animals-2571413930.html 2022-11-18, and for the Anthropocene and Great Acceleration, see https://www.anthropocene.info/great-acceleration.php. Accessed 2022-10-15.

3. See https://www.overshootday.org/newsroom/country-overshoot-days/ and https://www.footprintnetwork.org/. Accessed 2022-06-02.

4. See https://www.wfp.org/global-hunger-crisis. Accessed 2022-10-18.

5. On this risk/problem of scholars tending to blame the consumers, see Miller 2001; Rief 2008; Evans 2011.

6. A recipe for coping with worries and anxiety is constructive action/engagement—individual and collective—rather than inaction. About the complex relation between factors such as anxiety/worry, hope, and agency in relation to climate/environmental issues, see Ojala 2016; Ojala et al. 2021; and Ojala 2023. This research also suggests that overly optimistic framings regarding the climate/environmental situation may spur false hope rather than action.

7. For a recent overview that also defends a plurality of perspectives, see Warde 2022.

8. A broader framework is that of Manfred Max-Neef (see Max-Neef 2010; Smith and Max-Neef 2011) who list the following needs: subsistence, protection, affection, understanding, participation, idleness, creation, identity, and freedom. These can be satisfied by having, doing, being, and interacting (see also Rauschmayer and Omann 2015).

9. In this book, I use commoditization and commodification interchangeably, because I see no useful reason to distinguish between them. Commodification is

sometimes used to describe a process where supposedly nonsalable objects become salable (with the result that the assumption was disproved, at least from a descriptive point of view). See also Warde 2022.

10. Princen (2005) argues that a sufficiency principle has strong relevance in history and relates to terms such as moderation, thrift, frugality, prudence, temperance, and reverence. In contrast, an "efficiency principle" has grown along with industrialization and now dominates the market and politics.

11. I use the word "driver" as a synonym of the word "mechanism" commonly used among critical realists. I am inspired by a nondogmatic application of critical realism (see Sayer 2002), however I find that the word "driver" may be more intuitively understandable.

12. My thinking around institutions is particularly informed by Berger and Luckmann's (1991 [1966]) classical theory of the social construction of reality, including how our societal stock of knowledge—and understanding of reality—is patterned and reproduced via a dialectical process of internalization, externalization, and objectification.

13. I proceed from my analysis in Boström (2020).

14. Brand and Wissen (2021) uses the concept of "the imperial mode of living" to visualize how everyday life and consumption in the global North depend on an exploitive relationship with other parts of the world, causing both ecological destruction and human suffering.

15. See, e.g., Swedberg's (2003) discussion of how mass markets have been growing historically since the Agora, and even before, although it does not cover the recent growth of internet shopping. See also Rostow's (1959) analysis of the "stages of growth," in which "the age of high mass consumption" is the latest historical stage.

16. As humans, we may be evolutionarily shaped to have a propensity to overconsume. The human brain and the triggers of dopamine and other neurotransmitters evolved in a harsh environment of scarcity (Jackson 2017). The human brain is adaptive and can quickly learn and adapt to new levels of consumption.

17. However, in contrast to some versions of the social practice approach, I place greater emphasis on the importance of symbolic/cultural aspects of consumption.

Chapter 1

Social Relations, Everyday Rituals, and Consumerism

We consume because we feel a constant desire to establish, develop, and confirm our relationships.[1] We consume for reasons of love, care, family life, and friendship. This chapter focuses on how intimate and friendly social relations drive consumerism, with a key focus on one important social driver: interaction rituals. I begin by presenting Randall Collins's theory of interaction ritual chains. This serves as a theoretical starting point for demonstrating how everyday rituals of consumption are linked to the development of group solidarity, which in turn provides reinforcing feedback to continuous consumption. In everyday speech the word "ritual" can be associated with formalized religious, mystical, or other ceremonies, such as graduation ceremonies. However, cultural sociology and the sociology of consumption demonstrate that rituals are a much wider phenomenon. We all engage in numerous rituals every day, and we do so because they are loaded with social meaning. After the theoretical introduction, the chapter proceeds by emphasizing how love and care can be deeply embedded in various consumption rituals, and how everyday rituals such as birthday parties are influenced by broader processes of commercialization permeating intimate and family life. Topics such as gift-giving, collecting, compulsive buying, and the chasing of discounts are discussed, and an analysis of loneliness will demonstrate the critical role of social relations in consumption. All this shows that understanding the intersection of social relations, everyday rituals, and consumption is crucial if we wish to grapple with some important drivers behind unsustainable mass consumption in societies.

RITUALS, SOCIAL LIFE, AND CONSUMERISM

Everyday life is full of rituals.[2] We engage in many rituals to develop and confirm our relationships and maintain social life. We enjoy dinners together. We go to concerts and movies and enjoy sporting events. We celebrate achievements and milestones in life. We give presents. We sing and dance. We follow certain codes of conduct to show courtesy and respect when we converse. We engage in interaction rituals when attending lectures, seminars, and workshops, and respect norms of conduct for listening, debating and honoring the speaker.

Rituals have some affinities with habits.[3] These two phenomena overlap but are not the same. Some rituals are performed very seldom (such as marriage) and there are regular habits that usually do not function as rituals (taking vitamin pills in the morning) (Rook 1985). What sets them apart from each other is that rituals function as essential glue in social life. They enrich and energize our social lives and are instrumental in establishing and maintaining relationships. This is what sociologist Randall Collins stresses in his book *Interaction Ritual Chains* (2005). Collins develops a general social theory based on the work of classic sociologists such as Émile Durkheim and Erving Goffman. Rituals, according to Collins, involve a mutual focus of attention and a sense of an exclusive shared mood within a particular group. Participation in interaction ritual chains generates social solidarity and positive emotional energy for the people involved. A ritual would not be a ritual if it was not repeated, which is why Collins adds the term chain to that of interaction ritual. Before exploring the connections between rituals and consumerism it is instructive to look at the elements of an interaction ritual according to Collins's model (Collins 2005, 48).

First, there are four ingredients of rituals: group assembly, barriers to outsiders, mutual focus of attention, and shared mood. A ritual, according to Collins, takes place in a group assembly under conditions of the situational and physical copresence of the included members. The ingredient barriers to outsiders implies that participation has a somewhat exclusive character. Copresence is converted into a full-scale encounter. The interaction becomes focused on something. This shared attention gives rise to a shared mood, which in turn reinforces the shared attention. Collins thus stresses the importance of the physical assembly of a group (I will later discuss digital copresence) for conversation, having dinner together, attending protests, listening to concerts, watching football games, and so on. In such activities, participants may "play roles" and follow rules and scripts, with the result that rituals appear like relatively fixed episodic sequences.[4] The copresence is upheld by actions of bodily inter-orientation within the group such as applause, nodding to each other, toasting before beginning to eat, or marching together on the street, which contribute to an intensification of the shared experience. However, people also perform rituals when they are alone. Solitary activities—such as meticulous body and hair care routines in the morning—can be highly ritualistic. They are both personal and socially oriented highly focused activities involving deep-seated emotions and aspirations. They are backstage preparations for a successful front-stage appearance and interaction in social life.

This notion of energizing is a core theme in Collins's theory. He employs a term coined by Émile Durkheim, collective effervescence, to designate the emergent enthusiasm in a collective act characterized by copresence and conformity. It can be understood as a sense of heightened intersubjectivity, group excitement, or "electricity" produced in the situation. This is an immediate ritual outcome. There are also four somewhat more indirect ritual outcomes: group solidarity, emotional energy in individuals, symbols of social relationships (sacred objects), and standards of morality.

The first indirect ritual outcome, the development of group solidarity, is key to Collins's argument. To the classic sociological question often posed in the Durkheimian tradition, "What holds society together?," Collins's answer is rituals. "And the 'society' that is held together is no abstract unity of a social system but is just those groups of people assembled in particular places who feel solidarity with each other through the effects of ritual participation and ritually charged symbolism" (Collins 2005, 41; see also Kišjuhas 2023). Among the participating partners, there is a situational pressure to be in agreement and maintain the social solidarity. Rituals therefore exert pressure to conform. They show that one is a member of the group or society.

Emotional energy is a second key outcome of rituals and serves to motivate the members of the group to repeat the rituals. According to Collins, much of the glue in social life can be explained by the inner intensities, the energies, contained in rituals. Emotional energies are a result of achieving meaningful social meetings through rituals and help to form collective conscience and consciousness. Participants who are copresent and aware of experiencing, doing, and desiring the same thing as everyone else experience collective effervescence and strong solidarity with each other. Shared action, awareness, and emotion create bonds. Emotional energy is the individual energy that is created in and stored by such situations. Collins stresses that individuals are "emotional energy-seekers"—EE-seekers, or even EE-maximizers (drawing a parallel to rational choice theory). Individuals are guided by the emotional charges of various activities (rituals) or of symbols representing such events. Even if the energy is experienced individually, it is important to stress that it is socially derived.

The third important indirect ritual outcome comprises symbols of social relationships (or “sacred objects”). Any event of heightened intersubjectivity can stimulate the production of emblems that serve as markers of group identity, that is, symbols. These can be totems, flags, logos, artworks, role models, artifacts, slogans, T-shirts with certain colors and prints, and so on. Such symbols reify the shared experience and make it thing-like. Collective sentiments can be prolonged by such symbols and enacted again and again.

The final important indirect ritual outcome is standards of morality (or social norms). People participating in rituals feel morally right when they are acting and feeling the electricity generated by the heightened experience of the group. Rituals, and the symbols associated with them, are thus a source of the group’s standards of morality. Norms are invented and a moral conscience is established. It becomes difficult to break with the social norms and rituals. Symbols must be respected. Rituals must be performed with appropriate reverence, and when a ritual is disturbed, the person who is responsible for the damage, or even just watches it happen, feels moral unease. There might even be a set of appropriate feelings to express openly when participating in a ritual (Rook 1985, 252). As the ritual outcome are felt as positive or obligatory, the rituals will be repeated (symbolized with the feedback loop (arrow) in Figure 1.1).

Collins’s theory was developed before the era of social media, which makes it easy to understand why he might have overstressed the necessity of

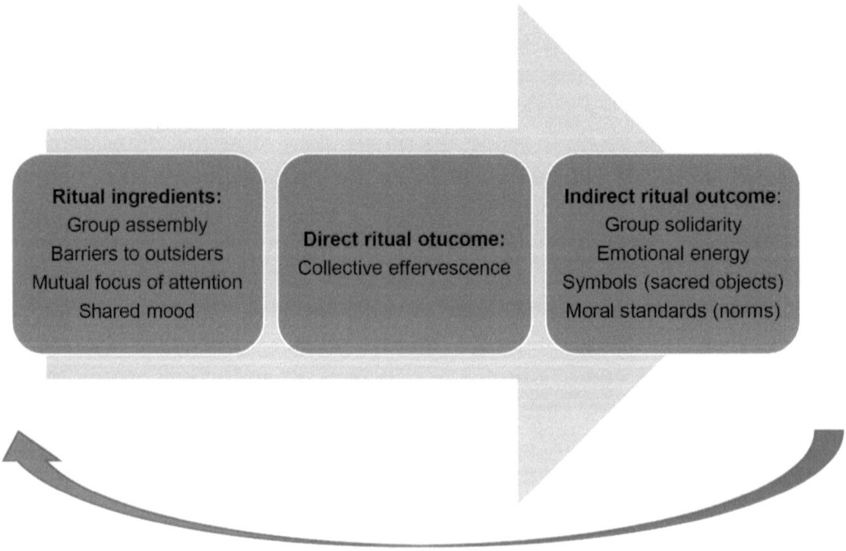

Figure 1.1. Interaction Ritual Chain. ***Source:*** **Author, based on Randall Collins’s theory (Collins 2005).**

physical copresence in interaction ritual chains. The COVID-19 pandemic, which brought a further wave of digitalized activities, both weakens and supports this part of the theory (Kišjuhas 2023). It weakens it because people learned to socialize and engage in "quaranteaming" via online platforms and invented virtual gatherings such as dinner parties, quiz games, religious services, weddings, musical performances, and much more (Kirk and Rifkin 2020; Echegaray 2021). The expanded use of digital technology even enabled reunions with distant families and friends (Sheth 2020). It supports it because "Zoom fatigue" and feelings of loneliness indeed showed that, for many, physical copresence has a greater capacity to generate positive emotional energy than digital copresence. People found themselves longing for physical contact beyond that available in the household.

So, what does all this have to do with consumerism and consumption? Based on Collins's model, I believe it is instructive to theoretically distinguish three facets of how consumption intersects with everyday interaction rituals and thereby contributes to our propensity to consume: (1) as a ritual ingredient (consumption act and object as focus of attention); (2) as a ritual outcome (consumption act and object causing emotional energies and bonds, and expressed via symbolically laden material manifestations, which are giving rise to consumption norms); and (3) as a context or requisite for the ritual.

First, the object or act of consumption might be what the members of the group mutually focus their attention on. This could be a physical object, such as a mobile phone, a name-brand article of clothing, or a sports car. The mutual focus of attention could also be a commoditized activity, such as going out for dinner at a restaurant, watching a football game, or visiting an amusement park. Consuming with someone else is different from consuming alone (Ramanathan and McGill 2007); it can modify and intensify the experience. Emotions are contagious. Inviting someone for a dinner is a gesture of belonging, and the setting offers opportunities to mutually enjoy and converse about such things as the meal, drinks, tableware, and background music. Whatever the particular item or service may be, it becomes the focal point that the group gathers around. Sometimes the core focus of attention is a person—for example, at a child's birthday party—while physical items—presents, the birthday cake—also take center stage. To this, we can add a temporal dimension, because rituals appear at different phases in relation to the purchase/appropriation of the particular good or service. *Before* the purchase, as a joint focus of attention, the social group may engage in daydreaming, wishing, imagining, and planning. *During* includes shopping, negotiating, exchanging, or performing the activity. There can also be a joint focus *after* the purchase when accommodating the object at home, or engaging in activities such as using, maintaining, repairing, discarding, and remembering, for example looking at photos from a holiday vacation. All these processes create a shared mood and can be emotionally energizing activities for the individual members of social groups such as romantic couples, families, friends, and work teams.

The second facet, ritual outcomes, often overlaps with the first one, as consumer objects become material manifestations of rituals. Consumer objects emerge as symbols of relationships, the "sacred" objects representing rituals. As such they play a role in prolonging the collective effervescence and the emotional energies in individuals, as well as bolstering group solidarity. A beautiful handmade carpet on the living room floor reminds about a couple's romantic holiday trip to a destination known for producing such carpets. A T-shirt with a picture of Zlatan Ibrahimovic serves as a symbol of the football team. A product with a particular logo serves to signal affiliation with a particular status group or brand community (see chapter 2). Meat, cars, and protein bars become symbols of masculine identity and solidarity. Aircraft have become a symbol for a political community and ideology that endorses economic growth, free trade, and accelerated global interchange. When adolescent girls trade clothes with each other, they share not only friendship but also identities; they become "soulmates" (Belk 1988). Goods differ. Some goods have a very strong symbolic value. They are symbolically sacred, and consumption activities involving them are surrounded by an aura of sanctity (Firat et al. 2013). Other goods are more mundane, yet still part of everyday rituals. Even an activity that may seem banal and purely practical, such as everyday shopping for food and other provisions at the supermarket, can bring a variety of symbolic meanings into play (Miller 1998; Sassatelli 2007, 63; Jenkins et al. 2011). These symbolic meanings ought to be respected, and thus a key ritual outcome is the bolstering of consumption norms (morality standards) in social circles and society at large (more on norms in chapter 5).

In the third and certainly not least important category, consumer items can provide the stage (context, setting, frame) and requisites for the group's mutual attention, that is, can serve as material resources facilitating the ritual. One such stage is the home (see chapter 4), which itself is a commodity that can constitute a focus of mutual attention, such as when one invites guests to view one's new house or renovation. In relation to the second point, it can be a symbol (a sacred object) for homeliness or a particular lifestyle. And it is also the setting of a variety of other rituals in everyday life. Another example is the café, the setting of frequent everyday rituals in which the mutual focus of attention is friendly conversation, which is often done after another ritual—shopping—and involves the mandatory procurement of something tasty: coffee and cake. Taking part in interaction ritual chains can involve considerable material expense (Collins 2005, 160–63). Thus, material goods can be essential parts of the background setting of an everyday ritual, even if the goods themselves are not the key focus of attention (Rook 1985; Miller 2010; Jenkins et al. 2011).

In real life, these three facets are often blended. An item that is the focus of attention at one point of time may later become a symbol and social norm of the group, or part of a context. A comprehensive explanation of mass consumption and consumerism must accordingly include both explicit (foreground, consumption as a goal) and implicit (background, consumption as stage and requisites) references to consumer items. Figure 1.2 incorporates how the ritual elements are linked with consumption into Collins's model.

Many interaction ritual chains are thus connected to consumerism, deeply associated with family values, or contribute to the creation of group solidarity among friends and colleagues (Miller 1998; Sassatelli 2007; Black and Cherrier 2010; Jenkins et al. 2011; Spaargaren 2011). For example, eating together—at home or at a restaurant—represents a collective act that symbolizes the continuity of the group. Each time such goods and services are used, the experience is contextually shaped by moral standards (norms), and contains expectations related to the renewal of emotional energy. Dining out entails a whole series of acts loaded with meanings and shared attention: wearing nice clothes, choosing a restaurant, observing the proper manners in the setting, looking at the menu and discussing the options, selecting drinks to share, gazing at the physical surroundings, interacting with waiting staff and learning something new about the food, tipping, and so on. They represent a scripted drama in which we all participate to enrich our social lives.

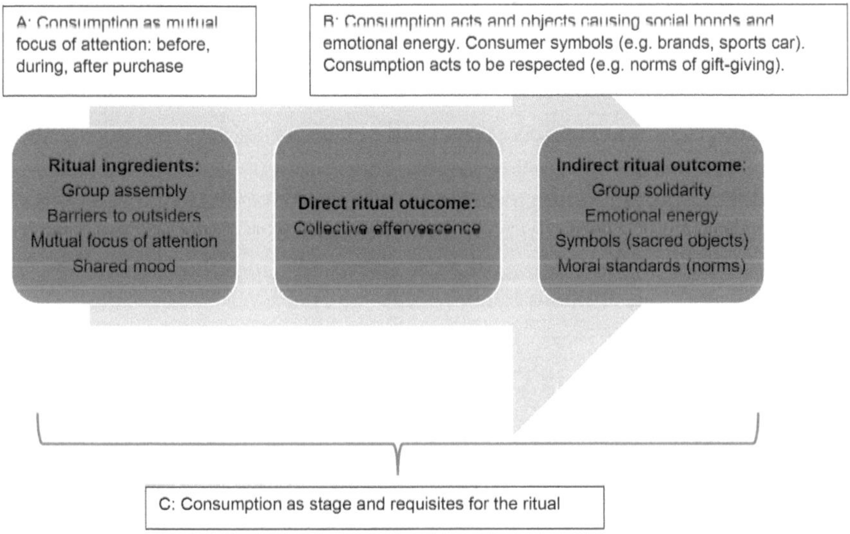

Figure 1.2. Rituals of Consumption. *Source:* Author, based on Collins (2005).

Consumption functions as relational work. We consume in order to build, maintain, celebrate, and modify interpersonal relations. An object that one procures—a gift, jewelry, dinner, toy, clothing, car, holiday trip—can represent a bridge to another person or to a collective with which one is affiliated. Sometimes the object is not directly related to any concrete person but stretches toward a more abstract entity: an idea, ideal, or imagined community. Such an imagined community could be the nation, a football team, or brand communities such as Apple users. For example, the sacred reference when buying fair trade products may be the "global community" and "an equal relationship between North and South."

Participation in rituals does not necessarily lead to positive emotions. Rituals can be draining, empty or forced, says Collins. Despite containing low emotional energy, such an interaction ritual can be maintained because of power structures. A forced mutual focus of attention may lead to negative emotions such as alienation, depression, anger, or fear. Such emotions are important to consider in relation to mass/excess consumption; for example they may relate to comparison anxiety (see chapters 2, 5, and conclusion). Negative and positive emotions can be mixed in one and the same situation. Failure to perform the ritual correctly, to properly respect the sacred symbols and associated norms, can lead to shame. This is the emotion of a self that is excluded or threatened with exclusion from a social group. Its opposite is pride.[5] It is important to remember that both the drive to experience positive emotions (high EE) and worry about experiencing negative emotions (low EE) are crucial to consider if we are to properly understand consumerism.

CONSUMERISM AND INTIMATE RELATIONSHIPS

The above section on everyday rituals and consumerism has provided a theoretical foundation for understanding the intersection between social relations and consumerism. The following subsections on love and care, commoditization of intimate life, difficulties of downsizing, and gift-giving will provide a more detailed understanding of how important (mass) consumption has become for building intimate relationships.

Consumerism, Love, and Care

A basic motivation behind many of our object-focused desires is to have social relationships with other people as well as to obtain desired responses from these people (Belk et al. 2003; Jenkins et al. 2011). A passionate longing for such goods as a house, a car, furniture, luxury items, fashion, and the latest iPhone or version of World of Warcraft, as well as commoditized experiences like a weekend getaway to a foreign city, can be something that unites a family, romantic couple, or group of friends. Feelings of connectedness or synchronicity during an act of consumption can intensify people's enjoyment of that act (Ramanathan and McGill 2007). Having aspirations in common makes for family bonding. Such longing is ultimately social. It binds. It expresses love and care and is part and parcel of the striving for new and better relationships and sociability within the family and among friends.

It is not just extravagant consumption that counts. Consumption is also involved in enacting more mundane social relations. Rebecca Jenkins and colleagues (2011) conducted phenomenologically inspired in-depth interviews of people in the South of England and asked about their imagined futures with regard to their everyday lives. Based on the findings and other sources, the authors claim that material goods play an important role in experiences and the imagination, even when they are not the key focus of consumers' attention. Social relations take central stage, but considerable quantities of material goods are implicated; they appear as part of the background context (as stage and requisites, see figure 1.2 above). Mass consumption is hence largely invisible.

This study by Jenkins and colleagues, as well as many other studies in consumer research, have been inspired by anthropologist Daniel Miller and his material culture perspective. In his book *A Theory of Shopping* (1998) he builds on ritual theory to emphasize how love and care for others is a basic motivation behind much ordinary shopping. Quite a lot of shopping is done for the benefit of others. Miller compares the practice of shopping to rituals of sacrifice. We may often associate shopping with indulgence and hedonistic materialism, seeking pleasure in the consumer objects and experiences; however, even if this is a core element of consumer culture (see Campbell 2018 [1987]), it does not constitute the lion's share, Miller argues. Rather, shoppers imagine and cultivate their most-valued social relationships by selecting all kinds of products, not just the most symbolically laden goods such as cars and fashion. Even the texture and color of toilet paper can bear social significance when a family member purchases necessities for the family household.

Miller's ethnographic study involved interviews and observations of mainly housewives on a street in North London. He interviewed the women at home and followed them to shopping outlets. He focused on mundane shopping, particularly grocery shopping, but also shopping for clothes and home furnishing. Miller found that much of the shopping was done with an eye to concrete or imagined others. Goods are means for creating relationships of love between subjects, and not just for achieving individualistic and materialistic goals. "The purpose of shopping is not so much to buy the things people want, but to strive to be in a relationship with subjects that want these things" (Miller 1998, 148). The ultimate benefits of shopping are not material. Even if shopping includes the procurement of material items, it is largely about creating and confirming relationships. Randall Collins stresses the same idea: individuals are not primarily seeking material gain; they are seeking high emotional energy.

Shopping is not best understood as individualistic, Miller says, even when it is done by one person, because shopping is rarely just self-directed:

> Rather the act of buying goods is mainly directed at two forms of "otherness." The first of these expresses a relationship between the shopper and a particular other individual such as a child or partner, either present in the household, desired or imagined. The second of these is a relationship to a more general goal which transcends any immediate utility and is best understood as cosmological in that it takes the form of neither subject nor object but of the values to which people wish to dedicate themselves. (Miller 1998, 12)

Miller's theorizing may have been colored by his empirical focus on housewives. Yet, an important lesson is that even if many of the purchases are not made jointly, the consumption can still be very social and relational. One must not disappoint the people that one is supposed to take care of. Love and care for others is expressed by procuring healthy food for the family, toys for the children, and respectable clothes for the husband, and not least, in volumes that conform to current standards of normality (see chapter 5).

People need scripts. To express love and care with consumption, one ought to adhere to various ideas, expectations, and trends in society. It can be difficult to deviate from institutionalized ideas because one not only rejects the ideas, but also faces the risk of disrespecting the relationship. Inferior consumption can be interpreted as a sign of rejecting other members of the group. Hence, ritualized consumption does not only generate positive emotional energy; because of the constant risk of disrespecting relationships by not sticking to standards of consumption, it also involves a great deal of anxiety. The strong role that such sociopsychological drivers play—both positively and negatively—are intuitively understood by the marketing industry and advertisers, which underscores the importance of taking into account theories of how market expansion and commoditization penetrate intimate everyday life.

Commoditization of Intimate Life

As we go about engaging in everyday rituals involving much consumption, both in the pursuit of emotional energy and family bonding and to express love and care, these drivers of social life provide a fertile ground for market expansion and exploitation. Commoditization is the social process through which things and activities come to be produced and exchanged as commodities (Sassatelli 2007).

Commoditization/commodification theory holds that the range of commodified goods and services is historically increasing. It should be emphasized that this is obviously not something new. Household and family centered consumption, as well as the introduction of shopping into social life, preceded industrial capitalism by a good margin (Hine 2002; Trentmann 2016). For instance, the introduction of coffee, tea, and chocolate into Western Europe in the seventeenth century triggered a shopping boom centered on cups, spoons, pots, linens, and other utensils of a new social ritual in both public (coffeehouses) and private settings.

However, in contemporary consumer culture, the market is increasingly colonizing the intimate sphere. This theme has been studied by sociologist Arlie Hochschild. Since her pioneering book *The Managed Heart*, in which she introduced the famous concept of "emotional labor," she has gradually widened her attention on such labor to encompass the creeping commercialization of intimate life (Hochschild 2003). Neoliberal capitalism is increasingly shaping and changing every possible aspect of everyday life. Much of our interaction with partners, families, colleagues, and friends has become commodified. In both activities and talk, consumerism grows in all aspects, including love, romance, intimacy, and parenting (Jenkins et al. 2011; Brook et al. 2013, 280). The fact that emotions are created in many such everyday commoditized interactions may even mask the fact that commoditization is involved. For example, the emotions of the romantic bond may obscure that a whole range of consumer practices are involved in enacting the romantic interaction, with consumption fulfilling roles as focus of attention, as symbols/norms, and as stage/requisites. Perhaps an overseas weekend trip is felt to be necessary.

Nearly anything can be sold, Hochschild claims (2003, 2011). There are few things or services that cannot be sold under any circumstances. Goods and services include everything from modern-day essentials such as childcare and eldercare to other more optional services like food delivery, birthday planners, life coaches, wedding planners, dating services, the sex industry (legal or not), parenting consultants, and highly specialized services such as plastic surgery and surrogate parenthood.

Birthday celebrations are a good example of commoditized family rituals. A birthday is an excellent opportunity for parents to gather family and friends in an emotionally energizing interaction ritual—a party—to create, confirm, and restore social bonds. It is also a kind of ritual that reflects and reproduces consumer culture; something which many parents have difficulty resisting even if they are aware of its excessiveness. Some birthday parties are prepackaged (for example, procuring paraphernalia for a Harry Potter theme) and outsourced to birthday party services (bowling halls, amusement parks), whereas others are more homemade (Schoonmaker 2006). Regardless of the form, consumerism is pervasive. Material things are key focus of attention (e.g., presents), represent sacred objects (presents as such) and norms of gift-giving, and appears as a background setting with all the needed requisites. In one article, Hochschild (2011) discusses a father who tried to overcome the estrangement (alienation) he felt when pressured to hire a birthday party planner by attempting to organize the event himself. He wanted to be a producer/creator, and not a consumer of his child's party. His alternative party was not anti-consumerist, which would imply less consumer stuff such as hamburgers, cakes, soft drinks, candies, presents, disposable plastic items, balloons, and other kinds of wasteful requisites. He did not resist consumption—but at least he thought that he could resist the commoditization of the party as such. The result was not a success (Hochschild 2011, 27)

His wife described the event:

> Michael dressed up as a cowboy from the Australian outback—like Crocodile Dundee [an alligator wrangler portrayed in a film of that name]. He put on a broad-brimmed hat, khaki shirt and shorts and tall leather boots. He stalked about on a pretend stage in front of the girls, describing this and that wild animal in a flat Aussie accent. And he went on for three or four minutes. Then he ran out of things to say. Michael hadn't thought out more to say. Worse yet, the children didn't think his jokes were funny. They began to examine his knobby knees. Then they began to fidget. Then the whole thing fell apart.

When Michael recalled the same event, he put it differently:

> Do you *know* how *long* two hours is? I didn't know it would be so *hard!* You have these people organize the kids into games and do tricks for them. And I thought, why not try it? So the day came, and I had all these little five year-olds. But they needed *constant* organizing, moving, entertaining. You have to know how to *do* this. It's a *skill* running groups of twenty or thirty five-year-olds. You can't really tell them what to do. You have to quickly engage them. It's like being a continual standup comic. You have about two seconds to catch their attention. If there's a gap at any point, they break up into little groups. . . . It nearly killed me.

This excerpt nicely illustrates a variety of pressures. First, it shows the power of common everyday rituals—birthday parties for one's kids—that are supposed to generate emotional energy and family bonding. Imagine how difficult it would be to arrange an anti-consumerist birthday party for that child in that specific community. Then there are the expectations that stem from previous experiences of birthday parties. Additional pressures result from the very existence of the possibility to outsource the job to those who know best—the experts. Then there is peer pressure, especially when one's own children are involved (see chapter 2). Finally, there are the more subtle pressures that arise when a community is becoming accustomed to rising standards—the creeping normalization of more extravagant birthday parties (see chapter 5). And it is very questionable whether this commercial escalation contributes to greater happiness (see concluding chapter).

Pressures such as these were also documented in a study by Sara Schoonmaker (2006), who interviewed parents from southern California with mixed class and ethnic backgrounds. Her findings showed that most parents savor these celebrations because they are an opportunity to do something their children enjoy, and are means to foster family bonds and children's relationships with each other. After all, is there not a painful lack of time for family togetherness? (See also chapter 3.) At the same time, parents struggle with an ambiguous relation to consumer culture, both embracing and critiquing it. Even if parents expressed a critical view of consumerism—with some trying various strategies to tone down the focus on material things and instead emphasizing relationships and activities—it was difficult to resist the overall materialist frame. Several of the interviewed parents felt ambivalence and embarrassment about the excessive materialism, and experienced birthday parties as "overkill" or "obscene," while nonetheless being unable to avoid the consumerism they involved. They were also embarrassed because they actually enjoyed the ritual. Birthday parties thus well illustrate the "tensions between being drawn to enjoyment of consumer culture while simultaneously critiquing it" (Schoonmaker 2006, 228). What parent, or grandparent, can resist the happy face of a child receiving presents?

Market opportunities escalate and appear overwhelming. They are not just opportunities; they add to the must-do lists, increase expectations about what the social group ought to do together, and provide an increasing range of things and activities that are difficult to resist in everyday social life. The work of Hochschild and others describes a general process of commoditization of intimate life. This development should not be interpreted as occurring in a deterministic way. It is possible for people to participate in these kinds of rituals and enjoy them, but at the same time to feel a sense of inner distance and develop creative alternatives. Indeed, the above-mentioned studies reveal much self-reflexivity and micro-level resistance among people, although they feel they can do little to counteract the macro development toward increased market expansion. But historical research shows that major developments need not be set in stone (see Text Box 1.1).

Text Box 1.1: Historical Changes of Commodification and Decommodification

In a historical comparison of cultural changes in Sweden, ethnologist Orvar Lövgren (2013) has shown that cultural macro-processes of "commodification" and "decommodification" (less dominance of commodities in private life) can shift in a dialectical fashion. The period between 1965 and 1975 saw a general informalization of private and public life, which included growing anti-consumption sentiments with a critique of status consumption and consumption that is extravagant, unnecessary, and wasteful. Starting in the 1980s, Lövgren observes a new era of market expansion that penetrated everyday life with "over-consumption" and "yuppiedom." This entailed a cult of "experience" and "romantic capitalism." Can everyday life again reclaim space from market colonization and resist further commoditization?

The Difficulties of Downsizing

I think every reader of this text can identify several personal consumption activities and objects that are important for one's relationships and would be difficult to relinquish. We might begin by thinking of the most obvious and spectacular objects. But think again, gaze at the material landscape around you and figure out if there are any more mundane aspects and objects of consumption that also are essential for your relationships, or that you may have bought when you were with someone in a situation that was especially exhilarating. The next level of the exercise would be to turn this insight into practice: avoid buying products, for instance by observing a temporary buy-nothing period. Such living experiments are likely to lead to surprises.

Experimental disruption of this sort has been a topic of research.[6] An effective way to discern the power of rituals is to examine efforts to change or avoid them. The omnipresence of consumption, including its importance for social interaction rituals, was detected in a study of a teaching project called the "Not Buying It" project (Grauerholz and Bubriski-McKenzie 2012). The researchers designed a study of a teaching project in which sociology students were to refrain from buying things for a limited period of time. Through an experiential exercise, the authors aimed to encourage personal and critical reflection about "hyperconsumerism" by asking students to document and reflect on their consumption habits. Despite the fact that students typically have limited resources to spend on consumption, the participants became aware of how pervasive consumption is in everyday life. They were able to perceive the subtle but very strong social forces that capitalism, media, and cultural values exert in shaping consumption patterns, including the participants' own consumption habits. One aspect of the study that is of particular relevance for this chapter on social relations and everyday rituals is that the students also experienced and learned how important consumption/consumerism was for *social interaction* in many different situations. Examples included the importance of shopping or visiting cafés to have fun and socialize with others. Here is an interview excerpt from one student in the study which I believe many people can sympathize with:

> Before completing this project I never considered how social shopping is. We buy things because we need them, right? I soon realized how often that is not the case. I don't buy a sandwich from Subway because I am in dire need of nutrients. I buy Subway because it is a convenient place to meet and socialize with friends over a meal. I don't buy coffee because I am thirsty, but because all my friends are. I realized how often I buy something just because I am with certain people in a certain setting. In today's society it seems rare that people can do something social without spending money . . . my friends and I hardly ever do something that doesn't require spending money. (Grauerholz and Bubriski-McKenzie 2012, 339)

The COVID-19 pandemic caused similar kinds of experiential learnings, as it made it difficult to engage in the kind of consumption described in the excerpt.[7]

Another way to demonstrate the powerful role of consumption in maintaining family life would be to investigate the socio-demographics of those who are able to significantly downsize their consumption or engage in activities known as voluntary simplicity. Indeed, the power of family life to reproduce mass/excess consumption can be discerned from the relative absence of downsizers in certain types of family contexts. I am not aware of any quantitative study that has systematically studied this precise question.[8] However, in some qualitative studies of downsizers (including voluntary simplifiers and similar lifestyle projects) there appears to be an overrepresentation of single people or couples without children, or couples who have found that having children creates extra difficulties (e.g., Schor 1998, 2004; Isenhour 2010; Walther and Sandlin 2011; Callmer 2019). This literature, including my own empirical research (Boström 2021c), makes it clear that the pressure to increase consumption, or to maintain high volumes of consumption, is experienced especially strongly by people with the role and responsibilities of parenthood. Parents raising children find themselves overwhelmed by consumer culture: diapers, safety equipment, toys and more toys, daycare services, birthday parties, mobile phones, home-entertainment facilities, a larger car or an additional car, and a wide range of other things that the family ought to procure that otherwise might not have been procured. In a consumer culture, it can feel like a profound social disability not to have enough money to purchase all the items the children "need," not least to keep up with their friends (Miller 1998; Schor 1998, 2004; Wilkinson and Pickett 2019, 141; Boström 2021c). For parents, failing to accommodate their children's wishes can feel overwhelming and spur overspending and larger debts. However, it should also be stressed that children and teenagers, perhaps inspired by Greta Thunberg, can exhibit creative agency and push for less consumerist family rituals, or modify existing rituals such as by switching to more vegetarian or vegan family diets.

The Obligation of Gift-giving

Tightly connected to the argument up to this point about the salience of consumption-laden everyday rituals is the strong role that gifts play in social relations. Gift-giving is an important social phenomenon in both historical and contemporary societies. Commodities are often reframed as "gifts" or "presents" for others, or sometimes for oneself, as self-gifts. Life starts with gifts. The newborn child is honored with gifts given to her, or rather to her parents, and this pattern continues with birthdays, Christmases, and many other occasions when people want to celebrate achievements, graduations, changes of social status and other milestones in life which anthropologists call "rites of passage" (Rook 1985). We have seen above how compelling a birthday ritual can be. The immediate joy that a toy can generate in a child makes it a highly desirable gift (Hamlin 2003). The child's happiness is a source of motivation for parents, grandparents, and others—happiness creates happiness—and therefore is a crucial ingredient in gift-giving rituals such as Christmas and birthdays.

Gifts can be enjoyable and emotionally energizing for both the giver and the receiver,[9] yet they can also be a source of anxiety. From social anthropology and Marcel Mauss (1990/1954) comes the classic insight that gifts create social bonds and cement relationship, but this involves both costs and benefits. There is no such thing as a free gift, says Mauss. A gift is inherently paradoxical; there is an assumption or obligation/expectation of reciprocity. The gift contains an implicit expectation of a gift in return; it is part of an exchange relationship. A gift in the form of consumption items will accordingly lead to expectations of continued consumption. A pattern of gift-giving becomes institutionalized. In contrast, if the receiver cannot give an equivalent gift in return, there is a loss of honor and a power asymmetry emerges. A situation of hidden and potential rivalry therefore lurks beneath the institution of gift-giving. Intuitive knowledge of such potential asymmetries and rivalries may also be a reason for giving something expensive (or at least not too inexpensive) or of high-volume giving. Many objects, and even entire shopping outlets, exist just because of the institution of gift-giving and the fear of not respecting gift-giving norms.

People sometimes give gifts to compensate for other lacks, such as a lack of time for a relationship due to a full and hectic work life (see also chapter 3). For instance, gifts to children can be a way for parents to cope with a shortage of time to spend with their children. As Text Box 1.2 shows, this theme is stressed in a historical analysis of the structure of toy consumption, including the role of Christmas.

There are rituals within rituals. The ritual of wrapping is interesting to reflect on. A decorated Christmas tree with many wrapped presents beneath it generates rising and almost unbearable excitement for everyone in the family. According to Thomas Hine (2002), the removal of the price tag and wrapping have been described as an attempt to disguise the industrial and commercial origins of the presents, as a way to "decontaminate" them from all signs of capitalism. But he also gives another interpretation:

> It seems more likely that wrapping is meant as a sign of caring. The wrap adds a personal and handmade element to a mass-produced product. The wrapping is not a disguise; it is tangible evidence that the giver thought about the recipient. It signals that the gift is really part of a personal relationship. (Hine 2002, 180)

This is a nice illustration of how mass markets and family rituals interact. Studies of reduced consumption reveal the difficulty of abandoning gift-giving practices. For example, in an interview study of voluntary simplifiers, religious environmentalists, and green homeowners in the United States, Janet Lorenzen (2017) found that each of these groups found it more difficult to reduce or avoid gift-giving than other types of consumption. Doing so entailed the most pervasive interpersonal challenge for reducing consumption, as gifts are highly symbolic of social relations. Successfully reducing gift-giving among family members and relatives requires mutual agreement, she found, and this normally was the result of a long-term negotiation process. Changes involved giving less resource-intensive gifts (such as concert tickets, though they are still a commodity) or giving gifts framed as "green" (also still a commodity). But attempts to refrain from gift-giving altogether were rarely successful (see also Callmer 2019, 94–95, 118). My own interview study of downsizers confirms how important gift-giving is and how difficult it is to abandon the ritual of exchanging Christmas/birthday presents with relatives and acquaintances (Boström 2021c). Altering the practices of gift-giving is provocative, contentious, and accordingly very demanding. Social solidarity is threatened. Emotional energies are at stake.

Text Box 1.2: Gift Rituals and the History of Christmas

The history of Christmas in Europe and North America in the nineteenth century was closely tied to the development of bourgeois middle-class ideology (Hamlin 2003). Christmas became a family affair emphasizing children. "Christmas redressed the balance between immediate expression of affection and the securing of long-term socialization interests" (Hamlin 2003, 862). The long-term interests Hamlin refers to concern the child's education, discipline, and cultural sophistication (social class distinction). But the intimate social and emotional bonds had to be secured as well, and Christmas became the key event. What is important here is that the toys were not supposed to be too closely connected with educational interests. Instead they were a tool for renewing emotional connections in the family. Happiness and immediate pleasure became the goal of the Christmas gift. Desire, manifested by the wish list, came to be accepted as a fundamental part of Christmas. Children must desire things. Otherwise, there is no way for parents to be able to give them things they believe they want. "Desire was to be stoked in others so that it could be satisfied with a gift ritual which solidified the emotional bonds of the family" (Hamlin 2003, 864).

People also give gifts to themselves—self-gifts. This was the topic of a well-cited paper by Mick and Demoss (1990), who empirically studied self-gifts in an American context. They found that people do it both as a reward (I deserve this; I am special) and as therapy (To cheer me up when I feel down; I need an escape). Like other gifts, a self-gift is highly symbolic. It represents a communicative act with oneself and relates to one's sense of identity (a topic discussed in Chapter 2). The item bought and perceived as a self-gift is often something extra and cannot be mundane, for example a fashionable article of clothing, a special haircut, a vacation. A self-gift can be something small, a "treat" (Miller 1998), such as a chocolate bar placed in the cart when buying groceries at the supermarket. Or it can be something large to mark a significant achievement, such as a graduation, which the achiever may feel should be celebrated with a new car. The theme of deserving a reward can even be generalized into a metanarrative and stretch over long periods of time: "I have spent my whole life working hard and contributing to society, and now I deserve my higher living standard." (On justification strategies, see concluding chapter.)

BEING ALONE AND CONSUMERISM

If social relationships are an important vehicle for excess consumption, then a lack of them—being alone—should arguably result in lower consumption. Indeed, due to their limited social networks, solitary people are not subject to some of the social triggers of consumption, as explained above and in later chapters. Roberta Sassatelli suggests: "The density of a consumer's purchases may reflect the density of his or her social networks" (2007, 85). Likewise, Daniel Miller (1998) found that one of the individuals in his study expressed how shopping became meaningless because of a lack of social relationships. "Concern for particular goods tends to come from the development rather than from the absence of meaningful relationships. An inability to relate to people usually means an inability to relate to goods also. As such, Christine finds little pleasure in shopping" (Miller 1998, 34).

It is difficult to generalize from this observation, however. Even if some solitary people consume less, others may do the opposite. Solitary people do orient toward groups, communities, and society at large, and consumption is a means for doing so. Indeed, the emptiness and loneliness felt by some solitary individuals in highly individualized societies are compensated by social aspects of consumption. Plenty of research shows that there are socio-psychological consumption triggers for solitary people as well. Such people may consume as compensation for a lack of social relationships, as a way to engage in social life, albeit in an artificial and superficial way, or to avoid the risk of social exclusion.

A recent literature review fleshes out these points. In the wake the COVID-19 pandemic, which has most likely caused isolation and loneliness around the world, Xueqin Wang and colleagues (2021) conducted a systematic literature review on the topic of loneliness and how it connects with consumption. They synthesized insights gained from loneliness studies conducted before the pandemic. Based on previous studies, they show that loneliness can trigger consumption in many ways. A key insight is that the act of shopping or procuring various goods and services can enable consumers to compensate for a lack of social interaction in their lives. One topic in the literature is how solitary consumers find a sense of involvement and some humanlike companionship by participating in brand communities, playing online games, or engaging in similar activities. For some, branded goods can be fetishized and serve almost as life partners, and social media can be used to cultivate such brand communities (Laroche et al. 2013). For solitary elderly people, nostalgic products can help them reconnect with the past and restore a feeling of belongingness with the social circumstances of the period that the product is associated with (Loveland et al. 2010). Segments of solitary consumers may adopt strikingly materialist lifestyles and see products as a substitute for interpersonal relationships. People at risk of social exclusion may also orient their spending in (often very excessive) ways that increase their chances of maintaining social relations (Mead et al. 2011).

For the socially excluded, technological innovations and the virtual world may come to the rescue. Digital gaming communities are one example, and another is the procurement of sex through online activities using digital platforms such as OnlyFans. Artificial intelligence takes these possibilities to another level. Some objects have built-in humanlike features. The concept of anthropomorphism is used to refer to the tendency of consumers to attribute humanlike features to nonhuman agents. These may "evoke consumers' sympathy and feelings of relatedness" (Wang et al. 2021, 11). Examples include humanlike brand mascots and smiling brand logos. Recent developments within AI can bring sophisticated humanlike features to the virtual world, with game characters able to speak seemingly natural language and capable of subtle nuances of facial expression. Hence, the solitary consumer may feel socially involved with the assistance of various internet and home-entertainment services such as games, gaming communities, streaming services, sex and intimate services, therapy, and communities related to these streaming services. Household robots are becoming popular and are given names. COVID-19 has triggered an increased demand for pets.

Some segments of solitary consumers may prefer the traditional marketplace and long for physical social encounters and brief conversations with service providers and salespeople. Market transactions do provide some opportunities for socializing with concrete human beings, albeit on a superficial level. This requires transactions, however. You ought to buy something if you go to the café. The crowded, noisy, and cluttered shopping environment helps to create some sense of social relatedness with society.

These examples show that solitary people also orient themselves socially by their consumption. Goods and services are procured as compensation for a lack of social interaction. At the same time, social interaction, even if distanced, artificial, or superficial, is what they are seeking with their consumption practices. The examples indicate that much of solitary consumer behavior can be interpreted in terms of Collins's model of social rituals. They are basically seeking the emotional energy contained in the consumption rituals. An imagined social solidarity and bonding can be found in the brands, games, conversation communities, and associated symbols. These sources of emotional energy may be of an inferior kind and be unable to do much to alleviate the psychologically distressing feeling of loneliness, but they are nonetheless sufficient to get solitary people to continue engaging with mass consumption society. Indeed, playing their part in the technologically mediated consumer culture is the only means many solitary people have for societal involvement. The many "virtual" products and services that are consumed online depend for their very existence on this mounting demand for high-tech electronics and home-entertainment technology.

SHOPPING RITUALS

The very practice of shopping—including searching for, trying on, and selecting products; chasing discounts; and engaging in the market transaction when purchasing the products—is crucial to consider in any analysis of everyday rituals in the area of consumption. Shopping has many ritual ingredients and outcomes. People shop for the sake of shopping, often together with friends and family members, as a way of spending time together with a mutual focus of attention—including with salespeople—and generating (for many) positive emotional energy (see also chapter 4 on malls and entertainment as well as digital shopping). In this section I will discuss shopping rituals in terms of four subthemes: (1) shopping with peers; (2) collecting; (3) compulsive buying; and (4) chasing discounts/thrift.

The first theme is shopping with peers. Miller (1998) has described how group shopping by family members and friends is often important for maintaining and building up relationships. Partners shopping together can figure out tastes they have in common, evaluate goods, pick up items they normally would overlook if alone, try to imagine new possibilities, and socialize in other ways.[10] By shopping, one can figure out if one is the kind of person who buys this or that product. Shopping can even provide an opportunity for solitary people to meet others and engage in conversation in the outside world, though on a superficial level. The interaction between consumer and seller may provide a short but potentially interesting and emotionally charged meeting. The product serves as the mutual focus of attention, something to discuss and become fascinated by: qualities, functions, attributes, aesthetics, variants, components, production history. The negotiation and deal can be thrilling. Also, in his book *Shopping as an Entertainment Experience* (2007), Mark Moss describes shopping as a social venue.

> As satisfying as shopping can be on a personal or psychological level, within the realm of entertainment and leisure, shopping also serves as a highly social function for many people. It brings them together in certain places, allows them to interact, and even connect, in others. (Moss 2007, 82)

Shoppers can even be emotionally attached to a specific shopping location, such as a mall, "through the interaction shoppers have with shopping pals with whom they have strong social ties" (Chebat et al. 2014, 77). The arousal that a shopping partner expresses for a specific good can be critical factor in inducing one's own spending. Through the acts of shopping and spending, people not only confirm their relationships with members of their social networks, but may also demonstrate loyalty to the shopping place as well as more abstract norms and discourses, including the economic growth paradigm, a desire to support local businesses, and the norm of consuming to help keep the economy going.

A second theme is rituals of collecting. Collecting can be a strong motivator for shopping excessively. People collect all sorts of things: stamps, art, books, fashion, tableware, vinyl records, alcoholic drinks, kitsch, stuffed animals, and—for the very rich—sports cars. This is also a ritual practice, even if it can take very individual forms. "Many collectors who are inhibited and uncomfortable in social interaction, surround themselves with favored objects upon which they project humanlike qualities. They practically talk to these objects; they find comfort in being with them and regard them as friends" (Goldberg and Lewis, quoted in Belk 1988, 154).

Collector's items are sacred objects, and as such are a source of emotional energy for the collector. They are something to show to one's peers—maybe a community of other collectors—and engage in conversation about. Ambiguities arise when rituals of collecting are viewed in relation to excess consumption. On one hand, collecting could be associated with carefulness, as a collector may search for a few very treasured objects and focus on quality rather than quantity. On the other hand, excessiveness is almost part of the very definition of being a collector. There is no sufficiency. One cannot have too many of the sacred objects. One is driven to achieve completeness, constantly chasing a larger share and trying to fill the remaining gaps. This chase is ritualistic and may become obsessive. Moreover, the practice of collecting appears to legitimize excess as such:

> One might be a collector of knickknacks in the form of a favored ("totemic") animal, of salt and pepper shakers, or of golden oak furniture. As with more widespread collections of family photographs, record albums, and clothing items such as shoes or hats, both the items included and the order imposed on them are expressive of one's identity. We may not be able to control much of the world about us, but the collection, whether of dolls, "depression glass," or automobiles, allows us total control of a "little world." Furthermore, collecting *legitimizes acquisitiveness*. (Belk 1988, 154; emphasis added)

Rituals of collecting may not be restricted to physical objects, but can also involve "collecting" experiences. People may "collect" places they have visited, like countries, cities, mountains, and so on, in effect contributing to the tourism industry and experience economy. John Urry (2010, 200) connects such "collectors of places" to his analysis of our contemporary, very mobile form of life, particularly among the richest segments of the global population.

Thirdly, compulsive buying is another consumer/shopping issue, with close connections to that of excessiveness, and which has attracted much attention in consumer psychology (see e.g. Dittmar 2008; Japutra et al. 2022; Muller et al. 2022). A classic paper on the topic is the one by Thomas O'Guinn and Robert Faber (1989). By surveying and interviewing members of self-help groups, they found that compulsive buyers derived much more positive emotion from the buying process than from the possession of purchased objects. The positive emotions were connected to the social environment and the exchange involved in the buying. The things bought were often perceived as having little practical utility after the purchase.

> Shopping for clothes, cosmetics, and gifts creates an interaction in which the salesperson dotes, telling buyers how attractive they look, what a good parent they are, or how much someone will appreciate them for giving this gift. These interactions provide the compulsive buyer with enhanced feelings of self-esteem. (O'Guinn and Faber 1989, 154)

Among compulsive buyers, a purchase can be triggered by various contextual circumstances in the shopping location, for instance discounts or a friendly salesperson who is skilled at demonstrating products. By shopping, such buyers hope to facilitate positive social interaction, and shopping appears to be a short-term antidote for feelings of anxiety, loneliness, and low self-esteem. Negative consequences abound, however: high levels of debt, frustration, feelings of shame and guilt, marital difficulties, loss of friends and loss of control over one's own life (see also concluding chapter). Compulsive buying could also be triggered by symbols of rituals such as brands. Research has indicated a relation between brand attachment and compulsive buying (Japutra et al. 2022). Compulsive buying is labeled "abnormal," but how wide is the gray zone of behaviors that we regard as normal today?

Finally, one more shopping ritual must be explored before concluding: the ritualistic chasing of discounts. Black Friday is perhaps the most obvious and dramatic example of this. Yet, the dramatic scenes where people, having already waited in line for many hours, rush and fight their way to the inexpensive products is just an extreme manifestation of a much larger phenomenon. In her book *Cheap: The High Cost of Discount Culture*, the American journalism professor, Ellen Ruppel Shell, highlights a critical question: Why are all sorts of products so cheap? Why are we so disposed to look for the "good deal"? She argues that Americans—and most of her observations would certainly hold for many populations elsewhere, such as in Europe—have developed something of a mania for getting a "good deal." Seeking out low prices has become an end in itself. Low prices are, after all, democratic and can be tied to such values as efforts to deal with income inequality and (relative) poverty (see also chapter 2). Everyone has the right to some everyday luxuries, the culture says. However, discount culture means that consumers become more focused on getting a "good deal" than on the object that is at the heart of that deal. The author has a name for this culture: the Age of Cheap. Cheap culture reproduces mass consumption because it affords high levels of consumption to the masses.

Daniel Miller (1998) provides more insights into the ritualistic aspects of the hunt for cheap goods. Even if there are strong cultural norms around thriftiness, which are associated with other values than immediate gratification of desires, saving can, perhaps paradoxically, be very much related to spending. As a personal experience, saving is not the same thing as actually spending less money. Thrift, Miller argues, is very much an end in itself, especially among elderly people.

Miller observed the notorious and systematic hunt for lower prices. We often relate shopping skills to the ability to engage in thrifty behavior. Paradoxically, however, the shoppers he studied generally lacked knowledge about prices at the same time as they were constantly looking for discounts. Few of the studied people knew the standard prices of most basic goods, although they looked for bargains. They sought out low-price brands, discounts, reflected on the size of packaging, and so on. There is no need to know the exact price, it seems. The point is to feel like one has gotten a good deal.

Shopping can even create an impression of saving money. A wide range of strategies can enable shoppers to have that impression, and it is even possible "to regard virtually the whole of the shopping expedition, not as an act of spending at all, but as an act of saving" (Miller 1998, 56).

The impression of saving by spending has some irrational aspects. It is possible for people to be aware of the contradiction and nonetheless be unable to resist it. Here is an illustrative quote from one of his interviews:

> **Q:** Why do you buy cheaper clothes?
>
> **A:** Because I like buying clothes, and I can't keep going out and buying expensive ones! Sometimes most of the clothes that I've got that were more expensive I like very much, and last longer, but somehow the logic still doesn't quite sink through. You'll still get tempted by the odd bargain that probably really isn't a bargain (Miller 1998, 60).

For some, Miller argues, the thrill—or emotional energy, as Collins would say—lies in the bargain. Thrift is the goal, not the means. People shop to have an experience of saving money. This behavior is observed among people regardless of income level. As Text Box 1.3 shows, this behavior can also be strongly related to hedonistic motivations.

Thrift must be viewed in relation to the situation, Miller says. Often, shoppers are balancing concerns about saving money against other factors such as a search for social status, which may require buying expensive goods. It is thus necessary to find a compromise between the perceived need to chase discounts and chasing status. The strategies of thrift are weighed against other motivations such as identity, class belonging, status aspirations, reputation, and so on, factors which will be explored in coming chapters.

Text Box 1.3: Thrift: Economic and Hedonistic Motivations

In an ethnographic study of "thrift shoppers" in a midwestern US town, Bardhi and Arnould (2004) build on Miller's theory of thrift, but with greater stress on how economic and hedonistic dimensions blend in thrift shopping. Searching for bargains can be a fun and exhilarating activity, even a hobby, and can coincide with rituals of collecting. Thrift—in the form of seeking unexpected bargains—can also be a way to justify indulgence: "consumers used thrift as a cultural resource to justify the realization of their desires and wasteful purchasing practice" (Bardhi and Arnould 2004, 231). Bardhi and Arnould also stress the social role of bargain hunting; there is often a social aspect of thrift shopping, as the thrift shoppers may keep an eye out for items they know someone else in their social network needs. Combinations of economic and hedonistic motivations were also found in an interview study of secondhand consumption in two economically disadvantaged regions in Romania, a country where the secondhand retail sector has been flourishing (Nistor 2022). Interviewees reported both economic (saving) and hedonistic reasons (leisure, bargain hunting, socializing, finding unique clothes) for their frequent practice of shopping in secondhand outlets. A few also supplied ethical-environmental motivations. One young woman said, "I've come to realize that buying in second-hand shops saves me more money so I can buy other things that are important for me" (Nistor 2022, 81), which illustrates why secondhand shopping may spur rather than prevent consumerism and excess consumption. A key conclusion of Nistor (2022, 90) is that "the lower price of products in second-hand shops allows consumers to really buy and to really feel part of consumer society."

Text Box 1.4.: Invitation to Reflect on Opportunities for Change

How can you foster social relationships by engaging in joint activities that rely less, or not at all, on consuming commodities? What kinds of everyday rituals would be as or more rewarding in terms of creating high emotional energy as well as bolstering group solidarity, while at the same time having a significantly smaller climate/ecological footprint than current practices? Think of walking, cycling, playing, vacationing, engaging in alternative gift rituals, slow cooking, attending cultural events like plays and concerts, engaging in sports, cultivating a skill, gardening, engaging in joint activities in civil society and the community, inventing rituals for sharing stuff and services, and so on. Do you think you would gain new insights about consumption norms and the embeddedness of consumption in social interaction and relationships by trying out a temporary buy-nothing period? How can society/communities facilitate social relations and ways of taking care of each other through forms of interaction—interaction rituals—that are less connected with consumption? Apart from consumption, what could be the focus of group attention and activities, and how can society/communities facilitate the contexts and requisites for such alternative activities? What types of digital or physical infrastructure need to be in place in cities, workplaces, schools, buildings, and structures? How can a culture that is less permeated by consumerism be nurtured?

CONCLUSION

This chapter has emphasized how consumerism and consumption are very much part of the establishment and maintenance of social relations among couples, families, relatives, friends, and colleagues. Consumption-laden everyday rituals give rise to many positive emotional energies and social bonds, as well as symbols and moral standards, and all these ritual outcomes create self-reinforcing feedback loops. Any attempt to explain and understand mass consumption must include this aspect of social life. Consumer items are central objects of attention, as important symbols for groups, and as contexts and requisites of social rituals. We cannot fully understand the omnipresence of consumerism in social life if we only view consumption as an end in itself. Social relations are key. Even solitary people consume in order to compensate for a lack of social relationships, as an expression of an aspiration to belong, or even as a way of enjoying something that is artificially humanlike. People may be subtly or acutely aware and critical of the dominance of consumerism in their everyday life and yet still be unable to fully resist it. They may also be aware of excessive levels of consumption yet continue reproducing them because their social relationships are too important to risk losing. Social norms and expectations are demanding. The risk of social exclusion is as life-threatening as any disease. The risks involved in consuming too little may be felt as particularly intolerable if children are involved. Whether the driving force is a search for positive emotional energy in social bonding, or fear of lagging behind in consumption standards, the conclusion is the same: intimate social relationships are a highly potent fuel for continuing consumption practices, and a serious barrier to cutting down on consumption. The theory of interaction ritual chains accordingly provides a good start for the analysis of how mass consumption is deeply integrated into social life. But social relations and social life affect consumption in other ways as well. The next topic to consider is drivers connected to social comparison. Before you turn the page, you can reflect on opportunities for change (see Text Box 1.4).

NOTES

1. I am grateful for constructive comments by Rolf Lidskog and Helen Peterson on an earlier version of this chapter, as well as to an anonymous reviewer.
2. For a recent overview of theories and examples of rituals in everyday life, and how these rituals are an important social glue, see Kišjuhas 2023.
3. There are affinities also with "social practices." Social practice theory sees social life as a series of recursive practices. It focuses on the habitual nature of agency and how agency is connected to social-material arrangements and situated in time and space. However, the cultural/symbolic dimension tend to be less focused on or even neglected (see e.g. Rinkinen et al. 2021). For an attempt to integrate ritual theory and social practice theory in consumer research, see Spaargaren 2011.
4. The dramaturgical concepts of script and role, derived from Goffman, are stressed in Rook's (1985) definition of rituals. However, they fit well into Collins's model, which is also based on Goffman's work.
5. This understanding of shame and pride is taken from sociologist Thomas Scheff, who argued that these are genuinely social emotions. Shame covers a range of emotions related to feeling foolish, awkward, stupid, ridiculous, incompetent, exposed, and so on. Pride is rooted in the process by which we internalize how we think others see us.
6. My own empirical studies of voluntarily reduced consumption include Boström 2021c, and 2022.
7. For research on this topic, see e.g., Boström 2021b; Echegaray et al. 2021.
8. There are several recent comprehensive literature reviews about the phenomenon of voluntary simplicity and downsizing, including analyses of the socio-demographics and motivations of the participants. See García-de-Frutos, Ortega-Egea, and

Martínez-del-Río 2018; Osikominu and Bocken 2020; Lee, Ortega-Egea, Manuel et al. 2020; Rebouças and Soares 2020.

9. One study, published in *Science*, showed that spending money on others led to more happiness than spending money on oneself. Dunn et al. (2008) used survey data of the American population as well as longitudinal and experimental evidence as support for that claim. These results, indicating a prosocial and otherness orientation in shopping and spending, link very well with Daniel Miller's ethnographic findings and arguments about how shopping can be viewed as an act of love and care.

10. See also Mangleburg et al. (2004) on how, among teens, shopping with friends can induce more spending through the mechanism of peer influence. Such effects are not limited to the physical shopping environment, but can be activated by social media as well (Hu et al. 2019).

Chapter 2

Social Comparison and Consumerism in Stratified Social Life

As human beings we engage in all kinds of comparisons about status, appearance, and achievements.[1] This inclination toward social comparison is one general driver of consumerism. A range of sub-drivers are also connected to social comparison within stratified social life. In the previous chapter, social life was pictured as a sphere of personal relations and everyday rituals. Social life is also stratified in more distant, indirect social relations. What I have in mind here is a social infrastructure (see Introduction) consisting of stratification in terms of social hierarchies and distinctions: occupations, classes, status groups, gender divisions, and more. This chapter will show how such differentiation and social comparison spur consumerism, and consequently promote ecologically destructive mass consumption.

In sociology, social stratification and comparison are not new topics. Sociology and social psychology have a long and rich tradition of studying how consumption and consumer culture relate to social inclusion and exclusion. On one hand, we consume to seek affiliation and integration within communities. On the other hand, we consume to demonstrate exclusivity and differentiation. All of this is based on social comparisons, and a society that is differentiated (vertically and horizontally) with regard to gender, class, ethnic group, age, income, education and occupation provides many reference points for comparison. Group belonging/distinction involves specific tastes and status markers and different shades of consumption.

This chapter explores theories, concepts, and research that help us understand the links between societal stratification, social comparison, and consumerism. I draw on general concepts such as identity, status, and inequality to uncover important drivers. This is combined with a range of empirical research providing evidence on the importance of comparison in stratified social life. The chapter starts by introducing three specific themes: luxury, brands, and social media. Each of these is important for understanding key aspects of social comparison. These subsections can be read as illustrative case studies and serve as a way to introduce aspects related to social comparison that will be further delved into in the following sections. The section then discusses the role of identity, including socialization. The concept of the extended self is employed to show how consumerism and possessions are important for identity formation at various ages. Identity relies on social comparison with reference groups and is a matter of both fitting in and appearing unique via consumption. The role of unattainable (gender) ideals is stressed. The next section draws on contemporary research and classic sociological concepts, such as conspicuous consumption and cultural capital, to review how the hunt for status and processes of distinction drive consumerism. The section on inequality continues this analysis, and with the help of theories of relative deprivation, it shows how an aura of consumerism and material values spreads to all parts of society.

THREE THEMES: LUXURY, BRANDS, AND SOCIAL MEDIA

Luxury

The search for luxury has been a basic driver in human societies for perhaps as long as humans have existed. In many eras and societies, the possession of goods considered to be luxuries has been a means to display oneself as distinguished and powerful. Luxury is a tool to show that one belongs to the most noble and exclusive group—those few who are powerful and really understand good culture. Another drive connected to luxury is hedonism: the enjoyment of the pleasures of life and chasing of novel experiences (Campbell 2018 [1987]). Luxury can also be associated with rewards and awards. It is the remuneration for lifetime of hard work, or for impressive or heroic achievements, such as victory in warfare.

A luxury item signals expensiveness, exclusivity, desire, beauty, pleasure, and enjoyment. Luxury is not a need, nor is it indispensable. One could do without it. Social groups may overtly or tacitly agree about what items that are luxurious, but a subjective element is also involved (Walters and Carr 2019). What is a luxury to one person may be ordinary to someone else. Also, what is broadly considered luxurious changes throughout history and across societies.

Luxury is a classic conceptual category employed to distinguish between high- and low-quality goods. People use luxury goods to communicate who they are (identity), and because society is stratified, it is important to display that you are among the successful ones (status). Historically, there has been an affinity between luxury and relatively durable, stable products (Sassatelli 2007). Examples are precious metals and gemstones. These luxury items stand for permanence and reliability. Almost by definition, such luxury consumption is meant for the most distinguished, for those few that can afford it. They serve well for the task of distinguishing: namely to exclude others. However, the drive to possess luxury items grew among broader segments of the population. Therefore, luxury became an important early driver of the emergence and development of capitalism and for what we today recognize as consumer culture (Campbell 2018 [1987]; Trentmann 2016).[2] Luxury helped to create new markets that paved the way for capitalism and industrialism. Everyday luxuries such as paintings, ceramics, and textiles, as well as ornamental personal accessories such as umbrellas, gloves, and buttons grew in importance as popular commodities from the second half of the seventeenth century. Food items such as sugar, coffee, tea, and cocoa played an even more important role in revolutionizing consumption (Sassatelli 2007; Trentmann 2016). The democratization of luxury gradually emerged as an important driver in class struggles. Other goods, such as sugar and sweetened bitter drinks became the first "democratic luxuries" (Sassatelli 2007, 40). A public sentiment grew in welfare societies that everyone should have the right to some pieces of luxury. Luxury created fantasies and became something to dream about, something to aspire to, and a cause of jealousy and crime.

There is somewhat of a contradiction between luxury consumption and mass consumption. On one hand, the idea of luxury appears to be associated with something that is only accessible to the few and distinguished, people with plenty of money and power. On the other hand, through its popularization or democratization, luxury is something to which the masses aspire. This second idea is perpetuated by widespread cultural frames about prosperity, progress, and the happy family life. Nonetheless, luxury goods are not associated with bulk and mundane everyday goods, but with more extraordinary goods, things that are expensive and rare. The relation between luxury goods and mass/excess consumption is therefore somewhat ambiguous. On one hand, the search for luxury feeds consumerism. On the other hand, expensive luxury goods may only retain their value as luxuries because they are rare.

Brands

Luxury and brands intersect in luxury brands.

> By wearing, displaying or purchasing some facet of the world of Ralph Lauren, one is demonstrating that one possesses "class" or more accurately, the

> disposable income to don these clothes. It is as if the polo, the button down, the tasseled loafers or the tweed jacket gives one a *pass* into a dream world of taste, manners, old money and refinement. From the golf photos to the picnics, from yachting to the antique cars, the shorthand implied is a level of status and taste that was once the preserve of the elite but that now can be available to anyone with the sense/cents to buy. (Moss 2007, 92)

Expensive branded goods and designer logos are to be desired by most people. There are markets that also have brands for people with less money. A logo has its paradoxical power because it combines mass consumption (similarity) and originality (difference). The logo solves the (capitalist) problem of how to mass-produce the perceived value of originality.

The system of commercialization of goods began to take its modern form from the beginning of the eighteenth century (Sassatelli 2007, 5) with techniques of product promotion, advertising, and shop display, among other things. The brand/logo gradually became more essential to consumer culture and capitalism. Branding changed the retail landscape. Brands offer standards of quality. They give goods an identity. They save time because people know what they demand and what they will get. There is a great deal of information stored in a brand:

> The declining authority of the store and its representative the salesclerk is almost entirely the result of the increasing authority of the brand. No matter what they are buying, today's shoppers arrive at the store with a clear idea of the characteristics, the quality, and the meanings of hundreds, or even thousands, of branded products (Hine 2002, 195–96).

> I can't sell a shirt without a logo. If I put a shirt without a logo on my selling floor next to a shirt with a logo—same shirt, same color, same price—the one with the logo will blow it out. It will sell 10 times over the one without the logo. It's a status thing as well. It really is. (Tommy Hilfiger, cited in Schor 1998, 46)

Brands and branding are central to contemporary consumer society (Thompson and Arsel 2004; Goldman and Papson 2006). Through branding, large businesses exercise enormous power to produce and specify identities, pleasures, rewards, joy, and aspirations (Holt 2002). They encourage the development of *brand communities* (Muniz and O'Guinn 2001), in order to create *brand loyalty* (Boström 2019). Consumers even self-organize brand communities and develop social ties, identities, and interaction rituals (see chapter 1) around brands (Pepsi vs. Coke, Macintosh vs. PC, Ferrari vs. BMW).

Brands and branding drive consumerism because they are so firmly integrated within consumer culture and the stratified social life. Even very young children can recognize brand names. Preferences for advertised brand names may be present in children as early as two years of age (Dittmar 2008, 175). Even well before the teenage years, children perceive brands with symbolic meanings as conveying status, prestige, and trendiness (Schor 2004; Piacentini and Mailer 2004; Banerjee and Dittmar 2008; Zhou and Wong 2008). Brands find their way into different consumer segments: luxury brands for distinguished segments, and other (imitation) brands for broader segments (Kim et al. 2018). There are brands for people who love the existence of brands, and there are brands for people that hate brands: "manufacturers can produce a product with 'loud' or conspicuous branding or tone it down to 'quiet' or discreet branding to appeal to different types of consumers" (Han et al. 2010, 15).

Some companies skillfully employ social media to foster online brand communities (Laroche et al. 2013). For instance, the company (brand) Jeep and its users are cocreators of an online brand community, with brand loyalty as the ultimate business goal:

> People join them [brand communities on social media] and other such sites and use words, videos, pictures, and avatars to stay in touch with their friends, make new friends, make plans with them, have fun and flirt with them, exchange pleasantries and argue, engage in intellectual discourse, conduct commerce, exchange knowledge, share emotional support, brainstorm, gossip, feud, fall in love, find friends, play games, create a little high talk and a lot of idle talks. (Laroche et al. 2013, 1757)

Social Media

People, especially the younger generations, spend hours every day on social media such as Facebook, Tinder, TikTok, Snapchat, Instagram, YouTube, Tumblr, Twitter, and more (Hruska and Maresova 2020). Social media has become a key platform for marketing and product promotion, via influencers, fashion bloggers, and celebrities. It is effective because social media users are active creators of messages; they exchange "user-generated" content. They actively engage with firms, brands, and other consumers to share insights and experiences and learn from others' experiences. People use social media to discuss, to compare, to seek, and to obtain social confirmation. The ability to create, share, comment, critique, and endorse makes social media an important social space for peer interactivity. Did I get enough likes?

Social media stretches people's reference groups, that is, groups that people look up to and try to imitate. Before the social media revolution, Juliet Schor (1998) published her book *The Overspent Americans*, in which she used the concept of reference groups. People traditionally found their reference groups within the same socioeconomic class as themselves and in the concrete networks of families in the local area. This changed with the growth of the advertising industry and media. Media stretched the reference groups vertically: "TV inflates our sense of what's normal" (Schor 1998, 80). TV and other media created reference groups consisting of role models and celebrities who were very much richer than the audience. Hence, TV fueled incentives for people to measure and boost themselves with reference to idealized groups with income levels many times higher than their own. This new mediascape increased consumer aspirations, but also a sense of dissatisfaction with what one has, thus creating a vicious cycle of spending. Social media has accelerated all this.

While TV may continue be important, social media is adding much fuel to the fire. There are unlimited opportunities for people to compare themselves with distant others.[3] Posts on Instagram, TikTok, and Facebook give the impression that others are doing better than oneself. Materialist and consumerist ideals around the "glam life" or "good life" are spread by fashion bloggers (Duffy and Hund 2015) and in Instagram posts (Loukianov et al. 2019). Studies have found that more frequent users of Facebook also engage more in negative social comparison; that is, having the perception that others are doing/having better and more than oneself. This can in turn lead to negative evaluations of one's social competence and physical attractiveness (de Vries and Kühne 2015), and such negative self-evaluation feeds consumerism (Dittmar 2008).

Thus, if groups with high status—like influencers, fashion bloggers, and celebrities—spread consumerist values and increase their consumption levels,[4] other groups will have to lift their gaze to a higher reference point, pushing the social game upward.[5]

IDENTITY

The above three sections on luxury, brands, and social media provide a starting point for elaborating a bit more deeply on consumerist drivers related to comparison. The first topic to look at is identity, and a good place to begin is the notion of the extended self.

The Extended Self and Unattainable Ideals

"It seems an inescapable fact of modern life that we learn, define, and remind ourselves of who we are by our possessions," says Russell Belk (1988, 160) in a pioneering article about consumption and identity. Belk argues that people tend to regard possessions as part of themselves, as their "extended self." He cites evidence from a variety of disciplines and sources from historical and contemporary contexts, as well as in different cultural contexts.[6] Objects that can be considered "mine" can easily be thought of as "me." Having is intimately connected with being and with the ability to do things. "People seek, express, confirm, and ascertain a sense of being through what they have" (Belk 1988, 146).

Belk found that people tend to view others—"my wife," "my children," "I have a relationship"—in possessive terms and as objects that are important in forming oneself and one's own identity: "you are the company you keep." The line between "me" and "mine" can be diffuse and difficult to draw. The loss of loved ones, by divorce or death, is often seen as a loss of an important part of oneself. The loss of valued objects, due to theft, damage, or destruction, can lead to grief and mourning. Victims of natural disasters that wreck properties or neighborhoods can express grief similar to that caused by the loss of a loved person. People miss not only the use value of things, but also the feelings and memories associated with them.

How can objects be so important to us? One answer is that in modern consumer culture possessions are an important part of identity formation early in life. Social psychologist Helga Dittmar (2008) has spent many years conducting empirical research on the link between identity, materialism, and (excessive) consumption. Building on Belk's concept of the extended self and several other theories, she argues that people are identity seekers, and consumption is a means for identity formation. Even if material goods can have a positive function by enhancing or maintaining our sense of who we are, there is a dark side of contemporary consumer culture and the aggressive advertising industry, she claims.

The concept of identity consists of both a personal and a social dimension. Each person has multiple identities, involving a diverse set of self-representations. Identity deficits can appear if one's self-image clashes with an internalized ideal identity. The "body perfect" and the material "good life" are two conceptual constructs that Dittmar developed to study how consumer culture negatively affects the mental and physical well-being of people. Girls are socialized into learning that their bodies should be used to attract others: "They learn to see themselves as objects to be looked at and evaluated by appearance" (Dittmar 2008, 13). However, men also show high concern with appearance and bodily attractiveness, guided by the ideal of muscularity.

Dittmar draws on symbolic interactionism (George Herbert Mead),[7] arguing that sense of identity stems from the human ability for self-reflexivity, that is, viewing oneself from the perspective of the other. This requires a capacity for self-reference and role-taking in a context of socially shared meaning systems. Young children learn the symbolic meanings of material goods by observing and imaginatively taking part in others' interactions with objects. Gendered body-perfect ideals are communicated very early to children through dolls (e.g., the classic example of Barbie) and action figures. Her studies show that the internalization of such ideals is linked to materialist values; that is, desire for affluence and possessions.[8] Fitzmaurice and Comegys (2006) similarly found that people who endorse materialist values are also more sensitive to the social acceptability and communicative ability of products and brands: "High materialists depend more on projecting an identity to others by relying on the social meanings of consumer goods" (Fitzmaurice and Comegys 2006, 289).

Material possessions, however, are poor and unreliable tools for repairing broken identities and producing subjective well-being. The problem is social comparison, people's tendency to evaluate themselves critically with reference to unattainable (gendered) ideals and more successful peers. Individuals may look at themselves as inferior, as having identity deficits, and thus hope that consumption can solve the problem and bring them closer to their internalized ideals. Because material goods symbolize various qualities, individuals buy these goods in an attempt to remedy perceived inadequacies of their self-concept, to complete their identity. The gap between ideal and actual identity is rarely closed, however. Attempting to repair identities by acquiring material goods generally fails as a long-term solution. Unattainable ideals mean that non-satisfaction and unhappiness remain. As subsequent sections in this chapter will show, the unequal and stratified social life provides the conditions for unfavorable comparison. The consumerist drive to incessantly acquire material goods continues. This nonstop driver is captured in Figure 2.1, where the vertical, half-transparent blocking line symbolizes the impossibility/difficulty of reaching one's ideal, which triggers continuing efforts (back-and-forth arrow) to bridge the gap anyhow.

Children are especially vulnerable. Early in life they internalize the ideals of consumer culture: the body perfect and the idea of the materialist good life. Girls as young as five to seven years old want a thinner body after being

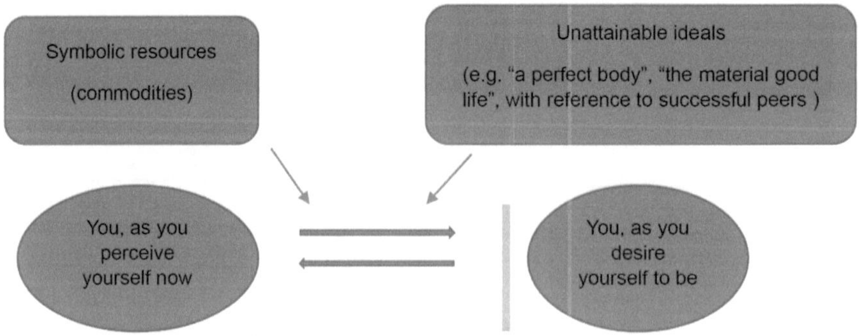

Figure 2.1. Identity Deficits and Consumerism. ***Source:*** **Author, based on Dittmar (2008).**

exposed to images of dolls such as Barbie (Dittmar 2008). Materialism is a significant aspect of eight- to eleven-year-old children's lives. Even young children are knowledgeable about the symbolic and status-signaling messages associated with branded consumer goods. Children learn what are the right games, clothes, shoes, and a host of other goods.

Particularly during the "identity crisis" of adolescence, young people embark on the process of seeking an identity by acquiring and accumulating selected consumption objects such as branded goods. Teenagers look to peers and social media influencers rather than their parents to find and define themselves, and consumption choices are crucial (Piacentini and Mailer 2004; Banerjee and Dittmar, 2008; Isaksen and Roper 2008; Solér 2018). Teenagers become increasingly concerned about self-presentation, peer-group norms, and social comparison and judgment.

Even if people's identities may become more stable as they grow older, the consumerist drive toward extending one's self can be important at all stages of life. For example, transitions in life are important. You move away from home. You get married, have children, find a new job. Your identities multiply, and each different part of the self—at work, at home, at a club—may have to be represented by a separate repertoire of personal decoration; hence, more stuff is needed. Getting your first job and an income of your own gives you fantastic new consumption opportunities. Something you could only dream of purchasing before is suddenly within reach. Consumer culture entices. You want to enlarge your extended self. Maybe it is finally possible to close the gap between ideal and the actual self. Or is it?

Belk argues that it is particularly during the middle years of life that people are likely to embody the most extended concept of self. It is as if you cannot be a respectable middle-aged person if you are not surrounded by a quite significant material landscape. The extended self must continuously swell. Not just for the sake of family rituals (chapter 1), but for confirming who you are: "A person who owns a nice home, a new car, good furniture, the latest appliances, is recognized by others as having passed the test of personhood in our society" (Csikszentmihalyi, quoted in Belk 1988, 148). You develop yourself as a respectable person by owning a nice house, a proper car, clothes with the right logos, *having* a family and rich social network, and so on. You should be able to talk about your experiences as well, such as the exotic trip to a distant destination, and post photos on Instagram. You focus on having, not being (Fromm 1976). Zygmunt Bauman argues that everyone is pushed to self-construction through consumption. I shop, therefore I am. I shop, therefore I am a sovereign individual, a subject (Bauman 2007, 17).[9]

In old age the extended self is still present, but possibly with fewer objects. Possessions are then often a means of storing memories and feelings from the past. Possessions remind one of valued life experiences and invoke nostalgia.

Late adulthood may be characterized by a retrospective life-review process (Dittmar 2008). Some objects, like photo albums, a piano, and other valued artifacts, remind one about important everyday rituals of the past and their associated emotional energies (chapter 1). Possessions are a record of one's personal history. Then we die. Many people seek to ensure that their selves, including their possessions, will extend beyond death by passing on their possessions as an inheritance to children and other cherished persons. Not everyone builds a pyramid, but quite a few try to shape the future destinations of their possessions.

The extended self is not only operating at the individual level, says Belk, but also at a collective level involving family, group, community, and subcultural and national identities. "Just as clothing, accent, grooming, and jewelry can distinguish an individual from others and express an individual sense of being, they can also indicate group identity and express belonging to a group" (Belk 1988, 153). Identity and self-expression through goods and possessions can be tied to personal values or religious beliefs, or be seen to represent one's profession, competences and achievements (Richins 1994). This collective dimension of the extended self meshes well with the insights about social bonding and emotional energies gained from the theory of interaction ritual chains discussed in the previous chapter.

A Paradox Drives Consumerism: Fitting In and Appearing Unique

Social belonging is a basic human need. As each of us fears social exclusion, social comparison plays a very significant role. Leon Festinger (1954) is famous for a few theories in social psychology, one of which is his social comparison theory, which emphasizes people's inclination to compare their opinions and abilities with those of others. People do so in a process of self-evaluation and to find groups in which to belong. We gravitate, he argues, toward groups whose members are relatively similar to us in terms of opinions and abilities. We form opinions and train our abilities for the sake of fitting in. This urge for uniformity may require consuming the right things, the stuff that a social group has defined as appropriate, respectable, and desirable.

Experimental psychological studies have shown that people who feel at risk of social exclusion are more likely to spend money on products symbolic of group membership as well as to tailor their choices to the preferences of an interaction partner (Mead et al. 2011). An interesting observation is that such experiences even increase the chances of buying unappealing products or engaging in risky behaviors such as drug consumption, if such consumption is seen as enhancing one's social connections. Lacking the "correct" possessions can lead to being bullied and socially excluded. This risk is naturally strongly felt among children and teenagers, who feel it is crucial to wear the right brands (Piacentini and Mailer 2004; Isaksen and Roper 2008). Banerjee and Dittmar (2008) found in a series of surveys that children (eight to eleven years in the UK) who experience "peer rejection" and pressure from schoolmates are more likely to develop materialist orientations such as desiring the right clothes, cosmetics, games, and other cool things. Chan and Prendergast (2007) report similar findings from Hong Kong. Certainly, fear of social exclusion is universal; it is human.

Accordingly, people who perceive a high risk of social exclusion may devote more thought and attention to how their consumption helps them to secure social connections. Their longing for respectable brands is primarily about wanting to fit in, and not to appear unique. Materialism is a compensatory strategy for a perceived lack of social connections or insecurity regarding them. Piacentini and Mailer (2004) conducted an interview study about symbolic aspects of clothing consumption among teenagers in Glasgow. One of the participants concisely summarizes what it is all about:

> Interviewer: Is it important for you to have branded clothes?
>
> Participant: Not really but I'd prefer to have it because it makes you mix in. You don't want to be any worse than what your friends have got and you don't want to be any better so you just get the same logos as your friends just to keep up with them . . . I wouldn't want to stand out of the crowd; I just want to be part of it. I wouldn't want to be the big man. (Male, fifteen years old, comprehensive school) (Piacentini and Mailer, 2004, 257)

The interview study showed, for example, that buying branded clothes was an important way to demonstrate that one was not poor (see also the section on inequality below). People look at reference groups to which they wish to belong and be associated with, but at the same time there are dissociative reference groups with which individuals do not want to be associated (White and Dahl 2006). These might, for example, be groups of people who do not consume enough or who have ugly clothes.

What complicates the matter is that a person in a culture that values individual expression also feel compelled to fit in, though, paradoxically, in a unique way. This increases the uncertainty and anxiety, which in turn feeds consumerism, because if you have more objects, you have a buffer from which you can mix appearances frequently. Moreover, what drives consumerism is that, in contemporary times (in contrast to the classic conception of identity as more of a life projected to be completed),[10] the "person," "personality," or "identity" is rarely assumed to be a finished project (see also chapter 3 on temporal aspects, including fashion). Consumption must remain an everyday struggle to incessantly re-create and develop one's identity. In terms of consumption, people are supposed to keep up with others, in order to fit in in a unique way. Dittmar unveils the individualistic myth contained in contemporary consumer culture and the paradox involved in individualized identity formation: "the idea that uniqueness can be achieved through mass-produced and mass-consumed goods is a paradox in and of itself" (Dittmar 2008, 213).

STANDING OUT: STATUS AND DISTINCTION

Part of belonging to a group is also showing which groups you are not associated with. I have already indicated the role of dissociative reference groups. Inclusion and exclusion are two sides of the same coin. An identity expresses both what one is and what one is not. There is a long tradition within the sociology of consumption of researching and demonstrating how status and differentiation fuel consumerism. Consumption is a tool for people to position and differentiate themselves in the social landscape. As seen above, luxury consumption, brands, and social media displays can help one fulfill this role.

A key sociological concept for exploring this phenomenon is social status. Social status represents one's rank in a social hierarchy and reflects the extent to which one is respected or admired by others. Status can be ascribed (by birth) or achieved (through work, profession, art, consumption, sports, etc.). According to the social psychologists David Dubois and Nailya Ordabayeva (2015), there are four ways of signaling one's social standing to others. First, obtaining status has to involve considerable cost (e.g., luxury brands) or be difficult (such as winning the world championship in long jump). Second, status signals rarely have practical value. Third, status signals are visible or recognizable by the members of the social group to which one wishes to signal one's status. Fourth, there is an agreement within this group about the value of a status signal. In addition, in order to qualify as "cultural capital," it must function as a status signal among a relatively large number of people in a society (Lamont and Lareau 1988).

Consumers use both explicit and implicit status signals (Dubois and Ordabayeva 2015).[11] They communicate their affiliations, including religion, gender, interests, favorite sport clubs, and hobbies, through where they travel and what they wear, eat, and drink. Volumes and frequencies may count too. People also express their values: "Through a sports car or casual clothes people may broadcast the message of the importance of their freedom and individualism" (Firat et al. 2013, 186). Status consumption can also be important to getting a job and finding a mate.

Classic sociology of consumption has provided key insights regarding the importance of consumption for boosting social status. "Fashion raises even the unimportant individual by making him the representative of a class, the embodiment of a joint spirit." wrote Georg Simmel (1971 [1904], 304–5). Fashion will be further discussed in chapter 3, while this section will focus more on the work of Veblen and Bourdieu. Thorstein Veblen's classic book *The Theory of the Leisure Class* (1994 [1899]) has become a standard reference, and is still very valid for the study of status consumption and for understanding contemporary consumerism despite being written more than 120 years ago.

Veblen's main interest was to provide a sharp critique of the nonproductive, conservative, and very wealthy leisure class,[12] which he argued was hampering social progress. Two of his famous concepts are *pecuniary emulation* and *conspicuous consumption*, both of which are important for the discussion here. As Veblen saw it, a basic motivation in social life, and a particular trait of the leisure class that has spread to the rest of society, is the striving for and display of social prestige or esteem: "visible success becomes an end sought for its own utility as a basis of esteem" (1994 [1899], 10). Striving for esteem in society is a competitive game. In modern society, property and economic wealth are what provide esteem. The concept "pecuniary emulation" refers to this effort to outcompete another person/group in terms of socioeconomic status, and the game is to be won by showing evidence of wealth. Conspicuous leisure or conspicuous consumption, that is, extravagant and wasteful consumption, provides the evidence. It is fundamentally important and "extremely gratifying to possess something more than others" (1994 [1899], 20). Veblen's concept of conspicuous consumption has been widely used in consumer studies, and the concept has often been interchanged with the concept of status consumption.[13]

A key driver for our understanding of consumerism and excessive consumption concerns social comparison and the restless, never-ending hunt for more:

> The end sought by accumulation is to rank high in comparison with the rest of the community in point of pecuniary strength. So long as the comparison is distinctly unfavourable to himself, the normal, average individual will live in chronic dissatisfaction with his present lot; and when he has reached what may be called the normal pecuniary standard of the community, or of his class in the community, this chronic dissatisfaction will give place to a restless straining to place a wider and ever-widening pecuniary interval between himself and this average standard. (Veblen 1994 [1899], 20)

This is a central observation in the work of Veblen. No one is really ever satisfied. If achieving status through consumption is a competition, then there is always a risk that one is lagging behind or others are catching up. The game must go on.

To signify wealth, consumption ought to be expensive and "useless" for practical purposes. Moreover, a member of the cultivated class must demonstrate excellence in drinking, eating, dressing, conversing, and so on, that is, give a demonstration of cultivated tastes. All this requires time and training.

While such norms of status consumption stem from the leisure class, they migrate downward in chains to the lowest strata of the social structure. The effect is that the members of each social stratum accept the ideals of decency in the next higher stratum, "and bend their energies to live up to that ideal" (1994 [1899], 52). Aspirations to live up to these ideals spread to the entire society, and everyone feels dissatisfied because the reference group is always a bit richer, except for the very few at the top. However, they too are dissatisfied with life, because they must incessantly work to maintain or increase the gap. Calming down is never an option.

Veblen argues that pecuniary emulation may not be as strong a motive for citizens in the lower classes. It is a motive that finds its purest expression in the leisure class. For the lower classes, conformity of norms—that is, fitting in, as discussed earlier in the chapter—specifically a normative standard of living, may be an equally important drive.

Veblen also points to the difficulty of deviating from norms and habits associated with the normative standard of living, as the latter serves to "prevent recession from a scale of conspicuous expenditure that has once become habitual" (1994 [1899], 65). Once habitualized, one's standard of living is notoriously difficult to relinquish. Any form of consumption to which one is accustomed is only reluctantly given up. The longer the habituation, the more difficult it is to break the habit. It is even harder to give up any habitual expenditure that is connected to the conspicuous consumption, to one's status and identity, because that would imply climbing down the social ladder.

When discussing the particularities of consumption, Veblen shows how various things, like clothing, shoes, art, furniture, architecture, rare animals (birds, cats, horses), food, drinks, and so on are not valued for their utility, but rather for their beauty, wastefulness, rarity, expensiveness, and even inconvenience (like high heels). Price is always important; an inexpensive item cannot be accounted beautiful. Dress has a particular advantage over most other methods because the apparel one is wearing is always in evidence and efficiently shows one's pecuniary standing. Likewise, "probably at no other point is the sense of shabbiness so keenly felt as it is if we fall short of the standard set by social usage in this matter of dress" (1994 [1899], 103). Clothing should be expensive in order to serve the purpose of conspicuous consumption, while a particular feature of dress is also that it serves so well to show "that the wearer is not engaged in any kind of productive labour" (1994 [1899], 105). Clothes should suggest leisure, exemption from personal contact with industrial processes and manual labor.

In the sociology of consumption, much criticism has been directed toward Veblen's theory; for example, it has been argued that he overstressed the significance of competition as a driver behind consumption (see, for example, the critique in Campbell 2018 [1987]). Nonetheless, even if he failed to cover all aspects of consumerism, the notions of conspicuous consumption, competition, and class struggle are essential.

Societies evolve. The objects selected for displays of conspicuous consumption shift accordingly. One aspect of societal development is increased social stratification. As a society advances in wealth, with further divisions of labor and specialization, the ability to pay is put in evidence by means that require progressively finer discrimination. It is here that the work of Bourdieu fits in nicely. In his classic work *Distinction*, Bourdieu (1984) basically confirms, with more empirical evidence, some of Veblen's ideas and provides some additional theoretical concepts, such as taste, habitus, symbolic capital, and cultural capital. According to Bourdieu, the way we present ourselves communicates our status in relation to others. Social classes acquire aesthetic preferences and, through socialization, teach those preferences to children. Therefore, aesthetic dispositions (including clothing styles) are internalized at a young age and guide human behavior. Bourdieu emphasizes that it is not just what we buy that matters, but (indeed like Veblen) also the cultural knowledge about how we use these goods. Cultural capital is a key concept and is understood as a basis of class position. It includes specific attitudes, preferences and behaviors that are conceptualized as "tastes" and are mobilized for social selection (see also Lamont and Lareau 1988). Hence, taste is not a personal and socially innocent category, but requires socialization and many (mainly unconscious) hours of training and cultivation. Bourdieu's work indicates that more subtle—even inconspicuous—aspects of consumption can add to the investment of cultural capital.[14] People with more cultural capital in a particular domain may prefer more subtle signals to distinguish themselves from mainstream. Subtle signals are only observable to people possessing the indispensable tacit knowledge needed to decode their meaning (Berger and Ward 2010).

Bourdieu focused strongly on art, but we perform all kinds of impression management with various objects: housing, clothing, sports equipment, TVs, what restaurants we go to. Even where we travel on vacation can be significant. Leisure can function as "conspicuous leisure," say Firat and colleagues (2013: 191), and thus functions as an indicator of status and social prestige. A quote from a German man in a study by Dubois and colleagues is illustrative:

> It is important to have a semester abroad in your CV. The companies think: Hey, this guy is motivated, he wants to learn, he is flexible, he has been to the US for a year. It sounds better, than saying: Oh well, yes, this guy is organic, he is

> climate-friendly, he decided to stay at home and not pollute the air. (Dubois et al. 2019, 149)

The most important signals of cultural capital differ between the social classes: "prestigious signals" are important for controlling access to high-status positions; whereas "respectable signals" would act to exclude members of the lower class from middle-class circles (Lamont and Lareau 1988, 157). Moreover, cultural capital is contextually shaped, as Lamont and Lareau (1988) argue, comparing differences between the contexts of France (where the concept originated, via Bourdieu) and the United States. They suggest that access to high-status goods is more important in American society; whereas cultural literacy or modalities of consumption (manners, dressing codes, how to consume, evaluate, compare, store, talk about wine, etc.) were more important in France. Sullivan (2008) adds to the picture by discussing the phenomenon of "cultural omnivorousness" and status distinction. Higher-status American groups do not restrict themselves to exclusively "highbrow" consumption—as in Bourdieu's analysis—but engage in high, middle, and lowbrow consumption. They seek the experience of all kinds of entertainment, sports, restaurants, vacation travel, and so on, thereby seeking an inclusive rather than exclusive consumption strategy. This facilitates developing "multicultural capital." In terms of volume, multicultural capital obviously requires more consumption of both expensive and inexpensive products and commoditized experiences, and not least frequent travel (by air) to various cultures. High status is related to the ability to converse about a wide range of cultural forms, and hence to have a variety of consumption experiences. We may assume that this tendency is not limited to American high-status consumers.

In our contemporary very stratified society, there are of course all sorts of differences. "Today, we don't merely have a variety of ladders, but rather a multidimensional matrix of taste and status, on which we can climb in many directions, and in which 'high' and 'low' culture intersect in unexpected ways" (Hine 2002, 158). For example, age can be important. Certain car brands can be loaded with symbols of prestige and success, suitable for a fifty-year-old man showing off by driving the right car (Shukla 2008); whereas certain clothing items, shoe brands, games, and mobile phones may be more important among adolescents. For middle-aged people who can afford it, owning a second home can bring both pleasure and status. For example, in a study of media representations in architecture/lifestyle magazines in New Zealand between 1936 and 2015, Walters and Carr (2019) show how the ownership of a second home was, and still is, the epitome of luxury. Initially only affordable for the upper class, a second home has gradually grown in importance as an object of conspicuous consumption for larger segments of society. It is presented as a marker of exclusivity, individuality, and luxury, and it is not just the object itself that functions as conspicuous consumption, but its size, location, atmosphere, interior design, and decorations. Status consumption may intersect with ideological positions. Kim et al. (2018) have studied the differences between conservatives and liberals in the United States. The desire for luxury goods and brands is stronger among conservatives. They feel a need to keep up their luxury spending habits to preserve their perceived high status. Others may have to procure other goods to climb the ladder in a particular social segment. For some, a Rolex is used to signal one's present status. For others, the ability to drink huge amounts of beer is critical to winning status among one's peers.

To summarize this section, we learn from the classic sociology of consumption that the drive to belong and the drive to distinguish oneself both contribute to consumerism, including both explicit and more subtle signals of consumption. The competitive drive to spend is driven both by the urge to climb the social ladder and the fear of falling down and becoming socially excluded. This competitive game is characterized by restless anxiety and is conditioned by many contextual factors, which generate constant pressure to consume more. For some segments of society and in some contexts, the drivers are channeled into a multi-cultural capital orientation, resulting in large ecological/climate footprints. In Text Box 2.1, I summarize ten interrelated aspects of status as a driver of consumerism.

Before completing this section, it is important to ask whether the hunt for status and social competition could work in the opposite direction and at least prevent excessive consumption. There are two possibilities. First, status consumption has also entered the area of conspicuous green consumption. Several studies using various methods show the possible status-enhancing effects of green choices such as solar panels, hybrid cars, or organic cotton clothing (Griskevicius et al. 2010; Elliot 2013; Carfagna et al. 2014; Dubois and Ordabayeva 2015, 353), and even secondhand consumption (Nistor 2022, 77). Conspicuous green consumption may however be a weak antidote to high-climate-impact consumption, for example, and could be exercised for dubious reasons (see chapter 5 on ethical fetishism and concluding chapter on justification strategies). Compared with green consumption, reduced consumption may be less able to bring social status,[15] even if frugality norms could grow in societies and in particular social groups and contexts. Secondly, and perhaps more promisingly, cultural capital is not just a matter of quantity (volumes). There is no obvious relation between mass consumption and good taste. Rather, these two things could even contradict each other, because good taste stems from more extraordinary consumption. Good taste, moreover, does put a brake on the acceleration of (cheap) consumption, because a prerequisite for it is the long-term experiential training of consuming the goods in the right manner. Here we can glimpse some opportunities for a possible anti-consumerism or slower ways of consuming, something to which I will return in the conclusion and the last chapter.

Text Box 2.1: Status as a driver of consumerism: Ten aspects

1. Status is expressed by symbolically loaded goods, which are difficult (and preferably expensive) to acquire.
2. Getting chances to impress others may demand a significant "extension of self" (Belk 1988) in terms of possessions. Clothing, housing, and cars are all examples of objects that can be acquired as a "second skin" that others may see when looking at us.
3. Because of competition, there is a drive upward.
4. Endless competition means that competitors are never fully satisfied with what they have. The game must continue. There is always the possibility of unfavorable social judgment. This reinforces a pattern of never-satisfied modern consumers (see also chapter 3).
5. Wastefulness is part and parcel of status (Veblen). It seems important to consume something which has low practical value. A logo is not useful other than to signal something. Wastefulness can be a status marker, showing you are able to spend on things you do not need.
6. More finely grained societal stratification makes the processes of status consumption more dynamic. Successively finer market and product differentiation is needed to distinguish oneself from others (see also chapter 3 on fashion cycles). As "lower" groups try to catch up, great effort needs to be invested to continue to stand out. This may result in adding areas of conspicuous consumption, which fuels further commoditization. Acquiring multicultural capital is also a strategy.
7. Status-seekers tend to underestimate the importance of status consumption, and attribute status motives to others rather than themselves (Schor 1998, 19). A reason for this is that our tendencies to distinguish ourselves via consumption are deeply internalized by socialization (into class belonging, good manners, etc.) and processes of normalization (see chapter 5).
8. Fear of social exclusion triggers status consumption. A variety of psychological studies show that people threatened by social exclusion will try to gain attention by showing off to others.

Researchers conducting experimental studies have found evidence that social exclusion, in the form of being ignored, increased the likelihood of conspicuous consumption (Lee and Shrum 2012), and that people spend and consume strategically in the service of affiliation (Mead et al. 2011).

9. The problem of social comparison and status consumption makes its way into the family context. Care (love) for others (partner, children) is expressed through consumption (chapter 1). Parents, or their relatives, are often eager to buy lots of things for their children, because they want their children to be able to match their friends in the acquisition of consumer status symbols (Miller 1998; Isenhour 2010; Schor 2004; Boström 2021c).
10. There is a general sentiment that develops when a group perceives itself as having less than other groups. Inequality—and relative deprivation/poverty—is a structural condition behind the incessant drive for status consumption and hence consumerism (see the next section this chapter).

INEQUALITY

Can inequality boost consumerism? Can it be a root cause behind the kind of extremely toxic and deadly excessive consumption we face on Earth, through the drivers of social comparison, judgment, display, and status consumption? Yes, it surely can.

Some classic sociological concepts, in addition to those of Veblen and Bourdieu, make important contributions to understanding the dynamic effect of inequality. Inequality—a term that is commonly associated with income and economic wealth—has increased dramatically in welfare societies in the last decades. The gap is widening because the rich are getting richer, while larger groups with lower incomes stay on the same levels. I will not dig into the explanation of why income gaps are increasing in many societies.[16] What is important for the argument here is that rising inequalities, in terms of income and economic wealth, have many serious social and psychological consequences that have an impact on consumerism.

Some People are Very Rich and They Consume a Lot

In studies of the climate impact of excessive consumption, it appears natural to focus on the wealthy part of the population. They consume more and have a greater climate and ecological impact. The richest 10 percent of people in the world account for almost half of all carbon dioxide emissions, while the poorest 50 percent account for less than 10 percent of emissions. What is even more absurd is that the richest one percent emit twice as much as the poorest half (Chancel and Piketty 2015; Kartha et al. 2020; Oxfam 2020). If we take traveling by air as an example, this is an activity that was performed by only 11 percent of the world's population in 2018. A small minority are high emitters by frequent flying. Only 1 percent of the world's population emit more than half of the global CO_2 emissions from air travel (Gössling and Humpe 2020). The very rich can be called the "polluter elite" (Kenner 2020); not only do they have the ability to hyperconsume, but they exert political power over the state to defend their interests and the operations of polluting industries (see Text Box 2.2).

Text Box 2.2: The Polluter Elite: Their Consumption and Political Power

In his book *Carbon Inequality: The Role of the Richest in Climate Change, Dario Kenner addresses the "polluter elite" in the context of the United States and the* UK. These two countries are becoming increasingly unequal and have strong vested interests defending the operations of the fossil fuel industry, including climate denial/delay campaigning by the rich. In the United States, the richest 1 percent possess 37.2 percent of the wealth, whereas in the UK the richest 1 percent have 19.9 percent of the wealth (Kenner 2019, 5–6). In 2013, this category emitted 318 tons of CO_2 per capita in the USA, and 147 tons per capita in the UK (Kenner 2019, 14–15).

Their high ability to pollute involves:

- Their luxury and status consumption. Referring to Veblen, Kenner stresses how their lifestyles are characterized by conspicuous consumption, including luxury mansions, multiple properties, and ownership of private islands where they can enjoy all kinds of fancy entertainment (sports, zoos, spas, etc.). They frequently travel to exclusive destinations with their yachts, private jets, sports cars, helicopters, and even submarines. "Being hypermobile is a key way to demonstrate membership of the global elite," Kenner says (2019, 18), and they are "competing over high-carbon lifestyles in areas such as the size of their superyachts" (21). Moreover, they have the resources to adapt and avoid the detrimental consequences of climate change and ecological devastation; they can always live in a bubble, in safe, exclusive residences.

- Emissions associated with investments. The richest 1 percent hold most of the productive and financial assets, with direct and indirect investments in the fossil fuel industry (Kenner 2019, 25–45). Accordingly, they have gained their wealth and continue to profit from activities that cause pollution. This also implies they have the capacity to shape the consumption choices of the general population and direct their lifestyles to remain dependent on fossil fuels.
- Political influence. The polluter elite use part of their wealth and profits from polluting activities for lobbying, funding think tanks and providing donations to conservative political parties that defend the interests of polluting industries (Kenner 2019, 64–101). The polluter elite gains and exerts structural power over the state, even capturing the presidency of the United States (Donald Trump). Politicians and policymakers accordingly accept the interest of companies as their own viewpoint. Despite technological advancement in the renewable energy sector, they block the transition away from fossil fuels thanks to a whole range of subsidies and support for the industry. They combat proposals for tougher regulations by threatening investment strikes and the relocation of domestic businesses and jobs to other countries.

So, is it not enough to focus on only the very rich, let us say the richest 1 percent or at least the richest 10 percent in the world, in a study of consumerism and its climate/ecological impact?

No! One reason for this is that there are numerous serious ecological consequences of the remaining 90 percent's consumption. Another more important reason is that in a stratified society, everything hangs together, as the discussion above has shown. What rich people do affects everyone; they own and support industries that shape consumption choices for the masses, they spread consumerist ideals to the rest of society, they raise standards (reference points) and inflame desires, their extended selves serve as role models, they fuel pecuniary emulation, they signal to "lower" groups that they should not be satisfied with what they have and thus cause identify deficits among them, they spread a culture of wastefulness, their lifestyles are displayed on social media, their desire to distinguish themselves from the ordinary feeds their own excessiveness, and so on (see Urry 2010; Kenner 2019; Wiedmann et al. 2020). A closer look at classic sociological concepts such as relative poverty and empirical studies related to inequality provides further insights and evidence about why inequality feeds consumerism in all social classes and groups, not just those at the top.

Relative Poverty Feeds Social Judgment which Feeds Consumerism

More than eighty years ago, the sociologist Robert Merton (1938) noted that a combination of limited resources (poverty), limited opportunity to climb the social ladder, and a commonly shared system of success symbols within a society produces what others had labeled "deviant" behaviors, such as crime. In contrast, Merton considered such behavior normal within a cultural context in which pecuniary strength is considered very prestigious, as in American society, at the same time as legitimate institutionalized means to achieve these goals are very unequally distributed. The problem is the wide gap between desires and available means. From this discussion, the idea of *relative poverty* or *relative deprivation* emerged.

Accordingly, in studies of poverty it is sometimes more relevant to speak of relative poverty (being poorer than . . .) than of absolute poverty (inability to satisfy basic needs). Huge inequalities between groups easily lead to feelings of injustice and envy, particularly in a society and cultural context with commonly shared goals. What matters is that people can observe what others have. The theory of relative deprivation is accordingly relevant to consider in a study of consumerism. People who feel relatively deprived perceive a lack of resources to achieve or maintain the quality of life that is considered standard or normal in their community, or in relation to their reference groups. They consider themselves worse off than the comparison groups. A more vertically differentiated social structure accordingly leads to a larger share of people feeling worse off. On the individual level, such a structure may contribute to identity deficits, as were discussed earlier in the chapter (see Figure 2.1). More people are driven toward unattainable goals, and the dissatisfied population will engage in compensation-seeking behavior framed in terms of materialistic goals, such as buying more things. Another important side effect, further elaborated in Text Box 2.3, is that inequality and feelings of relative poverty cause collective dilemmas and prevent responsibility-taking among the general population.

Epidemiologists Richard Wilkinson and Kate Pickett have written two celebrated books (2010, 2019) on inequality and why it is so harmful for the population's physical and mental health—for everyone, not just groups at the bottom of the income hierarchy. They provide empirical evidence from twenty-three welfare countries and argue forcefully that economic growth is no longer able to deliver health, happiness, and well-being in rich welfare states.[17] What matters for individuals in rich countries is not their actual

Text Box 2.3: Inequality and Collective Dilemmas

Equal societies foster a greater sense of collective responsibility, while inequality does the opposite (Wilkinson and Pickett 2010). This is yet another aspect of inequality that relates to the reproduction of consumerism. This topic is not primarily related to status consumption, but rather to collective dilemmas. Indeed, collective dilemmas play an important role in keeping consumers ignorant and steadily involved in individualized mass consumption habits. "Why should I sacrifice my prosperity and consume less if others don't?" This is another aspect of how social comparison plays an important role in reproducing patterns of mass consumption. (See also concluding chapter on justification strategies.) An individual may be very aware of how his ownership and use of a car and gasoline contributes to climate warming; however, this awareness is not translated into action because of collective dilemmas. The person looks at other people, the state, or businesses that he perceives as having more power and money to solve collective problems such as environmental degradation, and attributes more responsibility to those persons or entities.

income level and living standard, but rather how they compare with others in the same society. Wilkinson and Pickett thus employ the sociological idea of relative poverty.

The authors argue that social anxiety and insecurity are the most common sources of stress in modern societies. Social judgment and evaluations are central: How do other people rate me? "This vulnerability is part of the modern psychological condition and feeds directly into consumerism" (Wilkinson and Pickett 2010, 42–43). Greater inequality increases the importance of social status within a society, which in turn heightens people's anxieties about social evaluation. Larger income gaps make it harder for people to accept each other as equals. "As greater inequality increases status competition and social evaluative threat, egos have to be propped up by self-promoting and self-enhancing strategies" (Wilkinson and Pickett 2010, 45). Consumerism is one such strategy.

Differences in status and wealth create a social gulf between people. This prevents affiliative strategies such as cooperation and spurs dominance strategies including self-advancement and status competition. "The more we feel devalued by those above us and the fewer status resources we have to fall back on, the greater will be the desire to regain some sense of self-worth by asserting superiority over any more vulnerable groups" (Wilkinson and Pickett 2010, 207).

Diminished savings, increasing debt and bankruptcy rates, spending on advertising, and increasing working hours are all consistent "with the view that inequality does indeed increase the pressure to consume" (Wilkinson and Pickett 2010, 228). Anyone unable to raise their standards will be left behind. Inequality gets under people's skin.

Consumption may be even most important for people at the bottom of the social hierarchy. Miller (1998) discusses how care and anxiety are involved when a mother shops with and for infants. He describes a single divorced woman, Clary, who in her everyday life faces serious economic difficulties:

> The father of her two children is much better off, and she feels particularly vulnerable because she cannot compete with his generosity when the children go and stay with him, and she is worried about the indulgences they become used to while there. In effect, her love is manifested largely as anxiety about shopping, rather than in shopping itself. The social science literature on consumption often seems to echo most journalism in making the daft assumption that it is mainly the rich who are materialistic. Clary, however, like most people I worked with who live in considerable poverty, is much more materialistic than the rich, because of the miserable consequence of her lack of goods. For Clary, this is reflected not merely in her persistent worrying about goods she cannot afford but the deeper sense that she is a failure as a mother as a result of this. These anxieties constantly surface in conversations, as in a discussion about birthday parties for children at the school (Miller 1998, 31)

Varieties of Relative Deprivation

A whole range of studies give further support to observations such as those in the quote above. Materialism, competitiveness, and a sense of powerlessness have been identified in several studies as positively associated with conspicuous consumption.[18] Christen and Morgan (2005) found evidence for a positive relation between conspicuous consumption and inequality in a study on the relation between income inequality and consumer borrowing in the US context between 1984 and 2003. This was a period when household debt relative to disposable income increased from 60 to 104 percent. Over the last forty years, the boosting of consumer borrowing made it much easier to buy items such as cars, furniture, electronic goods, and jewelry (Christen and Morgan 2005). This was facilitated not just by credit card borrowing, which is only a limited part of the phenomenon, but by all sorts of financial solutions, including mortgage loans,[19] which consumers use to maintain consumption levels fairly comparable to those of people with higher incomes.

In developing countries, or in emergent economies, people are also likely to compare themselves with those who are economically better off. In a survey study, Guillen-Royo (2008) examined consumption and happiness in Peru, a country with serious economic and social inequalities. Here too, social comparison makes people pursue materialist goals by consumption, which can be frustrating, however, because of the scarcity of resources. In South Africa, with the end of apartheid, opportunities for advancement emerged for some segments of the black population. Chipp et al. (2011) found that conspicuous consumption among newly affluent black South Africans was associated with prior experiences of relative deprivation during the apartheid regime. Thus, past feelings of relative deprivation can result in conspicuous consumption when opportunities arise. The sample in their interview study included black people who had bought expensive sports cars, yachts, expensive clothes, larger homes, and second homes. Some quotes from their interview study are illuminating:

> It is because of the way we grew up, in poor environments. Our parents did not have cars and therefore it became a status symbol to own a car. Parents that had cars were somehow well off and they could afford to take their kids to boarding schools. We were never close to kids whose families had cars because they were rather prevented from playing with us in my community. It was because of social classes—we were seen as a lower class and therefore not worthy to play with the upper-class kids. (Male, 34 years old) (Chipp et al. 2011, 125)

> We as black people have a sudden madness for all these things because we never had any of the things that we have access to now. (Male D, 35 years old) (Chipp et al. 2011, 125)

The study reveals many sentiments, such as the feeling that one must correct past wrongs and the existence of widespread jealousy within the black ethnic group. Similar experiences can be found in post-Soviet countries, with experiences of forced frugality and scarcity of (Western) goods (Keller 2005). Likewise, in a country recently growing out of poverty with a rapidly increasing middle class, like China, citizens might look to references abroad, in countries that have been wealthy for a longer time. Something like this was found in a study of product conspicuousness and young Chinese people's interest in foreign brands: "In less affluent societies, conspicuous consumption serves as a major avenue for establishing one's social identity, making products and brands that symbolize affluent Western consumption culture highly desirable" (Zhou and Wong 2008).

Foreign brands can be seen as enhancing one's self-image as cosmopolitan, sophisticated, and modern. The younger generation in developing countries or recently transitioned countries can be eager to learn about and imitate global consumption cultures, as a way to appear independent and open-minded.

This type of driver can also be observed among teenagers from different class backgrounds. In a study comparing low- and high-income British adolescents, Isaksen and Roper (2008) noted that relative deprivation experienced during the teenage years (thirteen and fourteen years) had a negative impact on self-esteem. Such experiences made these teenagers more susceptible to interpersonal influence. Due to an inability to "keep up" with the latest fashion trends and buy branded consumer goods, the low-income teenagers had a less clear self-concept and were more susceptible to consumption pressures. These teenagers had a greater desire for branded goods and material possessions. They conspicuously consumed expensive brands as a means of disguising their relative poverty. Sadly, low-income teenagers are the ones least likely to be able to afford status consumption but also the ones most drawn to it, a desire likely to be perpetuated by the risk of being bullied and excluded by peers. The authors discuss the results in terms of a vicious circle:

> The inability to afford the things they want is likely to highlight (to themselves and others) their lower social and economic status, which again perpetuates their feelings of social exclusion, damages their self-worth . . . and results in greater susceptibility to interpersonal influence. (Isaksen and Roper, 2008, 1070)

This is certainly not to say that materialist aspirations do not matter among those who are better off. After all, they are the ones who consume the most. In a qualitative interview study, Piacentini and Mailer (2004) compared two different schools in Glasgow, one in a working-class area and another with pupils from the upper classes. The study was about the symbolic meanings that the teenagers connected to clothing consumption. In the former case, clothing choices were generally made to demonstrate economic competence. "Buying branded clothes was important to demonstrate that they were not poor, and brands were a useful way of 'keeping up' with others in the school" (Piacentini and Mailer 2004, 260). In the second context, it was more common to wear clothes that indicate affluence, such as being an early adopter of elite and rare brands.

If people in the lower levels of the social hierarchy cannot buy luxury brands, can volume and size perhaps be an important way to demonstrate status? Ideas like this are in focus in a series of experimental studies conducted by Dubois et al. (2012). They show that consumers' preference for supersized food and drinks does indeed seem to be connected to the status-signaling value of larger options. A consistent finding throughout their experiments was that a perception of powerlessness would increase the preference for larger-sized food and drink options. A lack of power led people to desire status, and this drive guided their food and drink choices. It is as if the supersized option could compensate a bit for one's tiny amount of social power. Also, the experiments indicated that consumption performed in public or among friends, rather than privately, also increased the likelihood of choosing a supersized option; thus confirming the element of a particular kind of conspicuous consumption. Their research suggests that even products without any apparent status connotations, such as soft drinks, could be viewed as having status when their large size becomes noticeable, relative to other options. This obviously relates to lower-income socioeconomic groups. For other groups and other product categories, it might be the smaller options that bring status (even if they probably live in larger houses and may have large boats).

A final study that is important to highlight in this section was conducted by Kim et al. (2017). They designed a series of survey studies in the US context and found a positive relation between social comparison, "personal relative deprivation," and materialism (understood as values, goals, and beliefs regarding the importance of acquiring money and possessions that convey status). They conclude that people with a tendency to compare their abilities and achievements with others are also more likely than others to perceive themselves as relatively deprived, which in turn leads them to express materialist values and goals. The authors noted that "even people who are objectively 'wealthy' can feel resentful about what they have compared with what others like them have" (Kim et al. 2017, 388), a finding that reflects Veblen's classic theory quite well. This reminds us that relative deprivation (also) has a subjective dimension. These different studies cover a variety of situations, but with some simplification they could be summarized in a model (Figure 2.2) suggesting a relation between higher income gaps, experiences of relative poverty involving perceived negative social judgment, and the seeking of compensation in consumerism and materialistic goals, especially in commodities perceived as loaded with status. Likewise, a structure of income gaps and relative poverty can spur a situation of unattainable ideals and identity deficits—related drivers of consumerism—as discussed earlier in the chapter (see and compare Figure 2.1).

Given all the findings discussed above, one may wonder whether reducing the income gap could be a key means to combat status spending and consumerism. The answer is yes, such a policy ought to be part of the remedy, but one needs to take into account that causes of phenomena in human societies

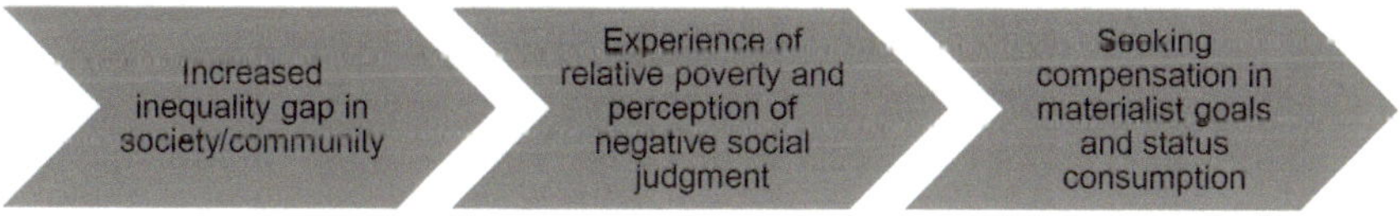

Figure 2.2: Inequality, Relative Poverty, and Consumerism. ***Source:*** **Author.**

are complex. Reducing the income gap could even result in status spending because of new perceived opportunities to climb the ladder, like the effects seen among the black community after the end of apartheid in South Africa, as described above. In a cultural context in which people care about social position, and in which status consumption is accordingly important, increased equality may very well lead to increased consumption, because more people see a chance to compete (Ordabayeva and Chandon 2011; Dubois and Ordabayeva 2015). In contrast, in a largely cooperative social environment, when people care about social position to a lesser extent, increased equality may limit status consumption. Counteracting status consumption is not only about reducing inequality. It is equally important to, politically and culturally, counteract the (neoliberal) norm of competition, and legitimizing the opposite.

CONCLUSION

This chapter has shown how classic and contemporary sociology and social psychology provide important concepts and evidence regarding the general role of social comparison in spurring drivers connected to identity (socialization, extended self, multiple selves, fitting in, appearing unique, unattainable ideals, incomplete identities) status/distinction (conspicuous consumption, wastefulness, [multi-]cultural capital, competition, fear of "falling down"), and inequality (escalating reference points, relative poverty/deprivation, negative social judgment, compensation seeking, collective dilemmas). As social beings, people tend to compare themselves with each other. For many people, if not for all, the important thing is to have more (or at least not less), better (or at least not worse), and/or more expensive (or at least not cheaper) goods (or commoditized experiences) than other people/groups. Levels of consumption should match up with an ideal, to close the gap between the actual and ideal self. The gap is never or only rarely closed, and therefore the consumerist aspirations continue. There must be a sizeable material landscape surrounding oneself—one's extended self. Institutional drivers (see Introduction) like capitalist commoditization, branding, the advertisement industry, the growth dogma, and cultural frames spread via the workings of mass media and via social media influencers, exploit this tendency of social comparison. Social stratification and increasing inequalities add fuel to the fire. The social judgment game affects all: rich and poor. You may win for a time, but you can always fall back down again. Even if you can resist the competitive status game, you may not be able to ignore your children's worries about social judgment. Because of social media and the smartphone you constantly bring with you wherever you go, there is ubiquitous visibility and you can be judged 24/7. And no one wins:

> Like standing up in a crowd to get a better view, it stops working once others do it too. In the end, the view is the same, but everyone's legs are tired. The more our consumer satisfaction is tied into social comparisons—whether upscaling, just keeping up, or not falling too far behind—the less we achieve when consumption grows, because the people we compare ourselves to are also experiencing rising consumption. Our relative position does not change. (Schor 1998, 107)

How can we stop the rat race? Take a moment to reflect (see Text Box 2.4).

Text Box 2.4: Invitation to Reflect on Opportunities for Change

This chapter has provided insights into why social stratification and growing inequalities fuel consumerism by spurring an atmosphere of social comparison and relative deprivation. From the conclusions in this chapter it follows that an essential area for transformative change is combating social inequalities and disintegration, including digital/physical circumstances that spur 24/7 social judgment, both on socio-psychological and structural levels. How can society/community/social groups supply alternative frames of reference and role models to help individuals expose and counteract the spiral of identity deficits and unattainable ideals? How can people learn to bridge the gap between their actual and ideal selves without resorting to consumerism and materialistic goals? What possibilities are there to expose the large climate/ecological footprints associated with multicultural capital and other kinds of conspicuous consumption and redirect aspirations to other more sustainable dimensions of experience? What are the options for cultivating new kinds of "good taste" based on slower ways of consuming? Which social groups will be front-runners in redirecting "cultural capital toward reduced consumption," and how can they influence other groups? Is the reframing of luxury to encompass more qualitative dimensions a way forward? Can social status and the associated emotion of pride be redirected to other aspirations than acquiring goods? With regard to more structural issues, the scholarly discussion of this topic is broad and varied, and a huge repertoire of measures are being discussed: progressive taxes, economic democracy, fair access to important infrastructure for all inhabitants, systems and facilities for service provision (see, e.g., Wilkinson and Pickett 2010, 2019). What possibilities are there to implement measures that could address these structures, and in turn dampen the drivers of consumerism? What are the key obstacles to change? How can we deal with the superrich: the current winners in the existing order? How can society/communities combat rising inequalities and facilitate a collaborative rather than competitive atmosphere, one that is less characterized by social comparison and judgment, one that can prevent the pursuit of extended selves, conspicuous consumption, and feelings of relative poverty? Last but not least, issues of equality are of fundamental importance because an increased inequality gap not only spurs unsustainable consumerism but also undermines a sense of individual and collective responsibility. How can society/communities stimulate a sense of shared responsibility?

NOTES

1. I am grateful for constructive comments by all participants at a sociology seminar at Örebro University, on an earlier version of this chapter, as well as to an anonymous reviewer.

2. Classic sociology, based on the works of Marx and Weber, emphasized different aspects of production forces as drivers, but it has been argued that the consumer revolution was equally important as a historical driver of capitalism (Campbell 2018 [1987]; Sassatelli 2007).

3. Lauren Greenfield's documentary *Generation Wealth* illustrates the point very well. Although the film demonstrates the most extreme examples and consequences, it makes the point that these tendencies exist everywhere in society. The film also illustrates very well the unhappiness connected to excess consumption (see concluding chapter).

4. Before the concept of "influencer" became popular, Fitzmaurice and Comegys (2006) found empirical evidence that "opinion leaders" tend to have higher scores on a scale measuring materialism. On fashion bloggers, see Duffy and Hund 2015.

5. A counter-effect, found in psychological studies, could be a perceived difficulty to imagine oneself in a success story like a reference person that one is reading about (Mandel et al. 2006). One just gives up.

6. Belk found some bias toward "societies that hold an individualistic concept of self" (Belk 1988, 145). In contrast, Lo and Harvey (2010), comparing Taiwanese and British consumers, found that possessions are an even higher value in Confucian societies. Members of these societies place even more symbolic emphasis on public and visible possessions than people in Western societies.

7. See Mead 1962 [1934].

8. Materialism refers to a desire for, and pursuit of, affluence and possessions, not to being affluent as such. It refers to what a person wants, not what s/he has. There can also be nonmaterialistic motives for making money, such as seeking financial

security. See Dittmar 2008, chapter 4. See also Fitzmaurice and Comegys (2006) on various conceptions of materialism and how it links to consumption.

9. A reminder is appropriate here. While the relation between identity and consumption seems crucial, we should not exaggerate this point. It should be stressed that we consume not merely to polish our identities. Daniel Miller (2010) argues that "stuff," such as clothes, has a lot more meanings than just something that symbolically represents us (contributes to our identities).

10. Identity was once something to be completed. It was more of a life project. One became a priest, doctor, lawyer, worker, etc., and maintained a completed role and identity. Identity was acquired and achieved through primary and secondary socialization (education). This too undoubtedly involved certain prescripted consumption habits. Later, identity become more transitory, argues Bauman (2007) and many other social theorists. The construction of identity appeared to be more of a never-ending project closely tied to the commoditization of people.

11. Experimental studies have shown that the presence of others, particularly the presence of desirable others, increases the likelihood of status consumption (Dubois and Ordabayeva 2015, 346).

12. The leisure class, according to Veblen, is the wealthiest class in society, an upper class exempt from industrial employment. It includes the financial elite, as well as citizens engaged in government, warfare, religious services, and sports. Today, the financial elite makes up a huge part of the richest segment of society; see Sayer (2016).

13. See O'Cass and McEwen (2011) for a discussion of how conspicuous consumption and status consumption overlap but could also have slightly different meanings.

14. Whereas Bourdieu implicitly builds on the intellectual legacy of Veblen, there are also differences between them. Lamont and Lareau (1988) argue that the key difference is that Veblen stressed how consumption was intentionally used to show off and win esteem, whereas Bourdieu focused more on how signals were learned unconsciously through socialization and are incorporated as dispositions, as habitus.

15. In a mixed-method study in the United States (using a vignette experiment and semi-structured interviews), Kennedy and Horne (2019) show that both conservatives and liberals link social status to green consumption (exemplified by rooftop solar panels). Investing in solar panels is tied with positive values such as being wealthy in terms of both money and time, being knowledgeable, as well as being ethical, because of perceived commitment to environmental protection. However reduced consumption (reducing emissions through behavioral change) did not have the same significance for providing social status.

16. I recommend the work of Sayer (2016).

17. They use measures of income gap in twenty-three rich and democratic countries. By referring to a wide range of statistics and measures, they are able to consistently show that health and social problems are only weakly related to national average income among people in rich countries. However, social problems are strongly related to the size of the income gap. Examples include the quality of social relations (trust),

physical health and life expectancy, obesity, mental health and the use of drugs, educational performance, teenage pregnancy, violence, and imprisonment.

18. See review by Chipp et al. 2011; see also Jorgenson et al. 2019.

19. Rising housing prices increase consumers' borrowing capacity, and combined with favorable interest rates, mortgage debt can be used as a substitute for consumer credit.

Chapter 3

The Temporalities of Mass Consumption in Social Life

A Lost Future

Words and phrases such as impulse buying, fashion cycles, obsolescence, seasonal vegetables, investments, durable products, and fast food all have a temporal connotation.[1] Much of our mass consumption has to do with time and tempo, with hurriedness and speed. Time and tempo are therefore important topics in an investigation of unsustainable consumerism.

We can speak of a number of temporal aspects. One concerns time frames, such as instantaneous, transitory, short-term, long-term, permanent, or eternal. Another has to do with tempo and related words, such as pace, rhythm, speed, and acceleration, which are implied in words such as "productivity" and "stress." We have issues of synchronization and timing, as in the phrase "just in time." We make periodizations of different kinds and distinguish between past, present, and future, or between before and after. Such distinctions are implied in words such as deadlines, seasons, irreversibility, and impulse buying. A term such as multitasking implies that we can do several things simultaneously such as eating a hamburger while driving and listening to the radio. Time is implicated in processes: life cycles, movements, routines, standstill, inertia, transformation, tipping points, and cycles of desire. From an economic perspective, time is a resource; we can have a scarcity of time or plenty of time. Time is invested and stored; work (in hours) is stored in products, physical infrastructure, and expertise. There are technological devices and services aimed for facilitating time-saving and time-shifting, like microwave ovens and freezers, which can help us plan and organize our time and deal with the problem of time-space coordination. Not least, there is our subjective experience of time in relation to such things as tempo, stress, urgency, time compression, and the like. Everyday life passes quickly or slowly.

In the study of the relationship between environment and society, it has been acknowledged that the temporalities of ecosystems often do no not harmonize very well with the temporalities of society (Lockie and Wong 2018). Short-term gains and ways of thinking triumph over long-term sustainability. The infrastructures, institutions, and social life of mass consumption are certainly no exception to this. This chapter will accordingly look into how temporal aspects intersect with consumerism and mass consumption. The theory of social acceleration, developed by Hartmut Rosa, serves as a point of departure and as an overall interpretive frame, and in the next section I will briefly introduce this theory. The following sections will discuss consumerism in relation to, first, the separation of work and leisure time and the hectic everyday life that comes about as a result of, for example, long working weeks. Secondly, I will discuss the cultural imperative of novelty, important features of which are cycles of desire, fashion, fashion anxiety, and rapid obsolescence. I will then explore the topic of impulse buying. Finally, in the conclusion, I argue that the future is discounted in favor of consumerism in and for the present.

THE THEORY OF SOCIAL ACCELERATION

There are several theories of time and tempo within sociology. One of these is social acceleration theory, a critical theory of modernity formulated by Hartmut Rosa (2013) that is useful for capturing a number of ways in which consumerism intersects with aspects of temporality. Rosa makes the interesting claim that people in late modern society are locked into increasingly high rates of social acceleration.[2] Acceleration is defined as increased quantity per unit of time. This is not just about moving more quickly over physical distances, but also about performing more tasks or filling life with more experiences within a given time period.

Analytically, Rosa distinguishes between three types of acceleration. Technological acceleration includes goal-oriented acceleration connected to transport, communication, and productivity. Acceleration of social change includes increasing frequency of change regarding jobs, social relationships, identities, memberships, political preferences, hobbies, activities, fashion cycles, and so on. We are constantly urged or forced to make choices of various kinds; more and more areas of life appear like a marketplace. Finally, acceleration of the pace of life includes the experience of a faster life, the general sense of hurriedness that permeates individual and social life in late-modern society. People feel that they have less and less time and are forced to use coping strategies such as multitasking, time-planning, time-shifting, or just doing things more efficiently or quickly, for instance with power naps, energy drinks, speed dating, and speed reading.

According to Rosa, acceleration is driven by both endogenous forces (acceleration has a self-perpetuating effect via feedback loops) and exogenous ones. External forces include, first, the economic motor. Acceleration is embedded in how capitalism functions through market competition and capital accumulation, which not least implies that (labor) time itself is commodified. In industrialized societies, this has resulted in an institutionalized separation between work and leisure, which has important consequences for consumption (see next section). Industrial, technological, and capitalistic developments have also caused enormous productivity gains, which in turn have led not to shorter working hours but to increases in production, income, and consumption. A situation characterized by work-rich, time-poor social life emerges, with important implications for consumerism, and this theme is developed in the subsequent sections.

Secondly, there is a socio-structural motor. Increased social differentiation leads to increased complexity in society. All social groups, organizations, and societal subsystems face increasingly complex surroundings, vertically and horizontally (stratification). In chapter 2, I explored how social stratification is linked to consumerism. A more differentiated social structure will, from the perspective of social acceleration, create an additional problem of time-space coordination (synchronization), which results in a demand for high-speed solutions. Technological innovations, for example digital administration systems or sophisticated systems for transportation, are supposed to solve coordination problems. However, new technological systems add to the overall level of complexity, which in turn leads to new synchronization problems, feeding a spiral of acceleration. In a section below, I will discuss this problem in relation to consumer products for time-saving and time-shifting.

Thirdly, there is a cultural motor driving social acceleration. Cultural frames are linked to ideas such as progress, development, and the "American dream," all of which in various ways celebrate the promise of growth and acceleration. The normative pressure from the cultural motor implies that a "successful life," the "good life," and being a "respectable citizen" are associated with high levels of consumption, and hence people are subjected to a constant pressure to perform via consumption. We can experience more things and (superficially) achieve a fuller and more happy life by consuming faster: "Cultural patterns of meaning and subjective action orientations" drive "the acceleration process through the desire to heighten the pace of life in order to increase the number of episodes of action and experience per unit of time" (Rosa 2013, 183). The cultural imperatives of novelty and fashion—as explored later in this chapter—correspond with this logic.

WORK AND LEISURE

The modern separation of work time and leisure time, originally associated with industrial, urban social life, is a prerequisite for the pattern of consumerism that we see today, including a shopping lifestyle. The following subsections discuss how contemporary work and patterns of everyday social life stimulate consumerism. The first subsection discusses consumption related to leisure time. Then follows an exploration of how the norm and practice of long working hours seen in wealthy countries causes consumerism, through both higher income and time scarcity. Three types of buying are then related to this: buying for convenience, for instant reward, and for future leisure.

Consumption and Leisure Time

In parallel to the historical development of industrial and urban life, a more distinct separation between work time and "free" time was chiseled out. This separation process took centuries, but the idea and practice of leisure slowly and steadily grew, first among the upper classes and later to broader segments of the population, and then after the world wars with the growth of "welfare societies." The separation—along with higher income, more free time, more generous holiday legislation—brought new expectations connected with leisure time. Labor came to be associated with discipline, whereas leisure time was associated with freedom and consumption (Princen 2005; Sassatelli 2007; Urry 2010). Leisure time was, first of all, the time for rest. It was the time for reenergizing (male) bodies—the task and duty of home-working women—so that they could remain a productive force for industry. However, a growing economy requires more than just a supply of productive workers. It also needs a growing aggregate demand, which is facilitated by higher salaries and leisure time for larger segments of the population (Trentmann 2016; Southerton 2020). The development of welfare societies implies, moreover, a growth of expectations. Men, women, and children in family or kinship contexts "deserve" compensation for time sacrificed in work, household work, and school. Leisure time is, hence, increasingly associated with fun, recreation, and reward, thus implying increased consumption in terms of travel, entertainment, and shopping. All this is supported by a flourishing consumer culture and ideology. This compensation is social-relational. It cannot (only) be for oneself, but needs to involve one's significant others. Time sacrificed for work is a loss of not just time for one's personal aspirations, but also of time that could have been spent with one's friends and family. The compensation might not necessarily need to be channeled through consumption; however, in consumer culture this has become the norm. Leisure has become closely associated with socially rewarding consumerist rituals, like the vacation or weekend trip (see chapter 1).

The division between work time and leisure time has led to mass consumption and mass entertainment being combined in the practice of shopping. This takes place at particular sites—to which one travels—such as malls (Moss 2007). Leisure time has come to be associated with ideas such as "freedom, naturalism, optional choice, deepness of thought" (Firat et al. 2013, 185), although in reality it has mainly been linked to consumerism, including commoditized entertainment. Therefore, shopping and consumption are considered by many to be forms of recreation and entertainment, and are packaged as such by the consumer culture industry (e.g., Uggla and Olausson 2012; see also chapter 4).

In terms of time, the very act of shopping can appear paradoxical. It has two competing modes or paces. On one hand, because of time scarcity, you want to shop conveniently and efficiently, any time, all the time. Without effort you want to quickly find what you are looking for. The growth of online shopping fits this mode well, because it offers 24/7 accessibility and there is no need to travel. On the other hand, shopping is associated with leisure. You shop for fun, for recreation, for experiences and without a plan, getting lost in all the abundance. Both of these modes exist, and they do not simply represent different categories of shoppers. Rather, one person may express both attitudes at different times and in different contexts. Also, shopping has several purposes. When you are buying everyday products, you may demand convenience, and when you are buying fashion items, you may look for entertainment. There is also a gender issue here: men often prefer efficiency whereas women seek recreation and socializing (Dittmar 2008).

Nonetheless, consumer culture includes the idea that consumption and shopping are fun, and that you do these activities during your free time. Going shopping has been framed as a playful activity (Moss 2007). Huge numbers of people have shopping in mind when they choose tourist destinations and plan free-time activities during weekends or vacations. There are even chartered flights and bus trips to markets.

Why are outlet malls situated in remote locations? To be sure, access to relatively inexpensive land is important. However, Ruppel Shell (2009) finds that the choice of such locations is a tactical business decision. Trips to outlets demand an investment of time, planning, and energy that often goes beyond what people invest in other spare-time activities. One must make an investment in time and other resources—like gasoline—just to get there. Once there, people are motivated to buy in excess to justify the costs of the expensive journey.

Leisure time may mean relief not just from work but also an opportunity to put a number of duties and responsibilities on pause. This is particularly the case for time reserved for extraordinary moments, such as a holiday trip. During vacation travels we may also pause our ethical/environmental consciousness. There is a "home and away gap" (Lamers et al. 2019, 357–59), which concerns inconsistencies between people's conscious ethical/environmental practices in their everyday lives at home and how they behave when traveling as well as where and how they travel. Barr et al. (2010, 2011) found that in a sample of British citizens, those with higher levels of environmental commitments in and around the home also tended to be those who flew farthest and most frequently (which also happened to be those with the highest incomes). Many also failed to transfer pro-environmental activities in their home environment to their holiday environments. Being environmentally conscious at home could even be seen as compensating for the lack of environmental consideration when choosing transport to a holiday destination or of taking care of the environment while on holiday.

On the other hand, leisure time, perhaps spent at one's summer house, could provide stress relief and more time to actually engage in sustainable habits, such as spending time searching for local food and engaging in "slower" cooking and baking rather than relying on processed foods (see Gojard and Véron 2018).[3] If activities done during leisure time indicate more sustainable practices, this pattern can be seen as an indication of how "ordinary time" is reliant on high consumption levels and fast options with higher environmental impact.

For busy high-status groups, leisure time is often dense in terms of activities and tempo. One strategy that members of high-status groups employ is "multitasking" of leisure activities. By studying time-use diaries, Sullivan (2008) found that these groups have more intensive leisure consisting of more varied and frequent activities. They are more voracious in their pursuit of leisure (they may foster their multicultural capital; see chapter 2). There is an "increasing acceleration in the 'consumption of experiences': the desire to do more, to do them more quickly, and to do them more simultaneously" (Sullivan 2008, 10).

Leisure time is also associated with time to relax from an otherwise demanding and stressful life. Could leisure time perhaps be a temporary escape from social acceleration? The rising popularity of activities such as yoga, retreats, mindfulness, spa hotels, outdoor life, and similar indicates something about the need to sometimes temporarily withdraw from high-speed social life. There is an ironic rapid oscillation between tempos in social life; times when we rush and times for calm (Shove 2003; Southerton 2020). We plan and find ways to manage these moods. People rush in order to have time to calm down. People need efficient (!) pauses to be able to bear the circumstances of the accelerated society. These strategies even function to promote social acceleration. Rosa (2013) calls such activities "strategies of acceleration-through-slowdown"; they reenergize people for high-speed society. These retreats are themselves commodified—they are part of the mass consumption landscape—and the infrastructure of the high-speed society is required to quickly, efficiently, and without hindrance integrate the yoga session into people's otherwise stressful everyday schedules. One person's retreat requires the rushing of other people delivering the services and systems of transportation and provisioning (Sharma 2014). People demand fast service in order to slow down their hectic lives during retreats.

A core reason why people demand speed is that they work so many hours, which is the topic of the next subsection.

Work-Rich, Time-Poor Social Life

Productivity increases. This has been a constant since the industrial revolution. What a fantastic success it would have been if the productivity gain had resulted in increased welfare *and* increased quality of life, with people seizing the opportunity to work less. Unfortunately, this has generally not happened. Admittedly, from the nineteenth century until the 1980s the aggregate working hours in OECD countries did decline steadily and significantly, but since the 1980s the reduction has been slow (Schor 2005; Devetter and Rousseau 2011), with an average of 1,893 hours of working time annually in the year 1980 going down approximately only 8 percent to 1,743 hours in 2019.[4] This is a small change, because it does not at all match the growth of productivity (GDP per hour worked), which needed only five years (2015–2020) to exhibit a corresponding 8 percent increase.[5]

Hence, productivity gains have led to more production, income, and consumption, and not to more leisure. People (still) generally work relatively long hours. Growth has ensued and aggregate income increased (as well as the income gap; see chapter 2). Due to higher production capacity and higher aggregate income, the volume of production has multiplied, creating an ocean of stuff available for consumption. Adding to the picture is the increased share of dual earners in households. Both men and women work many hours, and many work full-time.

The norm and practice of working "full-time" creates a stressful life for both men and women.[6] Their need to commute to work adds to time scarcity and an accelerated pace of life, which results in a "work and spend" cycle (Schor 1992, 1998; Knight et al. 2013; Solér 2018). Research has found that the number of hours a person spends at work is positively correlated with ecological and climate impact through consumption (Schor 2005; Devetter and Rousseau 2011; Knight et al. 2013; Jorgenson et al. 2019).[7] This is due to two mechanisms: the higher income and greater time pressure.

First, working longer hours obviously leads to higher income and hence to greater spending capacity. This is also known as the "scale effect" (Knight et al. 2013)—more work generates greater economic output, income, and consumption. To be sure, higher incomes may make people able to save money so they can work less in the future or retire early, but in mass-consumption society this is not the general pattern. For most people, the pattern is spending (often on credit, see chapter 4), not saving. Higher incomes moreover play a role in what types of goods people buy. For example, based on a survey of family budgets in France, Devetter and Rousseau (2011) found that higher numbers of working hours in a household result in sharp increases in consumption of clothing, furniture, household appliances, education, and housing. Consumption also increases in the categories of hotels, restaurants, and transport, while more working hours result in relatively small increases in consumption related to food, drink, and health.

The second factor is more directly related to time. Households with less free time also engage in types of consumption that have a higher climate/ecological footprint (Devetter and Rousseau 2011; Jorgenson et al. 2019; Persson et al. 2022).[8] Such consumption includes time-saving services and products (see below). Even leisure activities will be more climate intensive, requiring more energy and goods. In contrast, having more free time could stimulate activities with lower climate and ecological footprints, although the effect is not necessarily straightforward. In a survey study with citizens taking part in a workweek-reduction program in Gothenburg, Sweden, Persson et al. (2022) were able to confirm that a workweek reduction led to activities with lower carbon intensity (relaxation/sleeping, exercising, and socializing with family and friends). The effect was not definitive, however. Some spent the increased free time to take more holiday trips. If such trips include flying to distant countries, the freed-up time has no climate gains. The next subsection will continue to examine how "saving time" through various devices and services relies on consumption, and paradoxically can even increase the pace of life rather than slowing it down.

Buying for Convenience: Devices and Services for Time Compression and Time-shifting

We may think of convenience as having to do with functionality and ease of use. This is not wrong, of course, but Elisabeth Shove (2003) argues that this is the historical understanding of convenience. The word is still associated with these qualities, but in time-scarce social life, convenience is increasingly associated with time management. Think of washing machines, tumble dryers, fast food, automobiles, airplanes, processed food, microwave ovens, freezers, answering machines and text messaging facilities, email, apps, information systems, robot lawn mowers, and whatever the rise of artificial intelligence will lead to. With some of these objects you can get a sense of saving time. For example, by consuming fast or processed food, using a washing machine, or driving instead of walking/cycling, you can do activities faster or conduct several activities simultaneously. With regard to other objects, like freezers and email, they can (also) be seen as time-shifting devices (Warde 1999), because they enable you to manage your time: postpone the eating and communicating. Devices for time-compression (time-saving) or time-shifting are amazing, as they appear to make everyday life smoother—Shove (2003) calls these items convenience devices—but as this section will show, they can have paradoxical unintentional effects.

First of all, we need to purchase all these goods and services that are supposed to save time for us or make our everyday life more flexible and efficient. All the facilities should enable us to organize and synchronize fragmented practices (moving, eating, working, sleeping, cleaning, exercising, socializing, etc.) in a smooth flow of just-in-time delivery of services. Devetter and Rousseau (2011) found that consumption induced by time pressure was significant in the areas of housing expenses, transportation, and hotels/restaurants. Of course, there can be multiple reasons why someone buys things within these consumption areas. A car can be bought for reasons connected to masculine identity and conspicuous consumption (chapter 2) while convenience is also part of the motive (being mobile, demanding speed).[9] Time pressure reduces opportunities to develop slower but less resource-demanding alternatives such as repairing clothes and cycling to work. The longer hours people work, the more they use private vehicles rather than public transportation for commuting (Devetter and Rousseau 2011). After work, the stressed individual is tired and needs to get home fast and quickly energize his/her body if s/he has not already been able to eat on the run while driving home. Several studies have found that time scarcity and work-family imbalances result in fewer (slow forms of) family meals, and more consumption of fast and processed ready-prepared food as well as sweetened beverages and other "fast" items (Jabs and Devine 2006; Devine et al. 2006; Szabo 2011; Bauer et al. 2012; Gojard and Véron 2018).

Even if there is a rising culture of reengaging with food, such as gardening, cooking from scratch, slow food, and purchasing from alternative outlets such as farmers' markets, this encompasses only a small proportion of the population. Unless there is a sharp transition toward increased working from home as a result of the COVID-19 pandemic,[10] people's busy working lives will continue to produce high demand for convenient food options. The do-it-yourself dinner as a weekend family ritual—with fancy kitchen equipment—is saved for a few occasions.

Time stress thus contributes to a vicious cycle of consumerism. Lower income earners demand fast inexpensive products. Higher income earners pay for services, so that others, some of whom are living in very precarious circumstances, can do for them what they lack the time to do themselves (see Text Box 3.1). They will not slow down because "time is money." "Busyness" is even a sign of prestige, a marker of social status (Sullivan 2008). The (felt) necessity to work very long hours gives wealthy people so little time at the end of the day that they see a need to pay for home help and other services to do things that they otherwise would be able to do themselves, such as cooking meals, cleaning their homes, babysitting, and even arranging birthday parties (Hochschild 2003; Schoonmaker 2006; Sharma 2014; Alsarve 2017; Eldén and Anving 2019; Hickel 2019). Such extra services from people and firms outside the household have an ecological impact; they involve extra travel and gadgets in potentially substantial amounts (Devetter and Rousseau 2011).

There is accordingly a pattern in high-speed society of mass consumption of devices and services intended for saving and shifting time to meet this demand of convenience, and this comes with a significant socio-ecological/climate footprint. However, the problem is greater than just this. Such devices and services do not solve the root problem, time pressure, but deal with symptoms instead. People demand them in order to cope with time pressure, and they reflect individualized solutions (consumption) to a structural problem. The example of private motor vehicles illustrates the problem well. People believe they save time and feel they are more flexible and mobile when they have the opportunity to take their own private car rather than using public transport; they can travel door-to-door and are not reliant on fixed timetables. However, people's individual strategies together create adverse structural side effects or collective stalemates such as traffic jams. Another structural side effect is that the very existence of all the private, individualized strategies prevents public investment in collective goods such as public transportation. The net effect for the population is no time saved.

A paradoxical effect of the use of time-saving and time-shifting devices has to do with direct and indirect rebound effects (see Introduction). If a certain technology is more time-efficient, it may become very popular to use, and hence demand for it increases greatly (direct rebound), and saved time means time to spend on other things (indirect rebound). In other words, even if we can do things faster, more flexibly, and more efficiently with the help of time-compressing and time-shifting devices, the net effect is that we are forced to do more because of two factors. The first is the growth of interactions, tasks, and expectations that greatly exceed the efficiency gains. For example, think of how the transition from postal mail to email enabled an explosion of social interaction, meaning that people now spend more hours communicating than before this IT revolution. And now we not only communicate by email, but use all sorts of digital platforms that facilitate communication (social media, text messages, share points, etc.). The second factor has to do with the fragmentation of time in social life, which causes problems of synchronization and a vicious cycle of demand for new time-saving and time-shifting devices. This is explored in Text Box 3.2.

Text Box 3.1: Uneven Time: Business Travelers and Taxi Drivers

In her book *In the Meantime*, Sara Sharma (2014) criticizes some of the theories of speed and acceleration as painting an overly universal and simple account of acceleration in everyday life. What is often forgotten is how people in different strata of society experience the pace of life very differently, and how their different temporalities are structurally related to each other. By ignoring different experiences of time, we risk aggravating unjust temporal relations, Sharma argues.

It may be the richer segments of the population that mostly are experiencing the speeding up of society, while also tacitly embracing it. By accepting that the world is getting faster, the discourse of speedup can legitimize a certain temporal infrastructure for speed, which richer segments can use and others will have to maintain with their "temporal labor." In fact, there are multiple interdependent temporalities. Living among the busy and rich implies having the resources to get others to synchronize themselves with one's own demands.

Using ethnographic methods, Sharma contrasts some busy business travelers with taxi drivers. The former are served by an elaborate time infrastructure—environments like airport lounges to help them deal with jet lag, technologies, commodities, and services. Their temporal demands engage the "temporal labor" of many other people. The frequent business travelers Sharma studied were highly competent in cultural theories of speed and acceleration. They spoke of work-life balance, time control, and time-saving strategies. At the same time, they express an uncritical affirmation of a speedup society, viewing acceleration as a fact of life. There are always people willing to facilitate their lifestyle, many of whom have precarious working situations.

The taxi drivers' time is structurally related to the privileged time of others, like frequent business travelers, to whose demands they have to synchronize their time. In the context of Sharma's study, major metropolitan cities in North America, taxi drivers are almost always immigrants, and many are asylum seekers. Sharma uses the concept of temporal labor "to account for the experience of laboring within a temporal infrastructure while being cast outside it" (57). They worked very long hours, more than seventy hours a week year-round without holiday, yet without reaching the level of minimum wage. While taxi drivers recognize how certain populations live in their own fast worlds, they find themselves outside of that world. Speed is the wrong word to characterize their everyday life. Rather, they experience slowness and many hours of time spent waiting—waiting for busy passengers. Slowness switches to stress when others' demands for speed enter the taxi: "Speed has always frequented the cab. It comes dressed in suits, talking on cell phones, late for appointments, or about to miss a flight" (63).

Sharma's study reminds us that time is highly uneven and differently experienced. Time is lived and experienced at the intersection of a range of social differences that include class, gender, ethnicity, immigration status, and labor (see also chapter 2). One person's time is entangled with the time of others, and such relations of temporality and synchronicity have a great deal to do with inequality and relations of power.

Buying for Instant Reward

The "present" is strong in consumer culture. If much time is devoted to the "sacrifice" of working, then the person who sacrifices his/her time by working for a wage can expect compensation and reward. Consumption now! Immediate satisfaction of needs, wants and desires is indeed what people have been promised and what they expect of consumer culture. An almost definitional feature of consumer society is to buy now, and not to postpone the desire (Firat et al. 2013). Consumerism is oriented toward consuming, not saving; the present, not the future; enjoying, not investing. When people desire a reward after a hard day or week of work, after an achievement, or after any kind of suffering, the future is subordinated to present purposes and pleasures, even if people have adopted self-regulatory goals such as keeping a diet. "Faced with an opportunity to indulge, consumers may be motivated to distort their memories to fabricate progress toward a pertinent self-regulatory goal, allowing themselves to indulge in the present" (May and Irmak 2014, 624).

Text Box 3.2: Vicious Cycle of Demand for New Time-saving and Time-shifting Devices

In relation to household appliances, Shove (2003) emphasizes how time-saving and time-shifting devices cause a fragmented everyday life, which in turn leads to a vicious cycle of demand for new time-saving and time-shifting devices. Rather than reducing the number of hours spent on housework, household appliances change the way time is allocated and managed. People use strategies like multitasking and careful planning so that devices are used simultaneously, but this also causes a fractured timescape and ultimately results in no more free time. Likewise, Southerton (2020) maintains that difficulties of coordinating practices, in a context of highly fragmented and individualized social lives (historical weakening of collectively timed events), is a key factor behind the common experience of the "time squeeze." Time-saving and time-shifting devices and services can create even more time pressure due to problems of scheduling, coordination, and synchronization. The electronic calendar facilitates time management and individual scheduling, but causes temporal fragmentation of social life and difficulties of interpersonal coordination. People receive the means to control their own time and organize many fragmented time intervals, but find it difficult to actually spend time together. When we try to deal with time pressure without addressing root causes (like long working hours) we thus risk triggering a chain reaction that spirals out of control. This observation of paradoxical effects accords with Hartmut Rosa's general theory of social acceleration. Rosa (2013, 156) refers to the process as "the circle of acceleration." Time-saving technology (technological acceleration) tends to increase the rate of social change, which in turn accelerates the pace of life. An accelerated pace of life, in turn, means that people experience time scarcity and pressure, which in turn causes new demand for even more "efficient" time-saving and time-shifting technologies. The speeding up of society is, hence, partly a self-propelling process kept going via feedback loops (and also partly driven by the economic, cultural, and socio-structural motor, as discussed earlier).

Instant reward for all sacrifices made in working life and other areas of social life is a key symbol of all this. Daniel Miller (1998) discusses this theme in terms of "the treat," which he argues is an important part of the shopping activity. When someone spends time shopping, it is not unlikely that some portion of the shopping is seen as a treat. This could be some little luxury part of the consumption, perhaps a chocolate bar or toys for the children who must follow along. Miller argues that the treat is a minor part of all consumption; it is "an extravagance that lies outside the constraints of necessity" (Miller 1998, 40). The treat is for oneself as a shopper; it is a reward for carrying out the "burdensome" act of shopping. (Miller addresses shopping for mundane, everyday goods, not shopping as entertainment.) When the treat is for an accompanying child, it consists of going to a toy store, having an ice cream, or eating at a fast-food outlet such as a hamburger chain. This pattern may be repeated until it becomes a routine or even a ritual: "Most children are quite adept at turning what starts as a treat into a ritual, in the sense that this becomes an invariant element in all subsequent shopping expeditions" (Miller 1998, 43). Cafeterias rely on this logic, and it is carefully applied by supermarkets such as Marks & Spencer and retail outlets such as IKEA, not to mention the large malls which generalize the treat into an entire entertainment industry (see next chapter). The treat—or the instant reward, as conceptualized here—may accordingly be a much more general phenomenon than is suggested by Miller. A hard day or week's work may require a treat, provided for example by the fast-food restaurant (Bauer et al. 2012, 498). Dense leisure activities, as was explored above, reflects the same logic. For relatively poor consumers, a chocolate bar or a pint at the pub may serve as the reward. For rich or high-income earners, a weekend vacation trip abroad may be the equivalent.

There is still more to it, however. The idea of a treat, Miller says, has some similarities with the idea of shopping itself as a treat to be carried out when depressed. Miller quotes a middle-class female who is thinking back to what she used to do with her friends:

> "My god I'm really fed up, let's go shopping, and I need some shoes, and come along you can find something to buy as well," and we'd go and we'd both get a pair of shoes, or get our hair cut or whatever and feel a lot better. Completely superficial things but it was nice, it made a nice fun thing. We'd say "Oh I'm really pissed off this week, we deserve to go" and we'd do that. (Miller 1998, 47)

The treat works well as a (superficial) response to depression because it is an action that reaffirms the self. Yet, it may do little to cure deeper levels of unhappiness (see concluding chapter).

Buying for Future Leisure

What if we work so much that there is no time to spend all we earn, even if we intensify our leisure activities? What if some people in the community have more money than they can possibly spend on everyday convenience goods and services, instant rewards and pleasures? One option, of course, is to save money. Another is to buy stuff and accumulate it for future use.

Indeed, leisure is not just the time after work; it is part of our hopes and daydreams. Leisure is important in our plans for the future, for a "time-rich fantasy future" (Sullivan 2008). We expect much of our leisure. Our expectations often exceed what we have time for in the present. Sullivan and Gershuny (2004) point to the tendency to buy things in the present without using the stuff. Purchased goods may remain "in storage" at home as symbols of a potential but unrealized future. They found this tendency to be more common among work-rich, high-income, and time-poor social classes (in their study, in a British context). The contradiction and irony of this is that consumption expenditure is highest among groups whose leisure time is the shortest (and is getting shorter). These groups have plenty of money, but using goods takes time, time they do not have. Their (often unrealistic) hope is that they will have more time in the future to enjoy the goods they have stockpiled. Typical objects of this sort could be sporting and outdoor equipment, a boat, a second house, musical instruments, fancy kitchenware, electronic devices, or equipment associated with a particular hobby such as photography. Lots of stuff requires lots of space. You may need a garage or some kind of storage area for it all. One hopes to have time to engage with the objects later. Fantasizing about their use is important here, and is something that household members can do together as a kind of ritual that unites them as a group (see chapter 1). As an example, for family members, an "investment" in outdoor equipment may symbolize an aspiration that through the purchase becomes a bit more real. A garage full of expensive equipment symbolizes its potential actualization. "The desire to fulfil a particular idealized family role is symbolically represented in the purchases and the associated fantasizing about use, but the actual holiday is prevented by pressure of time" (Sullivan and Gershuny 2004, 93). Some satisfaction may be obtained in the time-pressed present by "the mere knowledge of possession, which symbolizes this imaginary future" (Sullivan and Gershuny 2004, 88).

Procuring goods could also be a way to deal with guilt and anxiety connected with an inability to sufficiently live up to an idealized role of parent or partner. If a parent feels guilty about not spending enough time with his or her children, buying goods for future family activities can play a compensatory role. It can be a way of confirming a (lifestyle) identity that one eventually hopes to achieve. Possessing goods that cannot be used right away can also generate self-confidence (Sullivan 2008), not least considering the mechanisms of identity, extended selves, and conspicuous consumption that were explored in chapter 2.

Even if this tendency to buy things for future leisure may be stronger among some particular income groups, I argue that it is reasonable to generalize this observation a bit more, considering the idea of social acceleration. Time pressure is felt among large segments of the population in welfare societies, and large segments of the population may accordingly buy and store goods for imagined later use. It is arguably common to have overly optimistic perceptions about having time to use all the goods later, and people are also likely to fail to consider the risk of goods going out of date.

In summary, the above sections show that the structural separation of work and leisure in social life and the common experience of time pressure due to long working hours—including commuting time—boost consumerism and high levels of consumption. Consumption represents a quick fix. Leisure time and commoditized experience in the mass consumption context serve to offer some reward for and escape from an otherwise hectic and overworked life. However, the escape itself requires a context of fast consumption. Leisure itself is intensified. When you work more, you can spend more, and because you experience time scarcity you need rapid—and environmentally impactful—consumption to handle your stress. Time-compressing and time-shifting goods and services come to the rescue, but they fail to address the root problem; in fact they perpetuate it. Moreover, living an overworked life implies having no time to engage in activities that can serve as a substitute for consumption, or slower types of consumption, such as cycling. Stress induces a narrow focus on the present—supported by consumer culture and ideology—and the search for instant rewards and pleasure. However, if you lack time to use stuff today, you can buy goods for the future; they can represent the fantasized time-rich future.

Let us now turn to another major temporal aspect of our mass consumption society, one that has a lot to do with how consumer culture and consumer capitalism work.

NOVELTY

A fundamental temporal aspect of capitalist markets and consumer culture is the celebration of novelty. Novelty is an often-praised aspect of consumerism, and it is even seen as a fundamental characteristic of modernity related to hedonism, pleasure seeking, individualization, progress, and similar values (Campbell 2018 [1987]; Bauman 2007; Sassatelli 2007; Jackson 2017).

Celebrating novelty means downplaying stability and neglecting such qualities as durability. Novelty is closely related to the rapid and accelerating turnover of products. Anything that appears new, fresh, innovative, or "modern" is automatically treated as something good, a symbol of innovation and progress. Novelty implies an accentuation of the present. The past is uninteresting and the long-term future (the consequences of present actions) is overlooked.

The urge for novelty and variety can be manifested in different practices such as the choice of a tourist destination, a restaurant for a weekend dinner, or how to dress for a party. One is looking for a new experience, a new landscape to admire, a new cuisine to try, a new appearance. Novelty is important in order to spur desire, surprise, and fascination. Novelty and variety can be seen as important parts of ritualized gift-giving (Hamlin 2003); you may not bring the same present to two different celebrations. Fashion is an area in which novelty is even definitional. This section begins by discussing a concept that is important for understanding this urge for novelty, and which explicitly takes into account a temporal aspect of consumerism: the cycle of desire. It then continues by exploring fashion and fashion anxiety, and I include a text box on rapid obsolescence.

Cycles of Desire and Insatiable Demand

In Colin Campbell's work on the culture and spirit of "modern" consumerism,[11] the core characteristic of this kind of consumerism is an endless process of wanting and replacement. "Wanting rather than having is the main focus of pleasure-seeking" (Campbell 2018 [1987], 141), and this is what drives the modern consumer. "The modern consumer will desire a novel rather than a familiar product because this enables him to believe that its acquisition and use can supply experiences that he has not so far encountered in reality" (Campbell 2018 [1987], 144).

Objects that have not yet been experienced are imagined as the sweetest: "Individuals do not so much seek satisfaction from products as pleasure from the self-illusory experiences that they construct from their associated meanings" (Campbell 2018 [1987], 144). This consumerism is therefore characterized as an incessant quest for novelty. It relies on insatiability. The "promise" is more appealing than the "actuality."

Campbell stressed the role of the imagination in driving the restlessness that characterizes consumerism in modern society. Belk, Ger and Askegaard (2003) proceed from Campbell's theory in developing their concept of the cycle of desire. Desire, according to them, is a cyclic emotion. The cycle of desire follows a typical never-ending course: desire-acquisition-reformulation of desire. It starts with seduction, when the consumer dwells on and craves the object. If the person fails to acquire the object, s/he may feel frustration and begin to desire other objects. An element of distance to an object and difficulty of acquiring it makes it more attractive; it triggers desire. Desire can be directed at fantasies about something better, even a life diametrically opposed to the one currently being lived. It is otherness that is sought for. That otherness could be a reference person (see chapter 2), another time, or another place:

> In addition to the otherness of past or future time, the otherness of a place is also associated with certain objects of desire. These desires involve traveling to exotic places, living in other countries, enjoying the exciting nightlife of glamorous world cities, or just having a flat instead of living with parents. (Belk et al. 2003, 336)

Goods and services that are just a bit out of reach—for economic, practical or moral reasons—have a special capacity to ignite the "fire of desire"; they trigger more desire, deeper longing, more engaging fantasies, a feeling of adventure, and so on. Longing can be a powerful, even obsessive feeling, as can be seen in a quote from a young man in the United States: "I wanted this car so bad I could taste it! I could hardly function throughout the day because I would make myself sick thinking about the Honda and how bad I wanted it" (Belk et al. 2003, 333).

Acquisition is problematic, however, because then desire ends. The journey is often better than the destination. Here, desire intersects with the demand for novelty. Satisfaction is short-lived. The acquisition and the realization of desire are often followed by mundane routine, even boredom. There is a feeling of emptiness. What one then longs for is the feeling of desire. There is a "desire for desire." There is also a fear of not having anything to desire: "to be without desire is seen as being a state of hopelessness tantamount to death" (Belk et al. 2003, 343). Desire connected with the chance to realize the object of desire creates a state of hope that itself is pleasurable. One even hopes for hope. It is this kind of energizing emotion that one is seeking. There is something of a paradox in being energized by a hope to acquire objects that are difficult to obtain. If they are impossible to attain, for pecuniary or moral reasons, they may fall out of one's gaze, and a "seemingly more obtainable object of desire takes its place in occupying the person's thoughts and providing a new focus of desire and hope" (Belk et al. 2003, 343).

According to Belk, Ger, and Askegaard, it is the state of desire as such, and not the short-lived satisfaction or disappointment when desired goods and services are consumed, that keeps the cycle going. It is "the desire to desire rather than disillusionment that energizes this the cycle of desire"

(Belk et al. 2003, 347). A quote from a young Turkish man in their study is particularly telling:

> It was a great effort to get my driver's license. I worked part time jobs and saved all of my earnings to buy a second-hand car but could never have enough money. My parents promised to buy one for my graduation. All my friends had cars. I thought I had to have one too. Upon graduation, instead of a second-hand car, they surprised me with a brand-new one; a good model, fast. . . . Now that I have it, it is no longer the most important thing in life for me. Maybe I got used to it. Now there is another fire awakening in me. I want a faster, better car. I have a sports car, but I'd like a Cabrio. If I have that, I might then want a plane. (Belk et al. 2003, 341)

If he gets a plane, perhaps he will want a rocket, to fly to space, to Mars . . .

This cycle of desire is depicted in Figure 3.1, which shows how the cycle is energized by both endogenous and exogenous drivers. The arrow representing social and contextual drivers indicates how the cycle can be initiated or accelerated by social dynamics external to the individual.

The above discussion seems to suggest that the cycle of desire is a fundamental human tendency. Can we humans ever calm down? Even if there will be always desires, the answer must be partly yes, not the least because the dynamics of individual desires are contextually shaped (external arrow in Figure 3.1). We could, in principle, reorient our energies toward "being" rather than "having" (Fromm 1976), or toward future-oriented, goal-directed

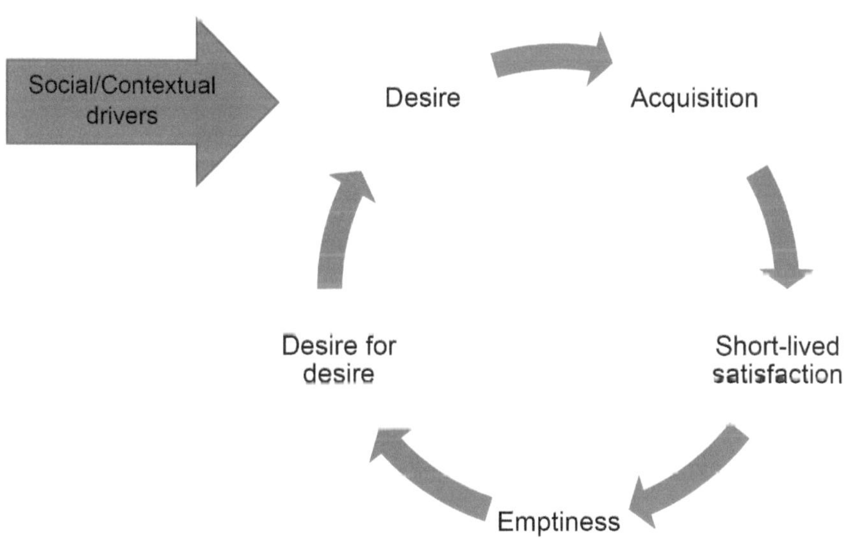

Figure 3.1: The Cycle of Desire. *Source:* Author, based on Belk et al. (2003).

self-actualization rather than toward material consumption and superficial commoditized experiences occurring in a chaotic, directionless present (Rosa 2013). Some social contexts will boost cycles of desire, whereas other can work in the opposite direction, or change the orientation of desires so that they become less materialistic, as well as slower and more long term. Even if the above analysis may suggest a strong focus on individual aspirations, Belk and his colleagues make it clear that desires are social; they are ignited by the kinds of social dynamics explored in chapters 1 and 2 of this book: social relationships and social comparison. The human propensity of desire also fits the dynamic nature of capitalism. Without the institutions of consumer capitalism, according to Belk et al. (2003), other objects of desire and hope would emerge. The internet and various kinds of online shopping, including secondhand shopping, can accelerate the cycle of desire (Denigri-Knott 2011), as will be further explored in the next chapter.

Zygmunt Bauman similarly emphasizes how consumer society fosters a sense that demands are insatiable. The fleeting nature of consumer life, expressed in his notion of liquid modernity, has been the focus of much of his work. The life of consumption, according to Bauman, appears condemned to be a life of rapid learning and swift forgetting. "The consumerist culture is marked by a constant pressure to be someone else. Consumer markets focus on the prompt devaluation of their past offers" (Bauman 2007, 100).

Bauman emphasizes this feature of consumer society, and discusses examples such as cosmetic surgery; people can constantly be "born again" through the plasticity of the human body. "The main attraction of consumption and shopping life is the offer of plentiful new starts and resurrections (chances of being 'born again')" (2007, 49). The quest for novelty logically implies that full satisfaction should be achieved through consumption, because the consumer will only be satisfied for a few days, hours, minutes, or seconds—depending on the product category. Satisfaction is a transitory experience. The cycle of desire continues.

Hartmut Rosa's theory of social acceleration adds an important insight. The supposedly good and full life is about experiencing everything the market has to offer, or at least much of it. Acceleration carries with it a fraudulent promise and perception that this full life is indeed possible to achieve. Unfortunately, any balance between one's own life and the supposed full life is never achieved. That imbalance or gap is itself a driving mechanism. Mass consumption is both a friend and an enemy here. In a context of abundant markets, technological acceleration provides opportunities to live faster and experience more things (though on a more superficial level). For example, you can intensify your leisure, as was discussed earlier. However, this very acceleration implies an increasing abundance of market opportunities for consumption, and therefore there are constantly more things that one is missing.

The cycle of desire then accelerates. There is an ever-widening ocean of stuff that one cannot have (or enjoy, because you have no time to use or experience the things you buy). There is a heaven of possible experiences almost within reach but which one never enjoys. All this adds to feelings of frustration, anxiety, unrest, stress, envy, hatred, and constant dissatisfaction. There is a constant fear of missing out (FOMO) on enjoyable experiences in social life, a fear that itself constantly fuels consumerism. The process is illustrated in Figure 3.2.

Fashion

Fashion is the classic manifestation of the urge for novelty, and it is a social phenomenon closely connected with cycles of desire (In Figures 3.1 and 3.2, fashion can serve as an example of an external driver initiating/accelerating the cycle). Fashion has long interested sociologists. Within consumer culture it is considered to reflect the spirit of modern life, individualization, good taste, and even civilization (Simmel 1971 [1904]; Campbell 2018 [1987]; Sassatelli 2007). Fashion reveals the restless nature of social life. Georg Simmel was a pioneer in analyzing the social logic of fashion (Simmel 1971 [1904]). He showed how fashion brings time and timing into consumption as a critical aspect of it. Simmel pointed to how fashion represents an accentuation of the present and a bracketing of both past and future: "Fashion always occupies the dividing-line between the past and the future, and consequently conveys a stronger feeling of the present, at least while it is at its height, than most other phenomena" (Simmel 1971 [1904], 303).

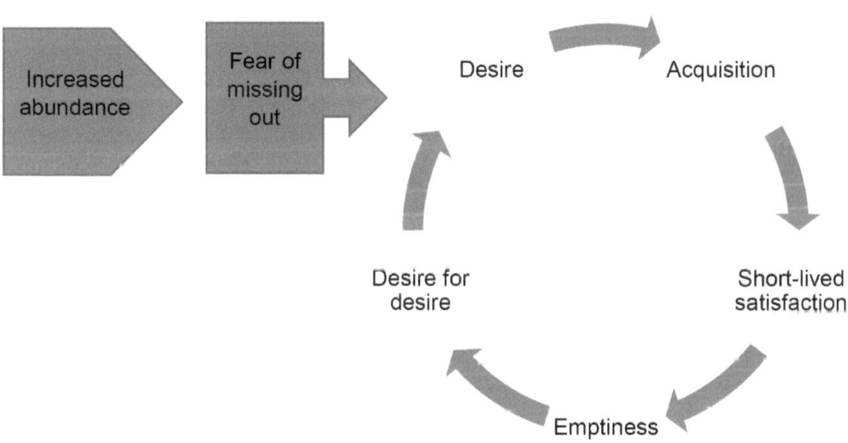

Figure 3.2: Increased Abundance, Fear of Missing Out, and the Cycle of Desire. *Source:* Author, partly based on Belk et al. (2003) and Rosa (2013).

Fashion is energized by the social comparison game (chapter 2). People enviously and anxiously glance at others, making comparisons, assessing themselves critically, adjusting to social class belongings and differentiation, and trying to both conform and stand out at the same time. People in all social classes feel the need to catch up and keep up with their peers and reference groups. Identities are never complete. The fashion-conscious consumer wants, paradoxically, to be someone special and original yet within a common frame: "fashion represents nothing more than one of the many forms of life by the aid of which we seek to combine in uniform spheres of activity the tendency towards social equalization with the desire for individual differentiation and change" (Simmel 1971 [1904], 296). The logic of social differentiation—between pioneers, adopters, mass followers—ensures that the cycle continue to spin:

> Social forms, apparel, aesthetic judgment, the whole style of human expression, are constantly transformed by fashion, in such a way, however, that fashion—i.e., the latest fashion—in all these things affects only the upper classes. Just as soon as the lower classes begin to copy their style, thereby crossing the line of demarcation the upper classes have drawn and destroying the uniformity of their coherence, the upper classes turn away from this style and adopt a new one, which in its turn differentiates them from the masses; and thus the game goes merrily on. (Simmel 1971 [1904], 299)

Thorstein Veblen (1994 [1899]) was interested in similar logics, and showed that fashion is a classic example of conspicuous consumption. He discussed its cyclical nature: "Dress must not only be conspicuously expensive and inconvenient; it must at the same time be up to date" (Veblen 1994 [1899], 106). The principle of novelty perfectly fits the law of conspicuous waste, he argues.

> The farther the community, especially the wealthy classes of the community, develop in wealth and mobility and in the range of their human contact, the more imperatively will the law of conspicuous waste assert itself in matters of dress, the more will the sense of beauty tend to fall into abeyance or be overborn by the canon of pecuniary reputability, the more rapidly will fashions shift and change, and the more grotesque and intolerable will be the varying styles that successively come into vogue. (Veblen 1994 [1899], 109–10)

As fashion spreads, it drives its own termination (regarding its content, but not the form itself). This restless fashion cycle, which these classic thinkers have described, is also known as the bandwagon and snob effects (Shukla 2008, 27). The term "bandwagon effect" is used to label a situation where consumers purchase products because reference groups are buying the same goods. "Snob effect," in contrast, refers to a diminishing demand for a product because others are purchasing that product.

Luxury was described in the previous chapter. Fashion appears to be a contrasting phenomenon, even though both are related to distinction, taste, and class struggles. According to Sassatelli, fashion is tightly coupled to a more mature consumer capitalism characterized by mass consumption, and can even be seen as a "democratization" of luxuries.

> If the desire for new and non-essential goods is one of the driving forces of early capitalism, the management of luxuries through their creation and domestication in the dynamics of fashion is one of the factors which keep the wheels of commerce in constant motion, stabilizing the capitalist economy in its mature phases. (Sassatelli 2007, 23)

Simmel too points out how the rapidity of the fashion cycle requires cheaper products, even for the wealthier part of the population.

> The more an article becomes subject to rapid changes of fashion, the greater the demand for *cheap* products of its kind, not only because the larger and therefore poorer classes nevertheless have enough purchasing power to regulate industry and demand objects which at least bear the outward semblance of style, but also because even the higher circles of society could not afford to adopt the rapid changes in fashion forced upon them by the imitation of the lower circles, if the objects were not relatively cheap. (Simmel 1971 [1904], 318–19)

Even if fashion is a phenomenon with a long history, the conditions that promote it expanded after World War II, when production capacity escalated. As a consequence, the capacity for producing inexpensive fashion items for mass markets also increased, thus favoring a broad process of "democratization of luxuries."

Fashion was primarily associated with the clothing industry, and perhaps still is. Other goods, like furniture, kitchen equipment, dinnerware, interior decoration, and watches have been considered durable products, even bought and invested in for one's entire life. These products were not meant to be replaced. From the 1950s onward, such goods also began to be marketed in fashion terms, implying that they should be bought now in order for people to be up to date, and be replaced again in a few years (Boström and Klintman 2019b). The same goes for more recent technologies in the area of electronics and mobile phones.

In our contemporary days, in the clothing sector, the concept of "fast fashion"—even ultrafast fashion—has gained popularity (Hiller Connell 2018; Camargo and Pereira 2020). Fast fashion, like "disposable T-shirts," signifies the social acceleration of fashion cycles, and a reliance on high consumption of low-price and low-quality garments (by outsourced, brand-driven production). Fashion has been increasingly reliant on rapid product obsolescence and continually growing throughput of resources. It has been estimated that in the United States, 67.9 garments and 7.8 shoes are bought every year per individual (Hiller Connell 2018, 294). While traditionally, the fashion industry was temporally structured around four seasons each year, the fast-fashion model has made this concept of seasons obsolete "with new merchandise continuously flowing into stores and fast fashion retailers speaking in terms of having fifty-two micro seasons per year" (Hiller Connell 2018, 295). Sustainable?

Fashion and Anxiety

What kinds of emotional energies are linked to novelty and fashion? Are they positive or negative? And how do these energies fuel consumerism? Novelty may well be linked to certain positive emotional energies that many people desire, for example curiosity and other hedonistic motivations, not least when daydreaming together (chapter 1). In cycles of desire, positive emotions (desire itself) and negative ones (frustration, disappointment, envy) are mixed. There is an "enjoyable discomfort" (Campbell 2018 [1987]; Belk et al. 2003). A mixture of positive and negative emotions fuels the cycle. There is also another important sociopsychological mechanism that underlies the demand for fashion and drives consumerism: *anxiety*.

The fashion-sensitive consumer is arguably equally much more driven by avoidance of feeling bad (social anxiety) than by the thrill of the chase.

> Fashion is one way to render the goods obsolete before their useful lives are over. Thus fashion plays an important role in adding feelings of scarcity and insecurity to a world of factory-made abundance. It can make a warm and useful coat unwearable, a sturdy and comfortable chair dowdy. It feels like a way of engaging the future, but its chief impact is to make people dissatisfied with the present, and especially with all the objects in it. (Hine 2002, 94)

A related problem that the fashion-sensitive consumer faces is that it is seldom clear exactly what is fashionable and how long it will remain so. Considering that s/he is fundamentally sensitive to social comparison, judgement, particular reference groups, and status (chapter 2), the consumer who is sensitive to trends and fashion must be alert. What is "in" today can be "out" tomorrow. This problem increases because of the diffuse character of fashion. Anxiety, which stems from fashion, is therefore also a driving force behind excessive consumption (Solér 2018).

Paradoxically, the diffuse character of fashion—"what exactly is it that I am supposed to emulate"—can make it particularly effective as a driver of buying excessive volumes. This is particularly clear regarding textile products. From the perspective of the fashion consumer, it is a problem that there are no clear-cut social conventions or explicit guidance from the fashion industry, magazines, advertisements, influencers, or celebrities on what to wear. This is also precisely the point. Everyone with a drive to follow fashion trends must employ her own tacit knowledge of what it is that one is supposed to imitate (or transcend). What the fashion industry actually creates is appearance anxiety (Miller 2010, 31–38). This anxiety, in turn, induces people to buy more clothes than they "need" because of their felt need to be able to pick outfits from a large wardrobe. There is a need to have a sufficient number of items to be able to fabricate one's appearance in a slightly different way each day. Moss discusses this in terms of the "rules of plenty":

> Having *just one* article is not enough. The lone polo shirt in the closet "hangs" in diametric contradiction to the rules of plenty. A form of addiction takes over and there is the unstated desire or even the overt intention for the consumer/viewer to purchase multiples and in quantity. (Moss 2007, 93)

To be sure, not everything that matters can be counted in numbers. People sensitive to fashion must acquire good taste (cf. Veblen, Bourdieu, chapter 2), which is more of a qualitative skill, and which may take a long time to acquire and the right kind of socialization. However, having a lot of something is practical or even necessary with some types of goods, because in the social comparison game, you may feel an urge to be able to frequently change your appearance.

The compelling nature of fashion can be revealed by voluntary or involuntary disruptions of consumption habits. Cosette Armstrong and colleagues (2016) conducted a study called Fashion Detox. Their textile students—who were probably interested in fashion—committed to abstaining from clothing acquisition for ten weeks and reflected about the experience on a blog. There were many interesting results from the study, reflecting both barriers and opportunities, not least in relation to the social comparison game. In this context, a psychological yearning for new and different things was common. Boredom or frustration were expressed in relation to not being able to buy clothing. Here is an illustrative quote from the study:

> This whole not shopping thing is really making me sad! Even if it's just a new ring or necklace, I just want something new!! I am really anxious lately, because neither my closet or my jewelry box is growing! I feel like I'm missing something in my life! (Armstrong et al. 2016, 430)

This pressure in relation to clothes is obviously not gender neutral. However, even if women may have a larger socio-ecological footprint in the specific area of textiles, men are not immune to fashion's capacity to generate such emotional effects as anxiety, and they too feel a need to be able to flexibly change their appearance with other objects selected from their stores of stuff: shoes, electronic devices, sports equipment, jewelry, and so on. Fashion links closely with a rapid obsolescence of desirability (see Text Box 3.3).

Text Box 3.3: Rapid Obsolescence

The logic of novelty (and cycles of desire) in general, and fashion in particular, implies a devaluation of durability. Destruction is built into design and prescripted into the consumer practices and experiences. Items are meant to break down, to be replaced. The spread of fashion and other urges for novelty involves an acceleration of product replacement. Fast fashion is a bizarre extreme. We could very well also speak of experience replacement, such as in constantly finding new (and more distant) tourist destinations, as well as personality/identity replacement (Bauman 2007; Rosa 2013).

This acceleration of product, experience, and identity replacement is obviously driven by economic and cultural factors. The big brand companies have much to win. Businesses have more to sell if product life cycles are shorter. But it is also important to consider the demand side. Supply and demand collaborate in devaluing durability. More than sixty years ago, Vance Packard (1988 [1960]) wrote about planned obsolescence. Whereas industry promotes obsolescence of function (an existing product becomes outmoded when a new product performs better) and also often uses the more controversial strategy "planned obsolescence of quality" (a product is designed to break after a set amount of time), an even more effective strategy, according to Packard, is "planned obsolescence of desirability"; which he understood as a psychological obsolescence in which industry uses fashion as key strategy.

Fletcher (2012) likewise argues that obsolescence is constructed and this takes different forms. The development of fashion gradually resulted in a "shift in the perception of clothes from a durable consumer good with an intrinsic material value, to a non-durable consumer good with novelty and brand value" (Fletcher 2012, 224). Garments had to become obsolete, at least in psychological terms. Psychological obsolescence, Fletcher argues, is indeed related more to aesthetic and social aspects than physical and technological ones:

> For fashion clothes, which already endure physically long past their period of use, putting resources and effort into enhancing the physical durability of seams and fabrics is worth little if it is aesthetics or social preferences—or even changing waistlines—not material robustness that determines a piece's lifespan. (Fletcher 2012, 227)

There seems to be no point in producing enduring quality products if they are expected to soon be perceived as obsolete. In addition to psychological, physical, and technological obsolescence, there is also economic obsolescence; it is often cheaper to buy a new item than to repair an existing one. Consumers forget clothes they have bought. They are quickly hung up in the wardrobe. Price tags may remain on clothes for years. When fashion-conscious consumers discover unused clothes in the wardrobe, they cannot be used because they are out of fashion. If you then donate them to a secondhand outlet, you may even feel that you have done something good for the environment.

ACCESSIBILITY, SUDDEN OPPORTUNITIES, AND IMPULSE BUYING

There is much in the infrastructural environment that facilitates consumption in and for the present. I will explore some sites of consumption in the next chapter (the mall and the internet) but here I will discuss a temporal feature: how market offers have become incessantly accessible. This concerns the possibility of having year-round access to such objects as seasonal fruits and vegetables, which is made possible by advanced technology and what Giddens (1984, 1991) call the "time-space distanciation" of modern life institutions, such as the stretching out of global supply chains. One side of this is the incessant availability of shopping in general. Increased availability, 24/7 retailing, shops everywhere in urban areas, online shopping, credit cards, and so on provide a never-ending stream of consumer temptations. There is always a chance for instant reward.

The phenomenon of impulse buying is interesting to consider here. As a temporal variable, impulse buying indicates an act of purchasing characterized by spontaneity or a lack of planning (Rook 1987; O'Guinn and Faber 1989; Lo and Harvey 2010; Ozen and Engizek 2014). Impulsive people often experience a "sudden and unplanned urge to behave in a hedonically pleasing manner" (May and Irmak 2014, 626). Marketing science, the advertising industry and various media and influencers do what they can to increase this type of purchasing. It is "easier than ever before for consumers to purchase things on impulse," wrote Rook (1987, 189) long before the internet revolution.

Even if a desire may exist latently, impulse buying is a sudden, irresistible urge to buy without giving consideration to negative financial, dietary, or ethical consequences. It is often associated with objects such as candy, snacks, and fashion, but it can also include more expensive items such as jewelry, furniture, electronic devices, vacation trips, and even cars (cf. Rook 1987). These may be bought for instant reward or for future leisure, as discussed earlier. Also common is impulse buying of secondhand objects on online sharing platforms (Parguel et al. 2017).

Mysterious forces are experienced as taking over the mind of the consumer. Objects are empowered with agency and will, and they seduce the consumer, who forgets time and common sense. Rook (1987, 194) compiled some apt quotes:

> I was standing in the grocery store checkout line, and the candy bar was staring there at me. (male, twenty-six years of age)

> The pants were shrieking "buy me," so I knew right then that I better walk away and get something else done. (female, thirty-five)

> I had gone on to a different department, but the sweater was following me. I felt like it was pulling me back to the men's department, where I finally bought it. (male, thirty-eight)

There is an emotional arousal, a sense of focus and being in the present. The present says "buy." Any object can trigger a sudden higher level of excitement which feels compelling and leaves the consumer out of control.

Impulse buying is certainly associated with conventional shopping and may be triggered when people can physically see and touch products and meet skilled sales staff. What about online shopping and the pattern of incessant accessibility of shopping? In some respects, the internet may be less prone to induce impulse buying (though not entirely; see chapter 4). If something is always accessible, it follows that it is always possible to postpone a purchase and plan more carefully. However, in both physical and digital sites, sellers can aggressively inform customers of a sudden discount or that an item will soon be out of stock: "only one item left." Impulse buying is hence triggered by the perception that if I do not buy this immediately, a unique opportunity may be lost. The discount offer is now or never.

CONCLUSION: ACCELERATION AND THE LOSS OF FUTURE

I opened this chapter by referring to the concept of social acceleration. It is an apt term for capturing much of what people are urged or forced to do and experience in the mass consumption context. Rosa uses the metaphor of a slippery slope to capture how the acceleration of social change can be experienced. People experience a constant time pressure—a faster pace of life—caused by the demand to be constantly a jour, up-to-date, and online in order not to miss all the opportunities, or just to adapt to requirements of synchronization. The faster the flow of information—and in this context we can add fashion, durability of products, and so on—the higher the slope. It should be clear that all three types of social acceleration—technological, social change and pace of life—interact in reproducing mass-consumption patterns.

The basic separation of leisure time and work time is a structural condition that fuels consumerism. Long working hours do not just provide income to buy things. Time pressure itself boosts consumerism. Consumption represents a quick fix. Leisure time and commoditized experience in the mass consumption context are there for reward and escape. Escape however requires speed. Leisure is intensified. Time-saving and time-shifting devices and services come to the rescue when it comes to coping with stress, but they fail to address the root problem; instead they perpetuate it. Overworked lives prevent the seeking of slower alternatives. Stress contributes to an obsession with the present—an endless cycle of desire. Novelty and fashion are celebrated, but novelty and fashion may cause more anxiety than curiosity, and such anxieties—particularly when they link with social comparison (chapter 2)—make people continue to spend and throw away obsolete stuff. The promises of consumer culture remain unmet. There will always be newer and fancier dresses to obtain. The unsatisfied consumer is the only constant in the equation.

The analysis suggests that the relation between perceived time pressure and consumerism is two-directional (see figure 3.3), and involves a vicious spiral of consuming. *Time pressure cause consumption*: due to demand for time-saving/time-shifting products and services, fast options, and so on. *Consumption cause time pressure*: due to the abundance of opportunities in consumer culture that one cannot miss, igniting cycles of desire, and ownership of more goods (clutter) that needs to be taken care of (see also next chapter).

Most of the analysis in this chapter also illustrates something very important from the perspective of long-term sustainability: the discounting of the future. You consume in and for the present. Yes, some consumption is done

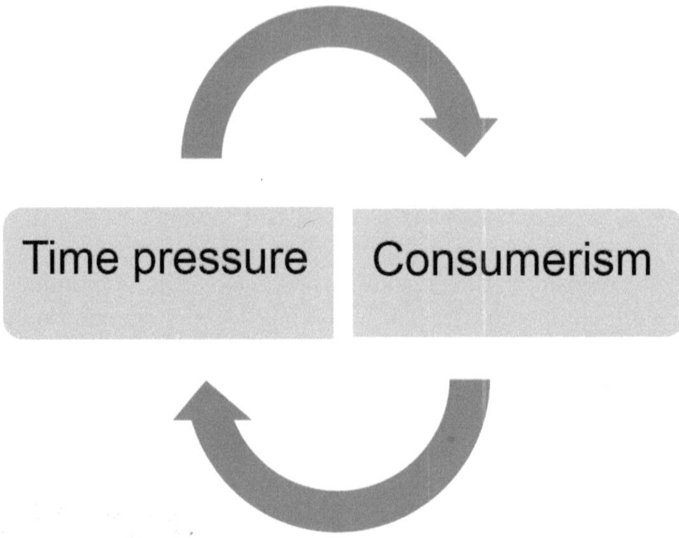

Figure 3.3. Time Pressure and Consumerism. *Source:* Author

to remember something that has passed. Yes, some consumption is done with the future in mind, such as when you buy for future leisure. However, even when you buy something for the future, it may take the form of a fantasized time-rich future. One rarely daydreams about a future characterized by socio-ecological destruction caused by present-day mass consumption. Buying for future leisure is also a form of present orientation in the sense that the future becomes the object of ritualistic daydreaming in the present. It is a way to spend (not save) excessive money (among high-income and time-poor classes) and to make possibilities in the future a bit more concrete. Much other consumption concerns more direct satisfaction of needs, wants, and (cycles of) desires for the present time. Indeed, even if humans can plan, build, buy, and invest for the future—an extraordinary if not unique feature of our species—the urges related to the present are compelling. The infrastructures, institutions and social lives of mass consumption generally favor the present. Concerns about the future can be postponed until the future. Future benefits are considered less valuable than present benefits (Lockie and Wong 2018, 335). Many results of the analysis in this chapter—demands for time-saving and time-shifting goods and services, the urge for novelty, the cycle of desire, fashion, fashion anxiety, instant reward, instant kicks, sudden offers, impulse buying (which has been contrasted with a capacity to delay gratification), compulsive buying, escalating consumer debts, rapid obsolescence, and social acceleration in a more general sense—lead to this observation. Whereas the present focus is highly permeated by the institutions of capitalism, it is important to also consider how deeply internalized it is in the consumers' minds and practices in social life. Our common future is discounted, devalued, neglected, forgotten, sold, lost; it is stolen from future generations, says Greta Thunberg (2019).

> We have everything we could ever wish for and yet now we may have nothing. Now we probably don't even have a future any more. Because that future was sold so that a small number of people could make unimaginable amounts of money. It was stolen from us every time you said that the sky was the limit, and that you only live once. (Greta Thunberg 2019, 58)

How can the future be won back? I invite the reader to reflect on opportunities for change in relation to the temporal dimension (see Text Box 3.4), before entering the next chapter, which deals with the spatial dimension.

Text Box 3.4.: Invitation to Reflect on Opportunities for Change

How can society/communities combat social acceleration or at least deal with the common experiences of hurriedness in contemporary social life? How can society, communities, and policies help people escape vicious cycles of desire connected with excessive material consumption and superficial commoditized experiences and redirect their aspirations toward slower, more future-oriented, and goal-directed self-actualization? How can society, communities, and policies attempt to block the two-way relationship between time pressure and consumerism which is driving a vicious spiral of spending and general neglect of our future? How can the long term triumph over the short term, rather than vice versa? The problem of time is extremely complex. It involves both structural and cultural issues, as well as issues of inequality, as Text Box 3.1 shows. No simple solution exists. As this chapter has shown, many commoditized solutions like time-saving goods/services treat the symptoms and fail to address the root problems of speed and acceleration. Nonetheless, there are initial steps that politics and policy could take; these include addressing work-life balance—for instance by facilitating home-based work and a general reduction in working hours. The latter in particular is a core degrowth policy, which in addition to reducing production and income/consumption can directly reduce stress and time poverty and free up time for cultivating alternative practices that are less reliant on consumption (Knight et al. 2013; Schor and Thompson 2014; Kallis et al. 2018; Olsson et al. 2021). At least for parts of the population, the COVID-19 pandemic offered some important clues, in that at least parts of the population got a taste of a slower pace of life. In what ways can policy and politics use these experiences for progressive and just transformative change? And what can be done to combat the cultural motor of consumerism with regard to its celebration of novelty and general insatiability? Do we need nothing less than a broad, global cultural counteroffensive on all levels of society? And if so, who is the change agent?

NOTES

1. I am grateful for constructive comments by Jenny Alsarve and Ylva Uggla on an earlier version of this chapter, as well as to an anonymous reviewer.

2. It may be sufficient to speak of high speed or rapidity rather than the bolder claim of constant acceleration (Boström 2020).

3. The COVID-19 pandemic triggered many such alternative practices, because people suddenly got more spare time at home due to lockdowns and social-distancing policies (Boström 2021a).

4. The references used data to up to 2010. See https://stats.oecd.org/index.aspx?DataSetCode=ANHRS (accessed 2021-11-20) also for the period 2010–2020, which shows a stable trend, although with some drops in 2020 (likely due to the pandemic). There are considerable variations between OECD countries, with the lowest being the Netherlands, with 1,440 hours in 2019, and the highest being Colombia with 2,172 hours in 2019.

5. See https://data.oecd.org/lprdty/gdp-per-hour-worked.htm (accessed 2021-11-20)

6. And particularly for women in some occupations, see for example Grönlund 2007.

7. Admittedly, this does not include people with precarious employment and those working long hours at low wages. For an illustration, see Sharma 2014.

8. Knight et al. (2013) label this the "compositional effect." Persson et al. (2022) use the term "time-effect" in contrast to the "income-effect."

9. Devetter and Rousseau (2011) discuss how consumption of time-intensive goods and services overlaps with conspicuous consumption (the Veblen effect). It is difficult to isolate what consumption is due to long working hours and what is due to conspicuous consumption, but they argue that these mechanisms interact.

10. Studies have also shown that COVID-19 created unexpected opportunities for many people to work from home, which facilitated slower food practices (See Boström 2021a). The involuntary disruption of many consumer practices during the pandemic serves as a good illustration of consumption related to time scarcity.

11. The title of the book *The Romantic Ethic and the Spirit of Consumerism* is a direct parallel to Max Weber's classic work *The Protestant Ethic and the Spirit of Capitalism*. Campbell's book is an attempt to complement Weber's historical

analysis about the origin of capitalism by giving attention to the consumption side of the industrial revolution alongside Weber's discussion of the production side. Like Weber, Campbell focused on the cultural meanings derived from protestant religious doctrines, and traced the roots of modern consumerism to some developments within protestant thought, via the Romantic movement. The romantic ethic evolved and could promote a spirit of consumerism just as the puritan ethic promoted the spirit of capitalism. According to Campbell, the bourgeoisie embraced both the Protestant ethic and a consumption ethic. There was a revolution in consumption as well as in production, and both were needed for the development of capitalism and the blossoming of a propensity to consume.

Chapter 4

Sites of Consumption

The Home, the Mall, the Internet

Consumption can be considered in terms of both buying and using an object.[1] In both senses, it takes place somewhere. We need to understand and emphasize how spatial aspects of consumption—whether buying or using—spur consumerism. Consumption and consumerism are contextualized by the sites in which they are performed. Consider an act of consumption such as having lunch; it can take place at home, at work, at school, while commuting by train or car, or at a holiday destination, and it can be done alone or with family members or friends. The spatial, temporal, and social circumstances surrounding one's consumption differ in the different sites.

Our choices are constrained by the many choices "society" makes for us (see Introduction), and one such constraint concerns the physical infrastructure where one is situated from moment to moment. One key spatiotemporal category that shapes consumption is the home. The home is both a physical and a social space, and is where we spend much of our time, even work time nowadays, in the wake of digitalization and the COVID-19 pandemic. The heaviest environmental impact of households is associated with housing, including the location of the home, heating, cooling, appliances, food practices, and mobility/transport. A very considerable part of one's income, and borrowed money, is spent on the home. I will show in this chapter that the home—and the many meanings associated with home and homeliness—is an important contributor to consumerism. The topics include how people seek to develop and enjoy cultural ideals of the "happy home" and the "happy personal/family life" by investing in the home and buying and using commodities related to it. Many of the emotionally enriching everyday rituals addressed in chapter 1 take place in the home context. Building on insights from chapter 2, we can view the home as an object for extended selves and for social comparison and the hunt for status. Houses and apartments are getting larger in response to a variety of urgent needs, and people fill their homes with a variety of goods, fueled by drivers related to both conspicuous and inconspicuous aspects of consumption, as well as to temporal factors. Hence, this chapter will show that the home environment is a crucial site for reproducing patterns of mass consumption in our society.

Another key place to consider in an analysis of mass consumption is the shopping site. I use the image of the mall to describe an important aspect of shopping in social life: entertainment. Shopping and shopping outlets have been designed and structured in relation to the idea—and compelling norm—that they should provide entertainment and be a place where we spend time on social interaction. Shopping and leisure are related, and people plan holidays and choose holiday destination for the opportunity to shop. Finally, the chapter will consider how the internet, as an abstract place, further boosts consumerism through many platforms and activities on social media.

THE HOME

The home is the physical and social place where we spend most of our time. A very considerable part of our income, as well as borrowed money, is spent on the home. In the preindustrial era, the home was a multipurpose site. The family held together as both an economic and a social unit, and most of social life took place in the home context. The gradual development toward industrialized economies and their associated forms of social life brought about a general replacement of the home-work model, with a spatial separation of work and other everyday activities including housework, caretaking, and leisure. This separation also had a significant impact on the urban infrastructure (Doling and Arundel 2020, 3), and a huge "mobility complex," facilitating transportation between these distant sites, was constructed (Urry 2010). Moreover, a distinct separation between the home as a private space and the public space of work was established. Work was supposed to be done at the workplace, and home was the place for leisure—to rest and reenergize oneself for work. The home became the privatized social setting, a family-based social organization aimed at fostering healthy individuals—particularly men, and later also women—suitable for a hardworking life. Hence, the home was shaped as a private space for consumption. To be sure, some income-generating work took place in the home, as did much unpaid household work, the latter mostly done by women. Although the distribution of housework gradually changed, some gendered patterns remain, and the changes are unevenly spread across different social classes and countries. Due to digitalization and the COVID-19 pandemic, the work-home division is once again becoming blurred, and the home is accommodating paid work, at least for considerable parts of the population.

The home is a "spatial conception, that is, both a physical structure in which we live, and a social idea imbued with feelings or meanings" (Madsen 2018, 332). The home is "socially constructed" by both macro-forces, including cultural values and political ideologies, and social-psychological processes of meaning-making (Miller 2010). Many institutional forces are outside of people's direct control, like those affecting prices, access, building standards, trends, and technologies. Most people move into houses and apartments designed and built by others. Broad ideologies and trends, such as modernism, functionalism and postmodernism, shape conceptions, building standards, and options regarding size, design, and decoration. Broad institutional and infrastructural factors interact with the social dynamics of meaning-making around the home.

The purchase or renting of a physical place—a house/apartment—can be seen as an investment that shapes subsequent consumption in a variety of ways. Once a person/family has invested in place to make a home, they are for some time "locked" into a particular material setting, including the building standards and technologies surrounding that setting, which sets some limits on what they can do there. The metaphor of path dependencies is applicable (see Text Box 4.1).

Text Box 4.1: The Home and Path-Dependent Consumption

If you have entered a path, you may be forced to continue on the track, or to make the inconvenient choice to turn back. This metaphor can be applied to consumption related to the investment in a home and the choice to live in a particular location, which both steer how you can travel to work/school and other activities. If a family buys a large house in a suburban community, this investment shapes subsequent investments, purchases, and practices for years to come: furniture, decoration, lawn and garden supplies, energy, means of commuting to work, and travel for shopping and accessing leisure activities. The physical setting of where you live may force you to consume in this or that way, and this may be difficult to avoid or reduce even if you want to, unless you move to another setting. A house/apartment that one owns may need to be continuously renovated—or even expanded—in order not to lose value. This perspective of path dependency indicates the significance of seeing how consumption is inscribed in the material surroundings, and may be hard to do without. Path dependencies are implicated in several of the aspects analyzed in the coming subsections.

In the following ten subsections, I will explore how meaning-making and practices associated with the home relate to consumerism. The sections cover five interconnected themes: (1) creating the happy home, (2) the home and conspicuous consumption, (3) the home and inconspicuous consumption, (4) expanding the home, and (5) borrowing money to create the happy home.

Creating the Happy Home

Many cultural meanings are associated with home, and they tend to have positive connotations. Achieving a successful personal/family life is strongly connected to creating a home for oneself (Morgan 2020). I use the phrase "happy home" to denote this meaning-making process, which is related to strong cultural values in society.

To begin with, homeownership is generally celebrated, normalized, and aspired to.[2] The house (or apartment) itself is often one of a person's most highly valued possessions (Richins 1994; Nethercote 2019). Even people who lack the financial means to buy their house or apartment often associate a positive value with the sense of owning one's home environment. The home is associated with control, privacy, secrecy, security, and safety. The home normalizes our ideas and expectations about private ownership and possessions. It must be recognized that owning a house is not only a source of excess consumption, but can also be a factor in countering it. A study showed that people renting a house had fewer opportunities to renovate the house and achieve the most energy-saving standards, because these decisions were up to the landlord (Dubois et al. 2019, 148).

The home is not just something static. It can be seen as a "project," constantly to be rebuilt and improved (Thorkild 2006), and as an identity-construction project (see Text Box 4.3). Making a home involves a process of "accommodation," which encompasses much more than just needing to find somewhere to live, permanently or temporarily. It includes not only forming one's home according to one's own aspirations, but also adapting oneself so that one's identity and aspirations fit the house or apartment where one lives (Miller 2010).

Creating the happy home involves a plurality of aspects. We speak of home comfort, which is related to physical and sensory aspects such as temperature, air quality, noise levels, and lighting. Other important factors are broader emotional, social, and cultural meanings. Location plays a key role, as we may associate the home with attachment to a particular locality. The home is, moreover, a site for daily family life, an object of emotional attachment, and a place for recreation and the performance of household routines; it further functions as a node in networks of social relations (Easthope 2004; Sassatelli 2007; Dowling and Power 2012; Ellsworth-Krebs et al. 2021; Morgan 2020).

Text Box 4.2: Consuming Culture from Home

In earlier times, more "cultural consumption" took place in the city—in the theater, the cinema, the concert hall, and the sports arena. Then TV arrived, followed by the internet. Increasingly, the home is becoming the central site of such cultural consumption (Sassatelli 2007). Bookshelves have always had their sacred place, while the TV, stereo, computers, audio equipment, and home cinemas are gaining ground. These commodities create space for rest, privacy, and detachment from work, but also for sometimes socializing with families and friends. Today, ICT is bound up with almost every dimension of social life and is integrated into the home environment (Sahakian 2017). Cultural consumption has become increasingly privatized and individualized in wealthy households. For instance, if the single TV set once united the family in the living room, now the device screen, as part of a multiscreen household, is an essential part of the private individualized space (Klocker et al. 2012).

It is the key site where the family—itself a core institution in society—confirms itself as a social unit. As shown in chapter 1, the family members confirm and celebrate their relationships—relatives, friends, neighbors—in everyday rituals, by relaxing and spending time together. The home is the key object expressing the unity and essence of the family. Home decorating can be a symbol of family-building, and through this activity a couple can express their love for each other and for their children (Gram-Hanssen and Bech-Danielsen 2004). The home is the primary site where the child is materially socialized into consumer society. The home and the objects in it are what the child will find "natural" (see chapter 5 on normalization). Housing preferences are embedded early in life (Nethercote 2019).

Feelings of safety, comfort, and homeliness are not simply scripted in the buildings, but are formed by family practices and homemaking practices (Morgan 2020). They emerge as "embodied knowhow" (Madsen 2018) related to all the practices and social interactions that take place in and around the home, such as baking, relaxing, showering, and taking care of family members. The home is where we feel at home. It gives us ontological security, a stable place for our routines and for spending time with our dearest relations. It is where we feel in control of our lives, serving as a base on which our identities are constructed (Easthope 2004) and sheltering us from external threats of various kinds.

Creating the happy home requires buying stuff for both the present and future. The home is a key site for instant consumption, where one expends acquired goods, an activity that requires a constant inflow of stuff and energy. For example, one type of consumption in the present that in contemporary times is done much more in the home context—not least, thanks to digitalization—is the consumption of culture (see Text Box 4.2).

But the home is not just for the present. A home is something in which one invests for a shorter or longer period of time. Sometimes the home is where one expects to live until the end of one's life. It also connects with the past. It can be seen as an archive of memories and nostalgia, as woven into the inhabitants' life stories (Jacobs and Malpas 2013) and identity constructions (see Text Box 4.3). For some, the home is less of a permanent place and more of a temporary station, while the occupants' activities mainly take place elsewhere (Thorkild 2006). Another widespread phenomenon is the trend of constantly

Text Box 4.3: The Home and Identity Construction

The home context can be important for creating and reaffirming one's self identity. According to Dittmar (2008), the home can function as an "identity shell," both in that it provides the physical location for privacy, social activities, and interaction, and because the objects within it are symbols of the self, reflecting one's values and stories. Especially if the homeowner personally built the house, made significant improvements on it, or invested a great deal of time and effort in maintenance, a strong sense of identification is established (Gram-Hanssen and Bech-Danielsen 2004). It can be important to leave one's own physical mark on the building. Certainly, it is not only the house or apartment itself that matters for identity; all furnishings, decorations and material objects in the home are important too, as well as the very homemaking process described in the section. To feel "at home," family members may make the home attractive by buying a variety of commodities—both the house itself and all the decorations. The many bookshelves or the expensive hi-fi equipment may have something to say about who the person wants to be. Jacobs and Malpas argue "what we call the 'home' is simply the most salient and significant externalisation of the self in its materialised articulation" (Jacobs and Malpas 2013, 285). It is a crucial part of one's extended self (Belk 1988; see also chapter 2) and of one's self-actualization (Hagbert and Bradley 2017).

remaking one's home, which connects to the theme of novelty discussed in chapter 3. The aesthetics of the home are shaped by fashion-oriented lifestyles and hence are subject to frequent change. These ideas are perpetuated by entertaining television programs focused on interior transformations, such as *60 Minute Makeover* (Powell 2009). Because of time pressure, people do not perform the makeover themselves. The growth of retailers such as IKEA has made buying home-transformation a more convenient and cheaper option than DIY.

The happy home and a happy personal/family life are what are expected of a home; obviously, however, in reality too many people experience (gendered) violence and other precarious situations on a daily basis. The home can feel like a prison (Morgan 2020). Many cannot afford what they want. Some are homeless. Different social classes and income groups have hugely different means to realize commonly held values around the home and homeliness. However, the point that I want to make here is that it is not how life is actually experienced that drives consumerism; it is the ideals, dreams, norms and expectations surrounding the happy home. An important driver is the gap between the actual and the imagined home.

The Home and Conspicuous Consumption

The home is a place for expressing oneself in relation to others. The house and its interior, surroundings and location reflects one's ambitions, cultural capital, and social class. Hence it is a common object of social comparison (see chapter 2) and a classic example of conspicuous consumption (Veblen 1994 [1899]; Miller 2010). Wealth, success, and a happy personal/family life are objectified through the home.

Conspicuousness requires visibility. A house or an apartment is visible in several respects: its exterior, including the garden and the surroundings, is visible to neighbors and passersby, and the interior to invited guests. Many aspects of the home/house are easy to compare: size, price, decoration, location. This is a class issue. Belk notes that the higher classes are status-seekers in connection to the home, whereas the lower social classes look for homeyness (1988, 153). Also, homeownership itself can be a key symbolic marker of class identity (Dowling and Power 2012; Nethercote 2019). The choice of location depends on practical (distance to work), emotional (attachment), recreational, and security/safety considerations, but social status can also be determined by living in the right or wrong city and neighborhood (Gram-Hansen and Bech-Danielsen 2004; Thorkild 2006). Location is easily comparable, and if one's home and its location seem inadequate for bragging purposes, owning a second home (or more) can be an additional means for displaying conspicuous consumption (Walters and Carr 2019).

The house is the place where one receives friends, colleagues, and relatives, and thus is where one can impress others and show off one's cultural capital. Large living rooms, furniture, expensive carpets, large kitchens, fascinating kitchenware, hi-fi audio systems, perhaps a home cinema and a bar—these are meant to be both used and socially displayed. Even if most potential observers, like neighbors, never or very rarely are invited into the house, the interior can easily be displayed on Instagram and Facebook. Indeed, homes/houses/apartments are arguably even more closely connected to one's status and identity than clothing, because a home is not something that one simply uses and discards.

The Home and Inconspicuous Consumption: Comfort, Convenience, Cleanliness, and Connectivity

Other drivers than those associated with symbolic and conspicuous consumption can also explain excess consumption in relation to the home. British sociologist Elizabeth Shove, a well-known proponent of social practice theory in consumption studies, has studied the "escalation of demand" for water and energy in relation to practices of comfort, convenience, and cleanliness (Shove 2003). One of her contributions is her highlighting of the role of inconspicuous consumption, that is, consumption that is not linked to questions of style, status, and symbolic dimensions.[3] Instead it involves consumption of resources that are less visible, or are indirectly connected to a variety of everyday practices such as eating, cleaning, or working from home. To be sure, conspicuous consumption can also have unnoticed effects with regards to heavy use of energy, water, and other resources.

In what ways can inconspicuous aspects of consumption be part of escalating demands? There are certain services connected to the home, such as lighting and indoor temperature, that people expect to be fulfilled. Moreover, there are standardized commodities connected to these services that people feel they need to have to make their "normal" home convenient, comfortable, and clean. The urge to buy such standardized commodities may be less a question of status-seeking or identity-construction than of a felt need to be, and appear, normal (see also chapter 5), to construct a standard convenient home, and to be entitled to enjoy what is considered a standard level of comfort in society. These commodities—technologies, equipment, tools—are found everywhere in the house, and are built into the design of buildings. These items drive the increasing demand for energy and water, and it can be hard even to be aware of one's consumption of such resources.

The standardization of indoor temperature is one such service that is often taken for granted. The construction of indoor climate, Shove argues, has mainly been driven externally by a network of science, universal standards for buildings and technologies, market forces, and standardized commodities. These external elements interact and create expectations that indoor temperature should be a bit above 20°C all year around, regardless of whether you live in a cold or warm place. Such standards legitimize objects/services such as air-conditioning.[4] A particular socio-material infrastructure is built around standards like these, creating naturalized expectations and locking people into technological dependencies. Simple strategies that people forget are opening windows or wearing more or less clothes depending on the indoor temperature (even though the cost of living and energy crisis in Europe and elsewhere during the fall of 2022 forced many inhabitants to adopt such measures).

Another at least partly inconspicuous aspect of consumption has to do with how all the things in a home fit together. Shove uses the term *coherence* when discussing this topic, which I see as an important driver somewhere in the gray area between conspicuous and inconspicuous aspects of consumption. People seek to create a coherent home environment. New items and technology may be sought after as a means of preserving coherence. Shove makes the important point that this drive itself creates a demand for new items. A new investment may lead to a demand for further items. The reason is that the new object—perhaps a sofa or an investment in a home cinema—causes existing objects in the home to look ugly, obsolete, tiny, or impractical.[5] Moving to a new apartment may result in a felt need to arrange one's possessions in different ways, causing a demand for new objects.

The regulation of indoor temperature is relatively invisible to the household. The sources that increase demand for energy-intensive investments are mainly external, even though the social practices, norms and taken-for-granted expectations around temperature, contribute to reproducing these patterns. With issues related to cleanliness, household members are more actively involved in reproducing the patterns. Cleanliness is often laden with moral and symbolic values. Excessive cleaning is part of the aspiration to keep the home—and the bodies in the home—presentable. This involves significant consumption of energy, water, chemicals, and other commodities.

The infrastructures of electricity, water, and sewage permit a way of life, including cleaning practices, that would otherwise be difficult to imagine. While these infrastructures have been influential in shaping the meaning and practice of cleaning, the user side also plays a major role. A person engaging in everyday practices of cleaning, laundering, and showering unconsciously contributes, by these very practices, to upholding norms related to cleanliness and dirt (see also Jack 2017, 2020, 2022). Bathing and showering are not just done with the aim to be clean. They are symbolic expressions and realizations of self in society. There are elements of both pleasure and duty in these cleanliness practices. The construction of additional bathrooms in homes indicates the strength of the culture of personalized and privatized spaces within the home.

Practices of bathing and bodily cleanliness have historically been invented by richer classes (Shove 2003). Such practices helped to differentiate between classes, and between the urban and rural, familiar and foreign, civilized and barbaric. Later they were reconceptualized as a matter of public health. From originally having been a marker of social status, regular washing became a basic condition of social acceptance. Referring to sociologist such as Erving Goffman, Pierre Bourdieu and others, Shove has studied the presentation and production of self in relation to bathroom rituals. The bathroom is a place not just for cleaning oneself, but also for many other activities such as pleasure, enjoying a sense of luxury, caring for one's health, stress relief, and even experiencing contact with nature. There is a related industry of equipment and health care products. Now some of the more luxurious homes have spa-whirlpools, waterfalls, massage jets, lighting effects, and music equipment in the rooms used for bathing.

The bathroom is not just a place for removing dirt; it is a place for retreat, stress release, relaxation, and backstage preparation for front-stage social life.

> Whatever the technologies involved, the social significance of daily washing has undergone . . . radical transformation, variously figuring as a curiosity, a symbol of social standing, a precondition of acceptability, a means of enhancing "beauty capital" and a way of marking the start and end of the day. (Shove 2003, 106)

Hence, what you do alone in the bathroom is profoundly social. You get ready for society, for social interaction, for presenting yourself in public. These social dynamics make frequent washing normal; it becomes a condition for social acceptance, and facilities for washing are a core consideration when building for and creating the happy home. Marketers, technologies, ideologies, and fashion interact to create the physical structure, the ideal and the image of the happy home and the body ideal.

Laundry is another illustrative case. Laundry practices are a coproduction involving those who do the laundry, including their values and ambitions, the conventions and standards of the day, and the tools and technologies people use. Shove asks why people actually wash their clothing. To remove dirt, obviously. But when asked this question, people give interesting answers. This reveals that it is a much more multifaceted issue than one of just removing dirt from clothes. It has to do with pleasure and sensation, with a perception of freshness, and the social value of appearing clean. Dirt can originate from external sources, as with food stains, or from the body. The latter is an even greater source of anxiety. Clothes must not be associated with the body (sweat, smell) of those who wear them: "Laundry is about decontaminating clothes that have been in contact with the body and restoring valued attributes of style, feel and image" (Shove 2003, 126).

We wash not because clothes are dirty, but because we can do it conveniently. The washing machine has historically transformed not just the work of washing, but also the meaning of it. It has modified the moral and symbolic landscape, and has enabled more frequent washing. The machine is there for the time-poor individual. Like so many other household appliances, it has to be immediately accessible. It should be in the home, if you can afford to buy it and have sufficient space for it.

Another, somewhat more abstract, aspect of cleanliness is connected to the ideal of the happy home. Even if the home is cluttered by commodities and shaped by the forces of consumerism, the inhabitants may want to "cleanse" the home atmosphere of a sense of commercialism. An important aspect of creating the happy home is to personalize it, giving other meanings to items than commercial ones. Commodities ought to be "detoxified" from some of their commercial traits. Sassatelli (2007) calls this process de-commoditization. We usually do not want to look at our things as pure "market goods," but prefer to see them as our personal and personalized belongings. Consumption therefore often consists of processes of reframing their meanings, by translating market value and "commodities" into other forms of value and meaning. A ritual of possession facilitates this de-commoditization: unpacking, removing price tags, arranging the object in the domestic space, combining it with all the other objects, reflecting on how well it fits, rearranging. Such a ritual of appropriation and de-commoditization serves to create a coherent, pleasing, and personalized domestic environment. It ends with enjoying the new item for the first time, hanging up a new painting on the wall, using the fancy new kitchenware for the first time, or enjoying a film together with friends using the sound system. This ritualistic process of de-commoditization—indeed cleansing—is certainly not something that runs counter to commoditization. Consumer culture thrives by ideologically negating it through domestication, de-commoditization, and personalization.

Whereas Elizabeth Shove addressed how comfort, cleanliness and convenience constitute sources of inconspicuous consumption, recent research has added another "C": connectivity (Gram-Hansen 2009).[6] The demand for connectivity with the outside world is obviously escalating, as more and more people are spending many more days and hours working from home. While the home was much more a multipurpose site in preindustrial eras than today, many of these features seem to be returning. Even before the COVID-19 pandemic, working from home was increasing in developed countries, and the pandemic accelerated the trend. There was a blurring of the once-so-strict division between work and everyday life, driven by such forces as new information technologies and changing economies with more emphasis on production of intangible assets such as knowledge, information, and software (Löfgren 2013; Doling and Arundel 2020).[7] During the pandemic, over a third of the workforce in EU countries worked from home, with the total exceeding half of the workforce in some countries (Doling and Arundel 2020). This change is likely to persist (Echegaray et al. 2021).

If an increasing share of the population works from home, this could imply less demand for transportation services, fast food, and fashion. But it could also imply more consumption in terms of communication equipment (Doling and Arundel 2020), energy, household appliances, and other stuff for the household (Jiang et al. 2021).[8] If working from home continues to increase as a norm and practice, there may also be a demand for larger homes, including home extensions, because of the perceived need to integrate space for the home office and due to more time spent at home.

Expanding the Home

Much of the analysis so far implies that considerable space is needed to create the happy home, space for extended selves, conspicuous consumption, social interaction, children's play inside and outside, privacy, working from home, entertainment, and so on. The home needs to be designed to manage and balance both the private life of each household member and the social relations within and around households. Space is needed to accommodate guests and have (big) parties sometimes. Hence the demand for additional square meters: increased floor space, a larger kitchen, additional bedrooms, outbuildings, an extended basement, a glazed terrace. Space is an important issue to consider in any analysis of ecological/climate footprints. All other things being equal, having more space per person involves more consumption of energy and material. A greater amount of space also indirectly causes a higher demand for commodities circulating in the home—there are more empty spaces to fill with stuff. Hence, size itself must be seen as an important contributor to consumerism.

A crucial point here is that considerable space is needed for families to live together and separately at the same time. A significant part of home comfort relates to expectations of privacy and synchronization. The number of bedrooms and bathrooms is key. People may make home extensions, a key reason for which is a growing family (more kids).[9] There may be a felt need to have at least two bathrooms so as to avoid conflicts in the morning when family members want to shower at the same time. Having individual bedrooms for each child and a spare room—or several—for overnight guests, has become a standard expectation in modern everyday life. There need to be individual zones and some silent places if other family members are noisy. There need to be separate spaces for kids and adults—toy-free zones—for play and silence, for individualized home entertainment. The inhabitants require some areas in the house to which they can retreat, where they can avoid conflicts, over which they have some control, and which they can keep clean and tidy while cohabiting. To this can be added the newly arisen demand for silent office space and room to store all the stuff which you do not have time to use today, but only in a fantasized future (chapter 3). Motivations like these are apparent in the demand for larger space. This interview excerpt from a study by Wiesel et al. (2013) on supersized dwellings in Sydney suburban areas is illustrative:

> It's nice having your own space. Sometimes my husband comes home from work and I'll have dinner, and he'll still go sit upstairs and eat by himself because we'll be doing homework and he wants to watch TV and the kids are getting distracting. . . . If you want to watch different shows on TV, I don't think we're selfish. Everyone's got their own movies, and you can watch your own stuff. It's just nice not being on top of each other. (Adele, Randwick) (Wiesel et al. 2013, 323)

Their study is about the tendency to knock down and rebuild older houses in Australia, a trend also labeled "mansionization." In their study the new buildings were more than double the size of the previous house.[10] Lifestyle expectations connected to consumption and space have changed over the decades, and this is a core reason for the demand for larger size. For example, houses built in the 1950s could have a single bathroom, which is no longer considered sufficient. However, an important motivation was also expected increase of sales value. That a supersized house could be seen as an investment was well illustrated by one of the informants: "'The potential when I die in 20 or 30 years—hopefully I'll last that long—my kids will have something that's rather more substantial to live in or sell on.' (Peter, Avalon)" (Wiesel et al. 2013, 322).

Although mansionization has received some public criticism for its excessiveness,[11] interviewees were nonetheless proud of being involved in what was perceived as suburban renewal, and saw themselves as involved in generational change.

The demand for more space is not only restricted to relatively wealthy social classes, as in the above examples, but is connected to broader trends. The kitchen has been in focus in several countries in recent decades. In their interview study of home extensions in Britain, Hand et al. (2007) looked at the reasons behind kitchen expansions (they also focused on the additions of bathrooms). Like the study by Wiesel and colleagues mentioned above, they found that there has been a profusion of appliances and commodities in the homes, which has led to a perceived need for more space. They also connect the demand for more space to dynamics of social life. "Although it is experienced individually, the pressure to extend, we argue, is essentially social: it has to do with accomplishing and achieving what people take to be normal ways of life and normal forms of social interaction" (Hand et al 2007, 672).

For instance, the kitchen is increasingly seen as a multifunctional living space. The introduction of dishwashers and many other appliances has caused demand for more space. Also of crucial importance is the perception of the kitchen as the symbolic heart of the home. The kitchen is not just a place for household work, but also a social place where informal social interaction take place. "Visions of kitchen-based sociality were, in every household, associated with a specific and simple piece of kitchen technology: the table. If the kitchen table is to fulfil its anticipated social function, people have to be able to sit around it—an arrangement that requires a considerable amount of space in its own right" (Hand et al. 2007, 675).

Ironically, kitchens have become larger at the same time as people use kitchens less for cooking and eating. At least until the COVID-19 pandemic, people gradually changed their habits toward more eating out. This phenomenon has been called "the cookery contradiction" (Sullivan and Gershuny, 2004). Especially among the work-rich, high-income, and time-poor groups (see chapter 3), people are eating out in restaurants more often. There is substantial growth in home delivery of preprepared meals, and supermarkets are providing an ever-growing range of ready-to-eat dishes. In parallel to this there has been a huge expansion in sales of expensive cooking equipment, which is accordingly drastically underused. Even so, there is demand for extended kitchens because of the opportunity they afford to interact with family members—sometimes. The "individualized" family members sometimes need to socialize. If the kitchen is to serve as a meeting place, even if only occasionally, it cannot be too small (Madsen 2018).

Demands for more space can be both a cause and an effect of increased consumption (Hand et al. 2007; Wiesel et al. 2013). They can be an effect because having more equipment and appliances requires more space, and a cause because more space leads to the perception that this extra space is waiting to be filled with stuff, for example because of the search for coherence discussed earlier in the chapter or just because one gets spatial opportunities: "Once built, supersized dwellings become homes for families that do consciously adjust their lifestyles in order to 'live up' to the potential of such a house" (Wiesel et al., 327). If you have a large garden, maybe there ought to be a pool in it? Hence, there is a potential vicious circle between stuff and space (see figure 4.1).

When the children grow up, the parents may stay in the large house rather than moving to a smaller apartment. Children's rooms become guest rooms. They redesign the freed-up space for individual activities such as painting,

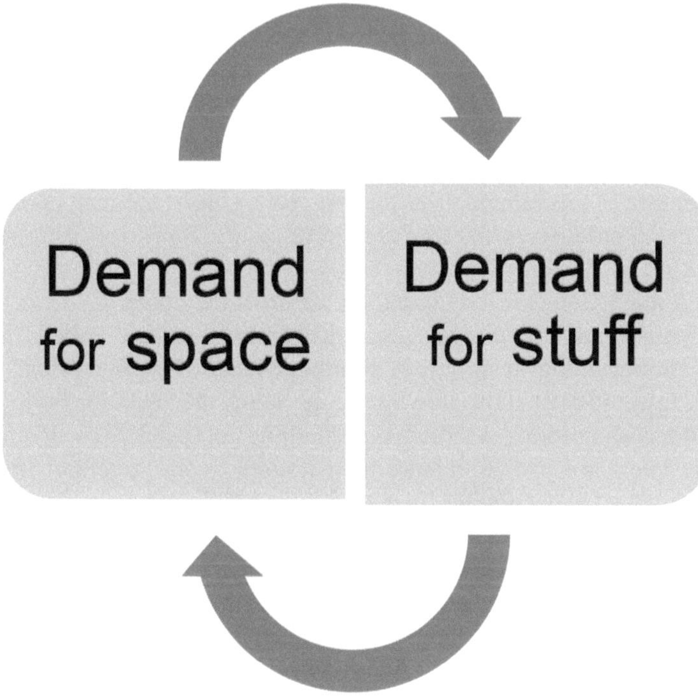

Figure 4.1. Demand for Space and Stuff. ***Source:*** **Author**

working, sewing or playing the piano. "This repurposing of children's bedrooms and play areas may be part of householders' justification for staying in larger family homes" (Ellsworth-Krebbs et al. 2021, 14). Then, large parts of the home are being left on "standby" most of the time (consuming energy).

Borrowing Money to Create the Happy Home

I will end my discussion of the home by considering how the creation of the (large and/or favorably located) happy home has been financially facilitated in recent decades. People usually do not have enough money of their own for it. Nonetheless (capitalist) financial institutions have made this feature of mass consumption possible, at least for the segments of the population that can convince lenders they have some long-term financial stability (though often with few restrictions). Creating the large, fashionable, and favorably located happy home costs a significant amount of money, especially in inflated housing markets, as has been the situation in many developed urban regions. The sum of money generally needed to purchase a (not even large) home is normally far beyond the reach of buyers. People must borrow to buy or improve their house/apartment, to add a second house or more, and to buy all the material stuff to make the home(s) safe, cozy, comfortable, and convenient. Internationally, since the first wave of financial deregulation in the 1980s, and later mortgage product innovation, there has been an explosion of mortgage-led consumption. The problem (from an excess consumption perspective) is that there have been few constraints (at least until the increase of interest rate in several countries the last year). One of the features of mortgage financial products is that they are discretionary. Borrowers can use loans for any kind of spending; not necessarily to reinvest in structural improvements and maintaining/accumulating the value of the home.

In a British qualitative study, documented in an article called "Debted objects: Homemaking in an era of mortgage-enabled consumption," Cook and colleagues (2013) show how mortgage loans are used for both investments and consumption. A home is something to spend *from*. People use mortgage loans not just to enlarge their houses or for structural improvements, but also for decorating their homes and filling them with consumer items such as kitchenware, leather sofas, and TVs. Indeed, investing in a new "kitchen" implies procuring the entire package; it is a structural improvement including many temporary consumer items. The study further found that mortgage loans are used for things and experiences outside the home: second homes, cars, and holidays. Social life and family values are key drivers, they argue, and the happy personal/family life is not just spent at home. There may be the "once in a lifetime holiday" and it may be felt "really necessary" to travel far away to find some "escape" from hectic everyday life and "build" and "restore" the family relationships.

Consumer objects such as an elegant TV or luxurious sofa can even be seen as investment, because they offer "a good selling feature" at the point of sale. Consumer goods and excessive renovations are not just procured or invested in to cultivate the family values or for conspicuous consumption; they are seen as means to generate capital gains. Objects symbolize improvements. The interviewed participants' narratives

> indicate how readily equity borrowing draws wealth away from either dwelling condition or investment returns and into consumer spending, with participants tolerating mounting debts in order to fund appliances, furnishings, and short-lived renovations (Cook et al. 2013, 302).

They also observed patterns that I discussed in relation to the restless nature of consumerism in chapter 3. People often experience feelings of unhomeliness and disappointment with their existing home, which can be an important trigger for new loans and renovations: "Debted objects can bridge the gap between the homely and unhomely in a myriad of prosaic and mundane ways" (Cook et al. 2013, 309). These debted objects are paradoxical—both alienating because of excessive borrowing, and endearing through the meanings they bring to the home. However, these meanings can be quickly punctured; new feelings of unhomeliness may arise generating new demands for borrowed money to renew one's home. The happy home is not completed yet, but within reach—it seems, in the eyes of the home creator—thanks to the bank. The cycles of desire go on.

THE MALL

I have discussed shopping in several parts of the book. This section discusses the activity of shopping in relation to the place where it occurs, and how the place itself encourages consumerism. Key issues here are not just making commodities accessible for people, but also a number of other social aspects that stimulate shopping. I call this section "The Mall," because the mall has become such a symbol of our mass consumption society. The consumerist drivers explored here are, however, not limited to this largest type of shopping outlet. Any type of physical or digital outlet (or places like city centers, cruise ships, amusement parks) can induce consumerism, but some do so more than others. The growth of malls and supermarkets—often located at the outskirts of a town with gigantic parking lots—is a common topic of debates about ecologically destructive mass consumption. These outlets are emblematic of unsustainable mass consumption.

Shopping is itself an ambiguous term with layered meanings, involving both desires related to recreational shopping and the more instrumental activity of satisfying needs and wants.[12] Much shopping, to be sure, is of a mundane nature, being how we procure mostly unfashionable everyday products. Even these examples of shopping are deeply social in kind; that is, you shop for others and with others in mind, which include practices and rituals of caretaking (see chapter 1). Shopping in larger malls and departments stores is also associated with other aspects of social life: entertainment, socializing, and status. Such shopping may involve goods that you buy somewhat less regularly and with more emotional involvement, like fashion, accessories, footwear, sports equipment, electronics, furniture, cosmetics, and home decoration. Even larger items, such as fashionable car brands, may be found in these shopping centers.

In his book *I Want That! How We All Became Shoppers*, Thomas Hine (2002) notes that the department store would have been inconceivable without mass industrialization, which produced a wide range of manufactured goods as well as the incomes required to purchase them. The greatest advances in retailing, however, were primarily psychological, he argues. The stores make people more comfortable as shoppers. The trick is to remove any barriers that would prevent them from buying. Associating shopping with entertainment and socializing are crucial triggers in this regard.

In a study of the historical development of department stores and shopping malls, Mark Moss (2007) provides some important insights into the role of shopping outlets and consumerism. Shopping is an entertainment industry, he argues, and the infrastructure of shopping malls and department stores has very much to do with this. Going to the mall and spending time there has become a dominant leisure activity in social life. Moss describes in his book how department stores, malls, and megastores such as IKEA outlets have been designed to get people to go there as a way to socialize. These facilities offer space and activities for families and friends to have fun together. Even if they do not shop, they can look and dream about all the fancy stuff in all the shops. Malls are entertainment centers, places full of promises, possibilities, and enjoyable experiences. They are constructed for many exciting non-shopping activities, inviting people to stroll around, window-shop, engage in sports activities, go to the cinema, engage in social interaction and live a public life. There are plenty of restaurants and cafés. "The bottom line is that even though these people did not decide to come and shop, most of them end up buying something" (Moss 2007, 48). Even more so, the bottom line is that these sites of shopping underscore how deeply integrated shopping is in social life, with all its ritualized form of social interaction (see chapter 1).

Hine (2002) applies the label "buyosphere" to places like these. The buyosphere is both a set of shopping opportunities and a state of mind. It is "the place that invites us to reward ourselves for all the bad things we put up with in life" (Hine 2002, 67). People come to malls and other large shopping areas—of course city centers generally also have such a shopping aura—not just to buy things, but also to socialize, have meals, go to the cinema, people-watch, and walk around. The shopping centers gives an illusion of community. Shopping is done with both close (the people one is shopping with) and distant others (all the other people present). A shopping center is supposed to be packed with people. People go there to experience the pulse. Even the lone shopper may feel less alone and can interact with staff in the stores. Such interaction can be rewarding because the staff is trained in pleasant social interchange. With reference to Arlie Hochschild's concept of "emotional labor," ethnologist Orvar Löfgren addresses how sellers in the growing "experience economy" (since the 1980s) are trained:

> To sell commodities and services was no longer enough, they had to be turned into a micro-event or a great experience. This called for employers who were trained to be good performers, in order to add that extra value of a pleasing atmosphere and an authentic exchange. In a sense it was emotional labour

> reinvented, directed mainly at the many service sector workers such as shop assistants, waiters and receptionists. Passion was needed to get the message across. In the Experience Economy, you constantly had to ask "How does it feel?" A lot of energy was devoted to producing not only material commodities and services but also to repackaging them with the help of atmosphere, images, auras and events. (Lövgren 2013, 291)

There is much more in the physical setting that may shape one's propensity to consume and enjoy than one might think. The physical setting includes smell, sound, lighting, and colors. There are accommodating sellers with whom you can have a nice conversation about any interesting object. Shoppers are supposed to be in the mood to consume. Moss comments on the early department stores in France, the USA and UK: "Their spectacular displays, luxurious trappings, fine selection of goods, and numerous leisure activities gave them an audience that almost rivaled the great cathedrals" (Moss, 2007, xx). Inspiration for the design of these places comes from many sources: cathedrals, museums, theaters, the sports arena, the bazaar, Disney World, the jungles. There should be amusement parks and places for the children. Nostalgia and retro-design are used to create the right ambience. Such references to tradition create a sense of authenticity, even giving the impression of being the antithesis of mass consumption. Waterfalls, fountains, the sound of water, and trees are all used to "pacify and soothe the tired consumer" (Moss 2007, 74). Furnishings add to a relaxed atmosphere.

> This is the magical sensation that people receive: they are excited, overwhelmed, calmed, focused, dreamy—all at the same time. Rightly or wrongly, morally appropriate or sinister in its calculation, shopping is so pleasing and so enticing because it transports people away from their mundane existences. (Moss 2007, 28)

Luxury—or rather the perception of it—is a significant part of the entertainment. Shopping is way to observe and fantasize about luxury items, even if you do not buy these expensive goods.

> Luxury and entertainment, enthrallment, and liminality could . . . be stimulated and created by the abundance of goods on display. Walking into the store and being overwhelmed by the quantity of goods available, the variety of textures, the multiplicity of colors, the selection of different things and the overall display, could certainly enchant the average consumer in a manner equal to seeing a film. (Moss 2007, 37)

The mall and department stores are not good or healthy places for people who are inclined toward impulsive and compulsive buying. Here is an illustrative quote from O'Guinn and Faber's study on compulsive buyers:

> But it was like, it was almost like my heart was palpitating, I couldn't wait to get in to see what was there. It was such a sensation. In the store, the lights, the people; they were playing Christmas music. I was hyperventilating and my hands were starting to sweat, and all of the sudden I was touching sweaters and the whole feel of it was just beckoning to me. And if they had a SALE sign up, forget it; I was gone. You never know when you're going to need it. I bought ten shirts one time for $10 each. (O'Guinn and Faber 1989, 134)

On the surface, all this might be associated with Western consumer culture, but malls are a global economic and cultural phenomenon, and the city of Dubai is perhaps the most emblematic of all places in this regard (Urry 2010). Particularly in economies growing their way out of a historical period of poverty and scarcity, the mall represents the new time and new promises. For example, malls can be fascinating places for citizens of post-Soviet countries to visit. The shopping center is the paradise on earth that the Soviet system promised but never delivered. Citizens of those countries used to experience coercively imposed frugality and shortage of goods. They could only dream about fascinating Western goods, unless they could make "under the table" deals with staff working in retail trades. Given such experiences of relative deprivation, they may develop a peculiar attitude toward the new opportunities that the mall offers. Today, the long-sought-after goods are suddenly accessible, although many nonetheless lack the money to buy them. Even those who cannot afford to buy anything may enjoy strolling around window-shopping, as Keller (2005) notes in her study of Estonian shoppers. Here is what one interviewee in her study had to say:

> We are pensioners, today we came simply to stroll, we are curious to look around what is available, what kind of commodities are there—just to know. Although we have no money to buy, we can look, can't we? . . . It is very pleasant here and very beautiful, we look at this beauty of the shop, but a pensioner cannot afford anything. (Keller 2005, 74)

Ironically, in Keller's study, some of the wealthier mall visitors expressed more criticism of westernized excessive buying, despite themselves spending time in the malls for recreational shopping. And yes, they do shop—often searching for higher-priced "quality goods" and thus contributing to the vicious circle of production of novel goods.

Historically, shopping is related to the rise of leisure time (see chapter 3), and therefore also to leisure. As leisure time increases, there is more time for vacations, and in contemporary times it is customary to plan entire holiday trips with shopping as the ultimate goal, including visiting the grand malls and megastores. This inspirational aspect involves a longer period of curiosity, planning, and dreaming about the place, and the abundance of luxuries, products, and possible bargains. Once there, consumers hardly even have to leave the mall. The mall was designed to mimic the town, complete with a main thoroughfare, side streets, gathering places, fountains, and so on.

Even if shopping is not the ultimate goal of the holiday trip, it is often seen as important. The almost perversely omnipresent nature of consumerism and shopping can be seen in all circumstances; it is everywhere downtown in a city. You may try to abandon consumerism for a while to engage in more "cultural" activities, such as visiting museums. But even museums are filled with commerce. For many tourists it is more important to buy and bring home symbolic representations of the art and architecture than to experience them in situ. Juliet Schor cites research that found that a considerable number of museum visitors did not actually visit the museum, but only got as far as the museum shop. For them, it was enough to visit the museum shop to buy (plastic) representations of (attractions in) the museum (1998, 48), perhaps to show friends and relatives that they were there, when they invite them for dinner to their house.

Obviously, not everyone associates shopping with joy and entertainment. With or without money, shopping can be joyful and painful. Not least in the cluttered and noisy environments of malls, it can be very stressful. Cecilia Solér (2018) discusses how the stimuli-rich marketplaces filled with sounds, scents, colors, lighting, symbols, and people cause not just feelings of joy but also feelings of information/perception overload and confusion. Such an environment, combined with social pressures, causes stress which the individual has to cope with.[13] For some, the stress can be felt as overwhelming, causing withdrawal from these environments. From a stress perspective, this can be understood as a "flight" strategy. However, in the context of shopping, Solér argues, most people use the coping-strategy "fight," which means trying to stay in the setting and deal with the overload. After all, people may want to obey the consumerist norm. A fight strategy can imply using shortcuts, such as sticking to one's favorite brands, relying on advertisements, or asking one's peers for advice ("support-seeking coping"). The latter coping strategy is a reason for shopping together as a social activity. These coping strategies tend to involve consumption rather than anti-consumption (fight rather than flight), adding to a vicious circle of spending (see also figures 3.1 and 3.2 in chapter 3 on cycles of desire).

Whether positive or negative, the experience of shopping can be partly gendered. Historically, the department store has been perceived as particularly relevant for the female consumer, Moss (2007) says, and sociopsychological research confirms this gendered nature of shopping. Much more than men, women see shopping as a way of socializing (which can involve mixed feelings, however). Dittmar (2008) observes in her sociopsychological research that shopping has a more psychologically and emotionally encompassing role to play for women than men. Whereas women associate buying with leisure, men tend to have more negative attitudes toward it. Women focus on the process of buying, whereas men focus on the outcome: obtaining the goods without fuss. This does not mean that consumption is less important to men. Women emphasize much more than men how shopping is a social activity that they do together with others. Obviously, gendered patterns in relation to emotional states of shopping may also play out differently due to the focus of the shopping, be it fashion, electronics, or cars, for example.

Entertaining or not, the investigations conducted by Moss and by others cited in this section show how the system of provision has created and constantly reproduces a culture of consumerism that is deeply integrated, and expected to be embedded, in social life. People are supposed to enjoy the entertainment that shopping entails. Entertainment via shopping is an idea, and as such it does not necessarily reflect an inner state of mind. People are *expected* to have fun, which is not the same as actually having it. Expectations can function as compelling norms, and as gendered ones. This relates to the drivers of normalization that I will elaborate on in the next chapter. Even if people hate these environments, visiting these places can feel like a social obligation. It can even be difficult to find alternative (non-consumption) spaces for social interaction outside the home. There is a shortage of public places and cultural options where people can sit down and socialize without being expected to buy things, even if only a cup of coffee.

THE INTERNET

Vicious circles of spending are nowadays obviously not restricted to the physical marketplace. This section discusses internet and buying, examines how sharing platforms may spur a cycle of desire, and continues the analysis begun in chapter 2 on how social media spur consumerism.

Internet and Buying

Hine reflects on the omnipresence of the buyosphere:

> Today, most of us spend our lives in a perpetual fair. Someone tries to sell us something nearly every waking moment, and we can buy casually, impersonally, with no wearying negotiation or personal contact. The act of consumption,

> which was once so exceptional an act in lives dominated by laborious production, is now commonplace and incessant. We are all in the market all the time. (Hine 2002, 59)

The home has ceased to be a place where you only accommodate the things that you have procured. The home incorporates more and more of everyday life. The internet revolution means that many of us can work at home, and unless you are on the wrong side of the digital divide, you can also buy most of the things you need at any time of day and night. The buyosphere is available everywhere 24/7. While some digital unfamiliarity/illiteracy may remain, in many countries it has largely been removed thanks to the COVID-19 pandemic. Digitalization paves the ways for hesitant IRL shoppers. Traditional types of shopping were, after all, not entertaining for everyone. Many people did not engage in shopping for the sake of social interaction.

As in the physical outlet, online sellers are doing what they can to make digital shopping an enjoyable experience. Again, entertainment is important. The internet offers an alternative to window-shopping. "Just looking" constitutes much of the traffic on the internet. Convenience is a key opportunity. Safe payments and free return postage remove obstacles and foster consumer trust. Of course, a drawback with online sales is that sellers lack the possibility to create a physical experience. In contrast to physical settings, not all the senses can be stimulated, so web designers must rely on visual experiences. These too can evoke aesthetic pleasure (Cachero-Martínez and Vásquez-Caselles 2021). With advanced technology, sellers can even create a virtual reality that substitutes for the perceived reality and simulates a real life shopping experience (Xi and Hamari 2021). Websites can rely on and encourage convenience (saving time, comparing prices, speed and efficacy of information processing) and intellectual experience (curiosity, creative problem-solving, customization, achieving product/service co-creation). Online buying may be weaker in terms of social interaction and physically sensing the commodities, but there are ways of dealing with this issue too; one can facilitate interaction with other humans through virtual communities, message boards, chats, or conversing with avatars. There are all sorts of techniques for encouraging consumers to buy something: repeated purchase reminders, pop-up/pop-under product information, instant offers, extra offers, and so on.

Internet shopping can trigger overspending, as well as impulsive and compulsive buying. The object is just a click away. Buying is both easy and remote, somehow detached from a sense of spending money. Especially young consumers seem more inclined to overspend when buying online (Dittmar 2008). Other segments of consumers are prone to impulsive buying when shopping online than in traditional shopping settings (Ozen and Engizek 2014). Research has found that people engaged in utilitarian (goal-directed) web browsing do not buy on impulse, whereas people exercising hedonic web browsing (for fun and distraction) do buy on impulse (Park et al. 2012). Special offers, smart use of sensory attributes, and virtualization technology can all increase such a propensity. The very plastic card itself, compared with cash, may make spending appearing less real, and thereby can induce excess spending (Lo and Harvey 2010), both in physical and digital settings.

Likewise, the internet provides a site for those who are not attracted to more social types of shopping. Clicks may be monitored by the algorithms, but the Internet can nonetheless enable one to make purchases when wanting to avoid interaction or being seen by others. Again, these patterns of social versus private shopping relate to gender structures. Dittmar (2008) observed that men find online buying more enjoyable and convenient (see also Kanwal et al. 2021 on gender differences and online shopping behavior). It triggers their curiosity. Women stress that they miss shopping as a social activity, which they do together with others to have fun together and to help each other with peer judgment. Other emotions that primarily women feel and are lost with internet buying were the thrill or excitement of an unexpected bargain, and possibilities for escapism, reward, or distraction. In contrast, men may gain such emotions through online shopping, including feeling a sense of privacy in the purchasing context.

A core insight from the research presented in this section is that the internet complements traditional shopping in that the different sites—physical versus virtual—reach out to different segments of consumers (gender, age, personality, etc.), who seek different types of goods/services, or have different reasons for shopping for the goods. There is always a way to buy, to associate buying with entertainment, whether more or less social. This is good for capitalism and sales, but bad for the planet.[14]

How Sharing Platforms Stimulate Cycles of Desire

The internet is not just a site where you can buy more; it is a site where you can share objects. Can sharing platforms, for example, create opportunities to buy less? Perhaps they can, but we need to consider indications of the opposite, and the drivers involved. It is commonly believed that second-hand peer-to-peer platforms will encourage sustainable consumption, as they offer a kind of second life to objects. However, they may very well lead to continuous consumerism. One driver of this is self-licensing (Parguel et al. 2017). A guilty conscience can be dampened by giving/selling excessive stuff secondhand and buying secondhand (see also concluding chapter on justification strategies). Because these sites, whether physical or online, are associated with sustainability, they offer a liberating context for the consumers, potentially triggering them to engage in impulsive and indulgent consumption: "Certain decision contexts lead to indulgent decisions as they offer a justification to give in to temptation, especially when conflicting goals are at stake" (Parguel et al. 2017, 49). Parguel and colleagues found support for such tendencies in a survey study of French consumers using secondhand peer-to-peer platforms. Based on the findings, the researchers even claim that "far from encouraging frugality, these are the ultimate places inducing indulgent consumption" (Parguel et al. 2017, 55).

Such websites can also promote consumerism, in that they stimulate affective reactions such as enjoyment, surprise, and the feeling of bargain hunting, thus promoting the same kinds of behavior as when shopping in a physical store. Such platforms stimulate temptation and impulsive buying. Similar results were found in a qualitative interview study of British users of the eBay platform (Denegri-Knott 2011). Drawing on the concept of "cycle of desire" which I discussed in chapter 3, Janice Denegri-Knott found that eBay sparked and accelerated such a cycle of desire among consumers:

> Because eBay never ceases to signal new possibilities in finding desired goods, it sets in motion accelerated cycles of revelation, characterised by unexpected surprises and opportunities where desired goods can be acquired quickly. This however, undermines the possibility of pleasure associated with a state of desire by radically shortening the various stages of the cycle. (Denegri-Knott 2011, 373)

eBay revitalizes a cult of the new through an ever-changing influx of goods. The interviews in Denegri-Knott's study revealed two types of browsing, similar to those described earlier in the chapter. One is more goal-directed and narrow, focusing on a particular type of object, while the other is more recreational, hedonist and diffuse, and characterized by aimless drifting. The latter type is motivated by the chance of finding and desiring something unknown. For the recreational type of internet buyers, web-browsing seems to be an activity in which a person can lose their sense of time, perhaps as a way to escape boredom.

eBay triggers consumer fantasies and ignites the *desire* for desire. Interviewees discuss the process of searching and occasionally buying as entertaining; the search for desired goods is itself seen as a joyful and meaningful activity. eBay even accelerates the cycle of desire. This is first of all due to the rapid acquisition of desired items. What was once rare or difficult to find has suddenly become easy to find and affordable. Secondly, it has to do with the removal of moral consequences tied to purchases. Thirdly, the platform can encourage rapid transactions by providing a sense of urgency; the product can quickly be bought by someone else. It encourages the setting aside of self-restrictions. Finally, the cycle is accelerated by disappointment, which is a common experience among eBay consumers. "Mistakes," however, can easily be sold off again, and desire refocused on another good. Guilt, disappointment and other negative feelings and consequences are easily offset by a quick sale. Features like these are smartly applied not just by secondhand platforms like eBay, but also by numerous other digital platforms in various sectors.

Social Media and Consumerism

As discussed in chapter 2 (see the case study on social media), people spend hours on social media sites such as Facebook, Tinder, TikTok, Snapchat, Instagram, YouTube, Tumblr, Twitter, and more (Hruska and Maresova 2020). Increasingly, social media sites are becoming important platforms for marketing and product promotion, via influencers, fashion bloggers, and celebrities. According to Hruska and Maresova (2020), "Facebook and other social media have opened up an excellent platform for marketers and companies to increase their product promotion through viral marketing that is viewed by more than one billion connected consumers" (Hruska and Maresova 2020, 2). They conclude that communication on social networks is highly effective because companies can reach specific target audiences. "The customer goes to social networks to relax and receives marketing messages much better. Content on social networks is primarily made up of people and is, therefore, more trustworthy" (Hruska and Maresova 2020, 14).

As discussed in chapter 2, the internet and social media can be a site of conspicuous consumption. They also bear much responsibility for disseminating ideals surrounding the good life, not least a happy personal and family life and the happy home. In a study, Loukianov and colleagues (2019) made a multimodal analysis of 150 Instagram posts tagged #goodlife. The good life could be associated with both future and present goals. Even if a minority of the posts explicitly mentioned material goods—consumerist ideals remain implicit—the authors of the study found that the background presence of material and intangible consumer goods reinforced consumerist ideals regarding the good life. Consumer culture appears everywhere, both explicitly and implicitly, in the background framing. Pictures of sunny vacations in exotic locations contribute to normalizing and legitimizing long-distance air travel as a good life practice.

Furthermore, many of the activities done in social media—and displayed by social media—imply a further commoditization/commercialization of intimate life. The market-oriented language—particularly on dating platforms such as Tinder—shapes how one finds and perceives relationships and a partner (including seeing partners as changeable and replaceable), as well as how one brands oneself as a really trim item for sale to be selected on the digital grocery shelf (Bauman 2007; Hochschild 2011).

CONCLUSION

This chapter has shown the important role played by some settings and sites in shaping consumption—both buying and using—and boosting consumerism. It has shown that our homes and all the meanings related to them spur consumerism in multiple ways. Both less and more conspicuous aspects of consumption are involved. A crucial factor is the urge to create the happy home and foster the happy personal/family life, which links back to the ritual dimensions of consumption discussed in chapter 1. Social comparison is also essential. The house/apartment is a crucial site where we can show off to others. Having a large home is important because of aspirations relating to conspicuous consumption, for separating spaces for privacy from spaces from social interaction, for carving out space for work, for accommodating guests, for expressing personal identity, and for storing things that you do not have time to use at present (see chapter 3). A lot of stuff is needed for the same reasons as are mentioned above, and for play, entertainment, rest, relaxation, recreation, cleaning, saving time, caretaking, working, communicating, and backstage preparation for front-stage social life performances. New stuff—including renovation, extension, and rebuilding—is needed to achieve coherence, follow the trends, and not let the house/apartment lose market value. The primary socialization of children into mass-consumerist norms and habits takes place in these settings. There is a constant demand for more space, facilitated by easily accessible credit. This wish implies greater consumption of materials and energy: a larger ecological footprint.[15] The happy home and happy personal/family life drive excess consumption both in terms of material consumer items and demand for energy and water. The totality of our homes implies a physical infrastructure that cannot easily and immediately be changed into something more ecologically sound. For everyone, the existing domestic material landscape involves path dependencies. We literally inherit an infrastructure; we are stuck where we are. It is possible to rebuild and crowd together a bit more, but such a change is not just a technological issue; it is deeply social and cultural. Also, it would not make ecological sense to tear everything down to build anew.

Your calm, happy home may be located a comfortable distance from your work and the noisy, hectic shopping outlets, so you ought to take your car to get there. In this chapter, I have focused on how shopping has been framed as entertainment for leisure time and vacations, and thus serves as a sphere of social life that aggressively promotes consumerism. This is a historical pattern that deeply shapes society today—as a culture and as a material structure—including the ways we interact with each other and move around in society. The mall represents the most extreme example, but the aura and aesthetics of consumerism are everywhere: in cities, in subways and on street corners. Entertainment and socializing are supposed to be channeled through shopping. This is an idea, a norm, an expectation that is hard to resist. Whether or not you are entertained, you are supposed to take part.

Then internet came, and the possibilities to create a nonconsumption space diminished even more. Via internet the mall entered the home, as did work, at least if you are digitally included. In digitalized societies, the buyosphere is accessible 24/7. Some shoppers find enjoyment in the traditional sites of shopping like the mall, and behave in a more instrumental, goal-directed manner when shopping online. Others practice the opposite. There is a site for everyone. The internet and social media are also responsible for new smart ways of spreading consumerism. Users are cocreators and co-disseminators of messages. Anyone is a marketer. Some—influencers, bloggers, celebrities—are more powerful than others, and they get rich by reducing themselves to "commodities." Even platforms that seem to facilitate sustainable practices—supporting secondhand shopping—perpetuate consumerism and develop new ways of accelerating the cycle of desire. Such "sustainable" shopping platforms stimulate self-licensing and help to justify consumerism. In all these ways, the internet further normalizes and legitimizes (helping to

Text Box 4.4: Invitation to Reflect on Opportunities for Change

In what ways can the multipurpose happy home be a site for countering consumerism and stimulating alternative forms of meaning-making that are less reliant on commodities and commerce? How can both conspicuous and inconspicuous drivers of consumption be revealed and dampened? Could you live well and combine the need for both privacy and social interaction with fewer square meters? Why is there a felt need for more space? If you spend more time in the domestic context because of better opportunities to work from home, how can this possibility to reduce demand for mobility be realized without at the same time spurring a vicious circle of demanding more space and stuff? Viewed more broadly, at community level, how can regional/local infrastructures, physical as well as digital, be rearranged to stimulate fine homes, living areas, activities, and interactions that are less permeated by consumerism? Could this involve building/creating homes and living areas that stimulate collective ways of owning/using/securing resources, prohibit/restrict ownership/use of cars, promote public and active (e.g. bicycle/walking) transportation, integrate blue and green infrastructure in cities (including community gardens), protect/restore local nature areas, decentralize supply/delivery of essential provisions, arrange facilities (premises, expertise, digital devices) for repairing and sharing resources, prohibit aggressive advertising, encourage digital spaces that are free from advertising and noncompetitive social interaction, limit access to easy loans, and so on? Much of this has to do with offering people possibilities to thrive and socialize together in the physical (and digital) community without having to resort to practices of excessive consumerism and commoditized experience. The COVID-19 pandemic provided the insight that a more locally tied, homebound life is possible (though increasingly exposed to digital consumer culture). But such insight needs to be integrated into community planning. Indeed, temporal, geographical, and infrastructural aspects, including issues of mobility and proximity, are closely connected to social dynamics, and not least to the possibility of maintaining healthy social relationships in real life. It is of key importance that people who aspire to reduce their consumption should have ready access to their social network and have the possibility to meet without using a car. What possibilities exist in the community to consider all of this in infrastructural planning and reform? Moreover, what kinds of infrastructural reform are needed to broadly support alternative practices in neighborhoods like sharing, repairing, and running alternative non-profit economies? Should malls outside of towns be closed or redesigned to be museums of consumer culture, with their parking lots replaced by trees and meadows? Can public policy provide recognition, protective space, and material/technological support to various civil society initiatives or alternative non-growth movements, including transition-town networks, alternative agri-food movements, eco-communities, cooperatives, time-banking networks, and convivialist movements? There is a need to recognize that all of these bottom-up movements seek to construct innovative, alternative nonprofit and nongrowth economies including novel ways to foster social sustainability in the local area (Schor and Thompson 2014; Kallis et al. 2018), while at the same time they need various form of societal support to be able to scale up their operations.

justify) our unsustainable mass consumption society. The question is raised: How can we redesign the home, the mall, the internet, and other sites to counter consumerism (see Text Box 4.4)?

NOTES

1. I am grateful to Karin Gustafsson and Helen Peterson for constructive comments on an earlier version of this chapter, as well as to an anonymous reviewer.

2. For example, in Britain between the world wars, 70 percent of families lived in rented accommodation. Between 1971 and 2002, homeownership increased from 49 to 69 percent (Powell 2009).

3. For a recent book exploring the links between social practices and escalating demand, see Rinkinen et al. (2021).

4. Between 1962 and 1992, the percentage of homes with air-conditioning increased from 12 percent to 64 percent in the United States (Shove 2003, 49).

5. Another term for this is the "Diderot effect" (Shove and Warde 2002). For a similar discussion, see also Sahakian (2017) and also the study "A Bigger Living Room Required a Bigger TV" by Aro (2020).

6. Kirsten Gram-Hanssen (2009) pays attention to all the standby consumption resulting from electronic devices and remote controls, which stands for a significant amount of the electricity consumed. In the study, she found several reasons why households were unable to cut down on standby consumption, even though the household members were aware of its significant volume and costs. She found that it is not just a technological issue, but also a practical and social one. The need to be incessantly "connected" with the outside world by internet is a barrier to reducing standby consumption.

7. It has been estimated that before the COVID-19 pandemic, an average of 5 percent of the workforce in the EU usually worked from home, with the percentage exceeding 10 percent in a few countries (Doling and Arundel 2020, 5).

8. In Sweden, total consumption decreased in several areas during the first year of the pandemic, but, in contrast, the area "furniture, household items, and maintenance" increased (3.6 percent, 2020) and continued to increase during the first part of 2021 (Holmberg 2022).

9. See for instance Dowling and Power (2012) about the demand for space. In another qualitative interview study in the Australian context, Klocker et al. (2012) also noticed this need for privacy in "extended family households," such as households in which an elderly parent lives with adult children. The sustainability gains of extended family living (with the potential for lower energy consumption per capita, forms of sharing, and pooling of material goods) were compromised by the cultural values of privacy and independence.

10. In developed countries such as Australia and the United States, households have decreased in size since the 1980s, counted in household members, while homes have grown bigger. In Australia, the average size of new houses has increased from 162 square meters in 1984/1985 to 239 square meters in 2006/2007, and in the United

States from 176 to 213 between 1987 and 2001 (see Dowling and Power 2012; Wiesel et al. 2013), or by 74 percent between 1910 and 2010 (Echegaray et al. 2021, 46).

11. Referring to public and scholarly debates in Canada and Australia, Wiesel et al. (2013) demonstrate widespread criticism regarding size, aesthetics, cultural values, extravagance, and environmental aspects. Dowling and Power (2012) also highlight social sustainability, as large houses require considerable urban space.

12. See, for example, Keller (2005), who discusses this complex meaning in relation to the Estonian term *soppamine*, which is an Estonian adaptation of the word "shopping."

13. Linked to her perspective on stress, Solér (2018) also discusses the chronic "role strain" influenced by the social and structural (marketplace) arrangements surrounding the individual. We are overloaded by the opportunities provided by the market, by the abundance of possible choices, which results in "identity overload"—the gap between one's actual and ideal self (see chapter 2, including Figure 2.1)—and "role overload," implying that the demands on people's energy exceed their capacity within a specific identity or role.

14. It is often claimed that digitalization is part of the climate solution package. For example, internet shopping may involve fewer trips to outlets. Under certain circumstances, online retailing may reduce the environmental impact of shopping (van Loon et al. 2015). Yet, this positive effect is questionable or at least moderated given the problem of digital rebound (Coroamă and Mattern 2019). Home delivery is often done by motorized vehicles, and this is not an environmental benefit if customers would otherwise walk, cycle, or take public transportation to the shop. In addition there is the problem of free return deliveries, particularly in the apparel sector.

15. Even though there has been a trend toward energy savings, the overall energy demand related to homes is increasing globally. It has been estimated that 40 percent of a nation's energy consumption relates to domestic buildings (Ellsworth-Krebs et al. 2021), and this will likely increase due to an increasing share of the population working from home because of the COVID-19 pandemic (Jiang et al. 2021).

Chapter 5

The Social Stock of (Not) Knowing

Normalization and Ignorance of Unsustainable Mass Consumption

Much of our consumption is something we just take for granted.[1] We do not generally question it. When we buy some item, the act of consumption seems obvious. We buy it because we feel a need or desire for it, or just out of habit. We do think about it, of course, but our reflections mostly concern mundane matters: price, function, quality, appearance. And why should we question the habit of consuming? Our culture tells us that as a "sovereign" consumer we can legitimately purchase the item.

This chapter deals with a cognitive dimension of consumption and consumerism. I am referring to our "know-how" about consuming, and even more to its opposite: our ignorance about consuming. In line with the general approach of this book, this cognitive dimension should not be confused with an overly individual or psychological perspective. As a sociologist, I am referring to the social stock of knowledge. What we know or do not know—what we take for granted or are able to question—derives from the society and culture in which we live and has its foundation in social life.[2]

By "cognitive," I am above all stressing what the sociology of knowledge refers to as "taken-for-granted" knowledge (Berger and Luckmann 1991 [1966]), practical consciousness (Giddens 1984), embodied knowledge (Bourdieu 1990) or tacit knowledge. The tacit knowledge in mass consumption society is related to a default mode of consuming whenever you encounter a need/wish/desire or practical problem of any kind. By default, you respond to desires and problems by the act of consuming (instead of making, being, reflecting). The cognitive dimension can also include a more discursive level of reflection. When habits are challenged—by sudden insights, problems, accidents, crises, aha experiences—then more focused reflections may enter a person's mind. Such reflection may lead to cognitive strategies like defending or justifying existing habits, but it can also pave the way for a more fundamental challenging of what so far has been taken for granted. The topic of justifying versus challenging, including the possibility of "transformative learning," will be dealt with in the next chapter.

Our ways of knowing are informed by overarching cultural factors in society (see also Introduction). Scholarly and everyday language have a wide range of words for these factors: ideologies, worldviews, narratives, storylines, frames, beliefs, discourses, discursive strategies, symbolic universes, paradigms and more. Cultures help people get cognitively oriented in the world. "Individuals orient their actions and selves to the overall narrative of the society in which they are socialized" (Brulle and Norgaard 2019, 11). The overarching culture can provide some "ontological security" to the individual self (Giddens 1984). That is to say, fixed ways of thinking can provide a sense of control and predictability in personal and everyday social life. Once a culture is internalized, a person will rarely question it, because doing so could be felt as traumatic.

These cognitive aspects have important connections to the key concepts in the title of the chapter, normalization and ignorance, but also to justification, which is considered in the next chapter. In the following sections, I will discuss normalization and ignorance in relation to the topic of consumerism and our unsustainable mass consumption society. Normalization (of much and more) has to do with mostly unconscious processes of "knowing" how to be and behave in society. For instance, we internalize what are normal, natural, or standard forms of consumption. Ignorance is about how high levels of consumption can continue because of a persisting lack of knowledge about the unsustainable effects of consumption. Not-knowing is a powerful force in reproducing unsustainable consumerism. Even if we become aware of it—as an increasing number of people indeed have done—a whole battery of cognitive strategies (arguments) is available that people can use to justify their current habits of overconsumption (see concluding chapter).

NORMALIZATION (OF MUCH, MORE, FASTER, BIGGER . . .)

Normalization (or naturalization) has to do with processes that make us inclined to see phenomena as normal (or natural). A phenomenon that we see as normal or natural is typically not questioned; it is taken for granted. Patterns and levels of consumption are good examples of this. Anyone can see that patterns and levels of consumption change throughout history, and thus can be at least superficially aware that there is nothing essentially normal or natural behind contemporary patterns and levels of consumption.

Nevertheless, powerful processes of normalization/naturalization are occurring that counteract this insight.

Socialization is key. A child born and socialized into a particular generation of mass consumption will unconsciously view contemporary levels of consumption as normal and natural. The consumption is implicitly legitimized and naturalized by the child's parents and by the everyday social life around the family, and its rituals and practices. It is not until much later in life that the older child or adult may begin to reflect on the historical prerequisites of her/his existing lifestyle. Nonetheless, what has been taken as natural and normal is always difficult to see as changeable, and it is difficult to consider the idea that what is could be otherwise.

These unseen processes of normalization are covered in various scholarly works on consumer culture. For example, in her book *The Overspent American*, Juliet Schor (1998) shows how the American lifestyle has been gradually expanding. A rather drastic upscaling of spending has taken place, but much of this process is unseen and not reflected on. What was once seen as a luxury for a few, is now taken for granted as a basic need for all. Such processes are also seen in larger historical works on consumer history, such as *Empire of Things* by Frank Trentmann (2016), whose analysis stretches back half a millennium in the contexts of Europe, the United States, and Asia. Historically, the big picture and long-term movement has led toward "more, better, and bigger" (Sahakian 2022), and "faster" (Rosa 2013). Expectations of comfort, convenience, connectivity, and mobility have been continually ratcheted up (Welch and Southerton 2019). In rich societies today, it is seen as perfectly normal and natural to live a life with an ecological footprint that exceeds by several times the planetary limits. Excess is normal (see Text Box 5.1). Excess consumption is expected from a normal citizen in a welfare society.

This historical movement relates to all the macro forces described in the Introduction and to the dynamics of social life that are analyzed in subsequent chapters. Historical macro factors such as industrialization, scientific and technological progress, incessant economic and productivity growth, as well as broad cultural processes that justify higher standards of living, all jointly produce normalization. Our thoughts are thus shaped by both the ideational (cultural factors) and material contexts (including infrastructure, technology, devices, objects) that surround us; and these ideational and material factors are often closely interrelated (Miller 2010). Normalization also occurs at the micro/meso levels of social life thanks to a variety of everyday rituals that help us to sustain group solidarity (chapter 1), as well as processes of identity and social comparison (chapter 2), including the perceived right to consume in ways and volumes that "everyone" else in society does. It relates to the hurriedness of everyday life (chapter 3)—for instance, if there is a fast-food

Text Box 5.1: Invitation to Reflect on the Normality of Excess and Compulsive Buying

You may reflect on to what extent and why the words "excess" or "excessive" are only applied to addictions such as alcoholism, drugs, and gambling. Isn't it more to the point to say that excess is mainstream? You may also reflect on the phenomenon known as "compulsive buying." Isn't compulsive buying best seen as only the most extreme manifestation of a much more general phenomenon in our contemporary societies? O'Guinn and Faber (1989,148) define compulsive consumption as: "a response to an uncontrollable drive or desire to obtain, use, or experience a feeling, substance, or activity that leads an individual to repetitively engage in a behavior that will ultimately cause harm to the individual and/or to others." Suppose the word "others" was replaced by "society" or "planet." Have we all become compulsive buyers?

restaurant along the route one travels home from work, it seems quite natural to many people to be a customer there—and it is related to expected and standardized home environments and their place in society (chapter 4). The following subsections will show in more detail how the drivers that are related to normalization function: (A) normalization and perceptions of necessity are inscribed in social practices; (B) normalization blinds us and prevents us from questioning or seeing that things could be otherwise; (C) it forms habits, tastes, and bodily knowledge; (D) it relates to our tendency to imitate each other, and (E) through cultural norms, it creates processes of stigma, shame, and fear of social exclusion.

Normalization and Perceptions of Necessity Inscribed in Social Practices

Historically, household consumption of water and energy has been constantly increasing. Why is it so? Shove (2003) employs the concepts of normalization and normality to explain "escalation of demand" of water and energy. As was discussed in chapter 4, key terms in her analysis include comfort, cleanliness, and convenience. Shove highlights the important role of "inconspicuous" consumption and links this to "normal" consumption. This refers to consumption that people usually do not reflect on and often are not even aware of. A technological infrastructure has been built up around certain standards, like those connected to indoor temperature, and these standards, in turn, create expectations. Inhabitants become locked into certain technological dependencies (heating and cooling technologies), which in turn perpetuate expectations in a mutually reinforcing cycle. The role of social norms and social comparison (which impose a certain level of comfort expected within a status group) as well as the drive to achieve coherence (e.g., making various elements in a house fit into a whole; see chapter 4)—work together with external arrangements (standards, technology) and are contributing factors to normalization. Continuing this line of argument, Rinkinen, Shove and Marsden (2021) show that high demands are rarely questioned by policy or by dominant social science doctrines. Demand, which historically has escalated, is seen as a given.

Practices around cleanliness (showering, laundering) also activate the user side a bit more—the household and its inhabitants. External infrastructures of electricity and water supply combined with particular technologies for cleaning (e.g., the washing machine) are very important, but so are also the users' role in shaping the meaning and practice of washing. For example, norms of cleanliness may relate to middle-class identities and respectability (see, also, Dowling and Power 2012; Jack 2020).

Practices can legitimize themselves in a cyclical way. For example, the very practices of laundering and showering convince people that there are norms one ought to follow: "It is the everyday activity of laundering or showering that convinces people there is dirt to remove" (Shove 2003, 85). If we fail to clean the home at regular intervals, we believe the home becomes dirty. Scholarship in social practice theory shows how such conceptions of normality are built into the physical structure surrounding social life. For example, houses are built with expectations that family members need both privacy and socializing, which requires considerable space (see chapter 4), or that everyone will shower daily, and so on, thus further confirming and cementing the normality of such practices and consequently increasing the demand for energy/water (Hand et al. 2007; Rinkinen et al. 2021). This also means that the material surroundings enable higher levels of consumption and resource use in somewhat invisible ways. Dynamics like these have been observed by Riikka Aro.

> The process surrounding new things and our daily proceedings has much to do with wider material surroundings, such as energy systems, the house and the technologies mediating consumption: kitchens, living rooms and utility rooms are designed and built for a wide range of equipment, the standard of which has risen in recent years both in size and in the number of devices. (Aro 2020, 507)

Aro (2020) conducted a qualitative interview study of members of well-to-do (high- income, well-educated) households in Finland about how perceptions of "necessity" were established and negotiated. Despite acknowledging sustainability issues, people find that there are many things they cannot conceive of doing without. An important observation in Aro's research is that these things are considered normal to have within a specific socioeconomic status group, thus highlighting the importance of social comparison. Higher income correlates with higher levels of perceived necessity of possessions and standards of decency. Aro's study also revealed interesting contradictions in phrases such as "the dishwasher is quite necessary" (Aro 2020, 507), the word "quite" indicating some ambiguity in the otherwise categorical word "necessary." Hence, not having a dishwasher appears negotiable in theory, whereas in practice it is not seen as possible to do without. Aro even found that the word "necessities" could be associated with such things as daily luxuries. The following quote serves well to end this section. Aro discusses one of her interview subjects, and the passage illustrates several ways that perceptions of necessity are tied to various social practices in the household; however, implicitly it also shows how important other aspects of social life (everyday rituals, identity, status groups) are for understanding processes of normalization:

> Susanna, a working mother with two schoolchildren living in a large detached house (309 square meters) provides insight into this in talking about their daily necessities. She explains how they have three refrigerators, two of which they "could not manage without," and three freezers, the biggest (chest freezer) of which is also considered "necessary." In categorizing these during the interview, the perceived need for the third refrigerator, for instance, "fluctuated" from being perceived as dispensable to being thought of as a luxury item with respect to different practices and its location in the household's spa/sauna floor where, she explains, it is "more convenient for us to get drinks and snacks while having a bath." The extra refrigerators are categorized as necessities for special occasions, such as when organizing social gatherings, and are regarded as having importance in the doing of family time and when socializing. Moreover, the situated and "fluctuating" nature of necessity is also represented by the five TVs in this household for different purposes (game console, movie-watching, family use, and while making dinner/eating) and for enabling simultaneous use by family members resonating with the specialization and individualization trend (Aro 2020, 512).

Normalization Makes Us Blind and Prevents Questioning

It is already implied in the above analysis that we generally do not perceive normalization processes. This is related to how the normalization of changing consumption patterns and levels is a gradual, creeping, and unconscious temporal process. It is related to our socialization and early internalization of the world around us, and thus it appears natural. In many ways, we do not take notice of all the material things around us until they disappear, when they are taken away from us or break. We can compare this with the common experience that we do not perceive a noise until it goes silent, like when the ventilation system suddenly and unexpectedly turns off. Daniel Miller explains:

> Objects are important, not because they are evident and physically constrain or enable, but quite the opposite. It is often precisely because we do not see them. The less we are aware of them, the more powerfully they can determine our expectations, by setting the scene and ensuring appropriate behavior, without being open to challenge. They determine what takes place to the extent we are unconscious of their capacity to do so. (Miller 2010, 50)

When something is very evident, it can be so omnipresent that we become blind to its presence. Much of the material landscape surrounding us appears somehow invisible to us, despite the fact that we can see all the objects. This also makes us unable to see that circumstances could be different. Imagine, for example, a city without cars. Quite a few people cannot even conceive of this.

A consequence of this is that normalization does more than just keep consumers at high volumes of consumption. It prevents consumers from being able to imagine that their lifestyles and consumption levels could be different. We fail to question needs because we are hardly aware of them and cannot comprehend or verbalize them.[3]

Again, practices of cleanliness are a good example. Cleanliness has long been considered to be closely associated with civilization and progress, and historically it was associated with the upper class. But over time, cleanliness standards have escalated, and this rise is largely unnoticed. People do not question many aspects of consumption related to such practices as showering, body maintenance, use of cosmetics, doing laundry, washing-up, ironing, and wiping because they have become such a mundane and essential part of presenting "normal" and "respectable" bodies and homes to others. People therefore also fail to question the high levels of consumption of environmentally sensitive resources like water and cleaning chemicals that are connected to cleanliness practices (Jack 2020).

Also, new technologies can create new dependencies, which we fail to see. Because of dependencies, we may demand more stuff, services, and energy than we think we want. Schor (1998) observes that people spend more money than they realize. There is a blindness embedded in spending, which is facilitated by the ease of borrowing money and the use of credit cards: "The painlessness of spending with plastic makes it hard for many people to control" (Schor 1998, 73). "Connectivity" and the felt need to be reachable 24/7 is another issue. Sahakian (2017) found in a study that there was a dominant norm that smartphones should not be used when people are socializing in restaurants, which however clashed with another norm that parents should be constantly available for their children. We demand access to certain stuff even if it is not wished for, and in this case, what is lost is the possibility to be unreachable.

The very existence of an ever-present supply of products creates a propensity not to perceive and not to question.[4] If products are available at a market they are, somehow, automatically legitimated. The consumer may assume the product is legal, safe, well taken care of, and ethical. The responsibility lies with the supplier, as well as with the state or non-state regulatory regime assumed to be monitoring that everything is in order. We do not ask questions, because of the existing supply itself. If someone supplies a commodity, it is already part of what is normal. Such processes of legitimation are further fueled by cultural frames around "welfare," "consumer rights," "consumer sovereignty," and so on.

Normalization and Embodied Knowledge

As already stressed, activities that have become normal are typically done automatically and without reflection. They are embedded in everyday social practices and are part of people's practical consciousness. Practical consciousness also shapes what is known as embodied knowledge (Bourdieu 1990). In late-modern society, our bodies are literally trained for consumerism, for a propensity to consume, for a consumption mode of life (Solér 2018). Habits are deeply internalized in our bodies, in our bodily memories; we just keep repeating the same habits. We buy the things we usually buy because our legs seem to walk automatically to the same shelves in the shop. The habit to constantly consume, and to consume a lot, even as much as we can get and as quickly as possible, is contained in the body. We do not think about it. We just do it in a way similar to how we do not have to reflect when we drive a car. The body knows where the brake is.

Good taste can serve as an example. Taste is associated with cultural capital, as Bourdieu (1984) taught us. It is important to stress that, on one hand, taste is socially and culturally mediated, that is, shaped by the social class or status group we seek affiliation with. But at the same time it is something physical and a part of our habitus. When we enjoy something, we really do enjoy it, tautologically speaking. Both body and mind are activated. For example, the consumer of inexpensive low-quality food has been trained to develop a taste for inexpensive low-quality food. Cheap food literally tastes better to considerable portions of the population, because it is what people have learned to enjoy. Strawberry flavor is better than real strawberries in the yogurt.

This discussion can be linked with various mobility practices. For instance, given time scarcity and assumptions about a need for high speed in social life (see chapter 3), there is a default mode favoring fast commoditized options, a "taste for speed," so to speak. People become accustomed to certain temporal rhythms in mass consumption society. The normalization of fast options becomes deeply internalized as body knowledge. There are opportunities for "transformative learning," however (Boström 2022; see, also, concluding chapter). My own study of voluntary downsizers reveals how a slower pace of life—involving much more walking, bicycling, taking the train instead of flying, and new activities such as gardening—involves elements of corporal learning. Such alternatives for mobility and other practices challenge previous "habits of mind." Mind and body can do things that were previously inconceivable. Home-grown foods become tastier. What was previously considered too far to commute on foot or by bike is now—or after a period of exercise—experienced as joyful, healthy, and refreshing. The problem is that consumerism—linked with assumptions of speed—prevents the cultivation of such practices, and hence impedes the development of associated embodied knowledge.

The topic of cleanliness (see chapter 4) fits in here. Our culture and advertising, together with our practical consciousness and deeper levels of body knowledge, inform us when we are clean or dirty. Cleanliness is not something we reflect frequently about, but we "know" or "feel" when we are clean and what we could do to get clean. In our contemporary society, (excessive) clean(ing) has become normal, it is something expected of every decent inhabitant (unless you are running a marathon), facilitated by washing technology.

Normalization by Imitation

Another way that normal consumption works is that it reflects our tendency to do what everyone else does. We consume what everyone else consumes. Daniel Miller questions the role of free choice:

> Consumption is often argued to be about choice, and in particular free choice amongst endless opportunities of difference. In practice, however, the largest measure of our consumption is not derived from a desire for more things or for more choice. It comes from the gradual expansion of a sense of what ordinary people may ordinarily expect as their standard of living combined with the growth in their incomes. (Miller 1988, 138)

The above could be illustrated with any kind of item. In the study by Aro (2020) discussed earlier, there is a description of a woman, Marianne, which illustrates how peer referencing contributes to decisions to purchase new technology:

> An iPad is the latest what we, around a year ago, bought. . . . There are, and will be, these things that you . . . wonder how you ever have managed without. . . . It would be very hard to give up. . . . I myself even woke up to the fact that "all of our friends, all of our friends' families, everybody has an iPad." And then we bought it. . . . Not really because everybody has one, but because we noticed that this thing seems to be a kind of home appliance that everyone should have. . . . and then we realised that this is actually amazingly good. (Aro 2020, 513–14)

This is rational choice turned upside down. After the item is purchased, it appears to have a useful function. Aro further argues that a "tacitly accepted standard of living has the negative power to prevent downscaling from any level of consumption once it has become habitual and normalized" (Aro 2020, 514).

Zygmunt Bauman uses the metaphor of a "swarm" to describe this phenomenon of imitating others. In our modern consumer society "the *swarm* tends to replace the *group*" (Bauman 2007, 76). He continues:

> In the case of human feeling and thinking units, the comfort of flying in a swarm derives from having security in *numbers*: a belief that the direction of flight must have been properly chosen since an impressively large swarm is following it, a supposition that so many feeling, thinking and freely choosing human beings couldn't be simultaneously fooled. As self-assurance and the sentiment of security go, the miraculously coordinated movements of a swarm are the next best substitute for the authority of group leaders, and no less effective. (Bauman 2007, 77)

Again, normality is both cause and effect. An action reproduces itself in a cyclical fashion. Normalization has to do with unconsciously doing the same thing as everyone else, very much like a swarm, as Bauman suggests. Other common metaphors are "following the herd" and the "chameleon effect." Imitation saves time; it is easier and faster to imitate than to think for oneself (chapter 3).

Everyone else can't be wrong, right? If everyone else seems to enjoy branded goods or going to Disneyland, how could that behavior be wrong? If other people desire stuff, we may believe that the stuff is worth desiring. Desires are therefore not just our own. We can speak of "mimetic desire" (Belk et al. 2003). Think about attending an amusement park. We may expect entertainment because it is *framed* as an entertaining social activity.[5] We are supposed to have fun there. The normality of this pre-framed activity is maintained by the sheer number of people involved in the activity. One's own participation, and the observation that other people appear happy and are screaming and laughing together in emotionally energizing rituals (see chapter 1), confirm that this framing was correct. Hence, because of this already pre-framed entertainment and desire, there is no need to reflect deeply upon what it actually is about the amusement park that attracts attention. It is self-evident (until perhaps one day you realize how much you actually hate that kind of activity).

The human tendency of "compliance and conformity" and susceptibility to social influences is well documented in social-psychological research (see, e.g., Cialdini and Goldstein 2004). In relation to research on non-sustainable consumption behavior, this was documented in an experimental study by political scientist Carolin Zorell (2020) who, by manipulating the "choice infrastructure," and making comparisons with an original pretreatment situation, was able to observe and find evidence that cafeteria guests strongly imitated each other when choosing cups. Even if they were "nudged" to pick the more sustainable coffee cup (by making the "sustainable" ceramic cup more visible and accessible than the "non-sustainable" disposable cardboard cup), people had a stronger inclination to choose the type of cup that their companion had already chosen. Individuals imitate their peers when choosing. Based on her observations, Zorell argues that people are susceptible to social influences and glean "cues" from peers about how to act properly and avoid uncomfortable social difference.

This is not just a matter of following norms, Zorell continues, but is a powerful subconscious force with social implications. Imitation is done unconsciously and has the sociopsychological function of easing personal and social tensions, as well as creating interpersonal bonds. Consider the well-known phenomenon of imitating bodily movements, such as touching one's head in a similar way as one's conversation partner. Consumption may be not very unlike that. Interpersonal mimicking can also spread and become contagious, says Zorell: "People stick to habits and they follow each other. This can be a vicious circle. As people mimic each other, predominant non-sustainable behavior can remain the common thing" (Zorell 2020, 13). It can be likened to a contagious disease: "Non-sustainable consumption can be portrayed as a contagious disease, which currently is treated through putting trust in people that they will do the 'right' thing. These people, however, are not even aware of them spreading the disease" (Zorell 2020, 13).

Normality, Shame, and the Fear of Social Exclusion

According to Cecilia Solér (2018, 53), there is a "social norm of constantly partaking in consumption activities and adhering to Western affluent consumer culture ideals." As the word "norm" is part of the word "normal(ity)," it also indicates in our language that what is seen as normal can become a norm. In reality, what has become normal is often also a norm, even if the latter concept can be seen as somewhat narrower. A norm includes an implicit requirement to behave in a particular way. According to Zorell (2020, 9–10), "Norms are implicit assumptions or beliefs about what seem to be common standards of 'good' or 'appropriate' versus 'bad' or 'inappropriate' behaviors developed as they interact in and with their social environments." Although the literature on norms may distinguish between descriptive social norms—relating to how practices are normally performed—and injunctive social norms—stipulating how practices ought to be performed—I would argue that descriptive social norms, or "normality," often lead to injunctive norms.

The key feature of norms, well known in both social sciences and everyday life, is the difficulty or impossibility of breaking them. People who fail to comply with "normal" behavior—whether understood as descriptive or injunctive—risk experiencing feelings of shame. They risk stigma (Goffman 1990 [1963]), being labeled as deviant, and thus social exclusion (Becker 2018 [1963]). This is what makes the power of normality so strong. One of the strongest fears among human beings is the fear of being stigmatized as deviant, as an odd person to be socially excluded.

Richard Wilk (2002, 11) uses the term "repressive naturalization." Wants and desires turn into "needs," partly through a process of stigmatizing alternatives to them. By displays of power, gossip, and slander, some practices are made unthinkable.

> A Maya man once told me about his first encounter with shoes when he went to school in a nearby town where he was the only Indian. His schoolmates laughed at his bare feet, and gradually he got into the habit of wearing shoes; by the time I met him he thought that going barefoot was unhealthy and disgusting. (Wilk 2002, 11)

According to Collins's model of interaction ritual chains (see chapter 1), shame is connected to a failure to recognize "sacred objects" or "moral standards" that are associated with everyday rituals (Collins 2005, 110). Shame is the emotion of a self that is threatened or depleted by group exclusion. Shame reflects a broken social bond; the social rhythm is impaired (Collins 2005, 120). Therefore, there is a strong pressure to consume what the social group to which one belongs considers normal, and, instead of feeling shame, to evoke the opposite feeling of pride.

In chapter 2, I discussed the importance of social comparisons, that people look upwards and strive for social status by consuming the right things in the right volumes. I also stressed that social comparison works "downward"; that is, people do not want to fall down the ladder. People feel a strong need to fit in, to remain desirable in all the different spheres of social life: school, work, friendship. Consumption is key in this respect. Fear of social exclusion makes people hesitant to deviate from norms of spending (Mead et al. 2011). Zygmunt Bauman (2007) discusses the imperative to be able to "sell" oneself as a "commodity" in several ways, for instance in order to get a job. This requires maintaining a high level of consumption. Having the CV and the right expertise is not sufficient for employability. You also must consume (the right) products.

The fear of appearing deviant and of acting outside the mainstream has been documented in several studies within environmental social science on (un)sustainable consumption practices. For instance, it is very hard to deviate from the social norm to consume significant volumes of various objects (Black and Cherrier 2010, 445; Isenhour 2010; Shove 2010; Armstrong et al. 2016; Boström 2021a, 2021b). Cherrier et al. (2012) use the image of a "glass floor" to represent sociocultural norms and standards that prevent climate-conscious people from achieving the goal of reducing their carbon footprint. The glass floor is seen as representing the minimum level of socially required consumption. "Under this threshold, an individual transgresses the socially dominant rules of the consumer society and faces risk of social exclusion and marginalization" (Cherrier et al. 2012, 401). It is again important to emphasize that these norms are often taken for granted. They are not seen for what they are, or are only very vaguely understood, because they are firmly internalized through socialization. This logic also applies to cleanliness practices, as discussed in Text Box 5.2.

The powerful role of norms relates strongly to other drivers described in earlier chapters. It is hard to overstate the importance of fear of shame and fear of being outside the normal as a fundamental driver of consumerism. Normality is strongly related to what we know or do not know about the world we live in. The next part of the chapter deals with this issue: how various examples of knowledge and non-knowledge contribute to consumerism.

MASS IGNORANCE AND ANTI-REFLEXIVITY

In this part of the chapter, I argue that ignorance is a powerful mechanism behind continued consumerism and unsustainable patterns of mass

Text Box 5.2: Cleanliness, Shame, and Social Stratification

The feeling of shame can be an important emotional factor in upholding high levels of consumption and resource use. Tullia Jack has conducted several studies of cleanliness practices related to the home, clothing, and bodies. Linking to the concept of inconspicuous consumption (see chapter 4) and employing theories of conventions and social practices, she has shown how accelerating cleanliness practices and standards have led to increased use of energy, water, and chemicals (see e.g. Jack 2017, 2020, 2022). The role of shame is crucial. In an article, Jack (2020) shows how the representation of cleanliness practices and ideals in various Swedish popular magazines mainly targeting women has contributed to a cleanliness culture connected to both the home and the body. The fear of shame is always there:

> Typical messages around bodily (mis)functions suggest that without perfect teeth you should be ashamed to smile, without the right deodorising panty-liners you should be embarrassed to stand near strangers in public, and sweaty armpits are embarrassing and should be avoided with strong antiperspirants. (Jack 2020, 337)

Jack, Anantharaman, and Browne (2022) conducted an interview study on cleanliness practices, infrastructure and social stratification in Mysore, South India. Men and women from the middle and working classes were interviewed. The growth of the middle class in India and associated increases in energy and water consumption serve as important context. The study reveals that expectations of cleanliness are general and normalized, while access to the infrastructure and resources needed to meet the expected standards differs significantly based on social stratification: gender, class, and caste. It is shown that dirtiness is used as a discursive exclusion strategy in Indian society, and that it is associated with perceptions of poverty, low education, and lack of responsibility. Cleanliness is central to signaling status and inclusion, something that can lead to overcompensation, especially from those who lack privilege and fear being stigmatized (compare chapter 2 on relative poverty). Altogether, this means that cleanliness practices and the strong power of shame contribute to the reproduction of social hierarchies, and the consumption of resources linked to the practices can be expected to increase further, because the authors of the study were not able to detect any questioning of cleanliness practices or resistance to them. The study shows how cultural norms/expectations around cleanliness intersect with social stratification.

consumption. Ignorance here means "not knowing" about the environmental and social consequences of one's action and decisions. One could say that ignorance is the luxury of not knowing about the negative sides of one's practices, and it is therefore empowering because it makes it easier to continue with the practices.

Our society of mass consumption is equally a society of mass ignorance (of the effects of mass consumption). There is generally a great lack of knowledge and understanding about the problematic aspects of consumerist lifestyles. Ignorance of the harmful consequences that one's habits have for others, for nature, and for oneself is a powerful force in reproducing them. The following sections will go into more detail about these patterns. First, I will elaborate a bit more on the concept of ignorance.

Ignorance is not exactly the same thing as what is expressed by the simile of what a fish in a glass bowl knows about its surroundings. It involves a bit more knowledge than that. Ignorance includes awareness: awareness of the limits of knowing (Gross 2010). Ignorance includes the knowledge that some unknown factors are involved. Ignorance can include the legitimate awareness of the impossibility of knowing everything of social and ecological relevance connected to a lifestyle, for example. It would be impossible to know everything that matters, considering the enormous scale and complexity of our globally extended industrialized society.

Thus, it must be stressed that ignorance is not necessarily something negative. Rather, it is better understood as an essential feature of social life (Gross 2010), given society's extreme degree of differentiation (e.g., its division of labor). We simply cannot know everything. The important question rather concerns how we view and exploit the condition of ignorance. According to Gross (2010), ignorance can be divided into non-knowledge and negative knowledge. "Non-knowledge" is knowledge about what is not known but needs to be considered in future planning. For example, we may be aware of the possibility of important unknown matters; the climate is expected to change, but we do not know how much, and we could guess about the consequences, but we do not know what they will be in the local context. And we can develop some preparedness to adapt to surprises. This can be done in planning and decisions, for example by applying the precautionary principle in the face of uncertainties. With an open attitude to learning, non-knowledge can be transformed into new or extended knowledge. "Negative knowledge" is things that are not known, but which are considered irrelevant or dangerous to learn more about. We may not want to know more about a topic because of anxiety about what that knowledge will reveal. Even such negative knowledge is not necessarily "negative" from a normative point of view. A person may not want to know more about whether he or she is genetically predisposed to get cancer, and may feel that his or her quality of life will be better without that knowledge. However, when negative knowledge is demanded by authorities or the culture, problems appear, for instance "don't worry, trust us, you don't need any more information," or "we can guarantee that this is okay, and you can continue as usual." This demand can be called anti-reflexivity (Boström and Klintman 2019a). There is a push from authorities or other sources to avoid reflecting and learning about matters of potential importance to us.

Hence, ignorance in the form of anti-reflexivity becomes problematic to the extent that such negation of knowing is systemic and is exploited to justify the continuation of unsustainable practices (for more on justifications, see next chapter). In terms of the ecologically destructive consequences of mass consumption, such negative knowledge is plentiful. It is relevant in this context to speak of mass ignorance and systemic anti-reflexivity in the current social life of consumerism. Furthermore, strong vested interests are involved in maintaining this state of mass ignorance and anti-reflexivity (McCright and Dunlap 2010; McCright 2016).

Earlier, I discussed how normalization makes us blind. Adding the perspective of ignorance, we can say that normalization contributes to mass ignorance of the social and ecological consequences of mass consumption. There are, however, some further drivers of ignorance, which the following subsections explore.

Distances and Complexity

One source of ignorance relates to the outsourced, distanced, and complex pattern of commodity chains. This pattern makes ignorance possible or even unavoidable. Consumer decisions and practices are very much detached from their consequences, all the way from the point of production to waste disposal. In past times, when most household consumption was based on domestic production, and people consumed goods produced in the domestic social context, they were more likely to know about the circumstances of production. They, their friends, spouses, or relatives worked in the local factories. To be sure, early industrial capitalism did not make life easy for the workers, and labor unions were not easily formed and mobilized. Nevertheless, (at least in some countries) it was possible to develop labor movements on the basis of workers' experiences of concrete, visible problems. It is more common today for the grandchildren and great-grandchildren of these workers to be employed in service occupations, buying material goods that stem from complex global supply chains, and consequently knowing vanishingly little about what it means to be a producer of a physical commodity.

Distances contribute to value-action gaps. People may want to express some degree of ethical and green consumption, but the pervasiveness of consumption in life only allows for the responsibilization of a few segments of one's consumption. "Green consumers" may be conscious and responsible in some domains of their lifestyle choices, while remaining ignorant and largely anti-reflective in others (Boström and Klintman 2008, 2019a), which tends to include failing to consider rebound effects (see Introduction).

Consumption of meat and dairy products is a good example of how the distance between production and consumption creates ignorance. People generally lack deep knowledge about the meat industry and animal husbandry. Meat production, including poor living conditions for the animals as well as their slaughter, is detached from meat consumption. This distance is even codified in language. We speak of eating pork, not pigs. Beef, not cows. The less people know about the identity of the animals they are eating, the easier it may be to eat them. The same holds true for other items. More than one hundred years ago, Georg Simmel (1903 [1971]) wrote about how consumption in urban, commercial, mass-consumerist contexts gives rise to a blasé attitude (see also Bauman 2007, 41). The substance that one is consuming is experienced as insubstantial, empty of content.

In consumer culture, the here and now is systematically prioritized above the distant and future (chapter 3). It is always easier to favorably value the close, present, and personal over the distant, future, and collective (Sörqvist and Langeborg 2019). The distant and the future are discounted, but even more so, we are not even aware of how present consumption may relate to distant production and future consequences. In a variety of ways, as argued in previous chapters, temporal and spatial frames and structures tie people to patterns of consumerism without them even being aware of it.

Disconnected, Deskilled, and Devalued

The historical processes leading toward commoditization, that is, bringing about the gradually increasing range of goods and services in social life, also imply a loss of skills to make and care for things on one own. Our society is a society of dependent people. It is a society with an unprecedented division of labor. This differentiation process has been under way incessantly ever since Adam Smith wrote about the wealth of nations. The differentiation takes many forms:

- Separation of production and consumption
- Division of labor, from the local to the global scale
- Gender divisions and other forms of social stratification (see also chapter 2)
- Separation of urban and rural
- Specialization of expertise

- Lost competence in all areas except one's area of specialization, which in turn devolves into a never-ending spiral of finer subspecialties

A consequence of this is that everyone has lost their competence to produce and create. People are condemned to commoditized consumption in order to survive. They have even lost the skills needed to work on the commoditized items, to care for them and repair them. Many skills requiring craftsmanship, such as repairing, gardening, sewing, and renovating, have been lost by the average contemporary citizen because of this extreme specialization and commoditization. Lay knowledge in many areas of everyday life has been replaced by technology or expertise. Knowledge exists somewhere else. Consumption becomes the default tool for solving a huge variety of practical and other problems.

This loss of competence is also driven by access to inexpensive goods. Cheap products lack durability, and people do not expect them to hold up. Because robust performance is not anticipated, the result is a habit of carelessness, and this habit grows into tacit knowledge, including the default mode of consuming. If goods fall apart, the consumer will buy new ones rather than spend time and resources to repair them. They do not even know how to repair them. Consumers know how the goods should function, but have lost capacity and skill to keep them working.

Symbolic Knowledge

To be sure, consumers do have a great deal of knowledge about products, but this stock of knowledge tends to be related to social and symbolic aspects such as rituals (chapter 1), identity, status, and cultural capital (chapter 2), fashion (chapter 3), and how to create happy homes (chapter 4). Knowledge about products is knowledge about the how, when and why of buying/using the products in the proper ways in social and everyday life. It is not about the conditions of production or detailed knowledge about the material and energy that go into goods or services. The knowledge is centered on the rituals/practice of consuming, not on what makes this practice possible. Due to the cultivation of "tastes" within brand communities, fairly detailed and esoteric knowledge can be accumulated about what various fascinating goods can do, for example how a new model of a product (mobile phone, car, kitchen appliance, game console, laptop) supersedes a previous one. However, effort to gain such lay expertise is exerted more for the symbolic reasons listed above—perhaps especially for cultural capital—than in order to get insight into the social and ecological life cycle of the goods.

Some scholars have used the concept of fetishism—somewhat abstractly—in discussing some peculiar tendencies in our twisted relationship to goods.

Chapter 1 included an analysis of the importance of rituals. Much of the stuff around us tends to be symbolically sacred. We may view the concept of "fetishism" as adding a cognitive aspect to this topic. When commodities become fetishes, they seem to take on a life of their own, becoming almost metaphysical and divorced from their production context. They are glorified, mystified. Consumer culture celebrates the goods, but fetishism is partly about forgetting how they were made. There might also be a little "story," coming from the culture or advertising, that presents an overly romanticized picture of how the product was made. Fetishism can perhaps be viewed as a kind of ignorance, but with added ideological content. By means of fetishism, the hard labor and other circumstances behind the production of the stuff are denied and made invisible. Karl Marx famously highlighted this tendency within the capitalist mode of production and consumption. Lengthy and distant production chains provide fertile ground for such fetishism.

According to Bauman, we can even speak of "subject fetishism" (Bauman 2007, 14), which has to with concealing how the consumer herself is commodified when s/he creates a supposedly authentic identity out of all sorts of commodities and "sells" herself with her CV, on dating apps, and so on. An illusion of pure subjectivity emerges, but as with commodity fetishism, the circumstances behind the production of the subject—using commodities—are bracketed.

There can even be a category of fetishism connected to environmental or climate friendliness which has been labelled ethical/green fetishism (Guthman 2009; Boström and Klintman 2019a). Campaigns addressing responsible consumers can easily invoke such fetishism, thus creating a "moral licensing" (Stolle and Micheletti 2013, 276) or giving the impression that one is doing something good by paying a premium price for eco-certified consumption. The consumer proudly celebrates how green s/he is. The notion of ethical/green fetishism is further elaborated in Text Box 5.3.

One-dimensional Thinking

On a general level, our culture lacks the capacity for "social imagination," that is, the ability to see that what "is" could be different, to see that we can "create history."[6] I believe it could be illuminating to end this part of the chapter by reflecting on Herbert Marcuse's (1964) classic work *One Dimensional Man*. Even though this book and its post-Marxist way of theorizing and arguing have a number of problems (abstract reasoning, lack of empirical evidence, defending a paternalistic distinction between "false" and "true" needs/consciousness) it still contributes some important insights.[7] In brief, Marcuse argues that technological rationality and consumer capitalism forcefully cause a totalitarian development of one-dimensional thinking and a

Text Box 5.3: What Is Ethical and Green Fetishism?

Ethical and/or green fetishism adds to the notion of commodity fetishism the idea that the consumer does not only believe that the commodity has some mystic intrinsic value unrelated to the production circumstances. Instead ethical/green fetishism involves a double fetish (Guthman 2009; Boström and Klintman 2019a). On one hand, a fair-trade or eco-labeled product could be seen as an attempt at de-fetishization. One presumed intention behind the labeling is to reveal that the labeled and certified product has been produced under more socially and environmentally sustainable conditions than other equivalent products. Thus, in this sense eco-labeling is seen to reveal the "true" value of the commodity by making exploitative and unsustainable conditions of production more transparent and politicized (that is, an option for political/ethical consumers). However, if some problematic circumstances still remain in the eco-certified practice, albeit without the consumers' knowledge, one might even argue that a double fetish is in play.

> If negative social and environmental impacts in the production relations still occur, but under a false flag (an ethical label), green consumers are fooled in a double sense. Ethical values are then created as if they were objective and intrinsic, while these labels ignore or conceal the severely unsustainable conditions that may persist under such labels. (Boström and Klintman 2019a, 370)

Of course, people may buy eco-labeled goods and services while upholding a critical, reflective attitude toward the labels, thereby not creating "fetishes." Even if consumers do not create fetishes of their "eco-friendly" purchases, this type of shopping can be distracting in other ways. For example, as was mentioned earlier in the chapter, it is difficult to include all areas of consumption within a reflective mindset. The rebound effects can be difficult to assess and prevent. Indeed, it is particularly easy to ignore or deny the climate and ecological footprint in relation to the *volume of one's consumption.*

one-dimensional society. Marcuse argues that what "is" ought constantly to be compared with what "could be."[8] This cognitive and moral ability to negate "that which is" is shrinking, and one important part of the reason why it is shrinking is consumer capitalism.

Two-dimensional thought is dialectical; it includes the ability to negate that which is: the actual, existing society. Critical thinking, which is two-dimensional, requires negative thinking.[9] Such thinking seeks alternative ways of thinking, and rejects thought derived from existing beliefs, norms, values and practices.

One-dimensional thought is maintained by something Marcuse ironically calls the "happy consciousness," which is "the belief that the real is rational and that the system delivers the goods," and this "reflects the new conformism, which is a facet of technological rationality translated into social behavior" (Marcuse 1964, 84).

Through consumer capitalism and rising standards of living, citizens are manipulated, indoctrinated, and pacified into loyalty and consensus. They do not think or feel that anything could be different. Translated into the terms used here: they are socialized into mass ignorance in the form of anti-reflexivity by the institutions of mass consumption. They do not see that there could be any alternative to consumerism because of the overwhelming omnipresence of mass consumption. Social life is colonized by consumer capitalism.

The increase in technological rationality, welfare, and stratification of the labor class which serves to integrate the laboring class with capitalist society, along with consumer capitalism, explains these tendencies. In the one-dimensional society, the subject is assimilated into social structures and loses the ability to discover any alternatives. The individual fails to see any liberating possibilities, and even if she does, she does not engage in transformative practices to realize them. According to Marcuse, consumer capitalism causes people to sacrifice freedom and individuality for the sake of satisfaction. "The people recognize themselves in their commodities; they find their soul in their automobile, hi-fi set, split-level home, kitchen equipment. The very mechanism which ties the individual to his society has changed, and social control is anchored in the new needs which it has produced" (Marcuse 1964, 9). He continues:

> Commodities of lodging, food, and clothing, the irresistible output of the entertainment and information industry carry with them prescribed attitudes and habits, certain intellectual and emotional reactions which bind the consumers more or less pleasantly to the producers and, through the latter, to the whole. The products indoctrinate and manipulate, they promote a false consciousness. (Marcuse 1964, 12)

Without accepting these sweeping generalizations, the use of deterministic theory and the paternalistic ideas of false needs and false consciousness, his theory nevertheless makes an important contribution to understanding the mechanisms of mass ignorance, (ethical) fetishism and anti-reflexivity. Because of the convenient, comfortable and "happy good life," the rising standard of living, the pre-framed entertainment, the massiveness of all the stuff, and all the facets of normalization, citizens remain sufficiently satisfied not to critically reflect on important matters in life. Consumption is all that remains of what is deemed important.

> If the individuals are satisfied to the point of happiness with the goods and services handed down to them by the administration, why should they insist on different institutions for a different production of different goods and services? And if the individuals are preconditioned so that the satisfying goods also include thoughts, feelings, aspirations, why should they wish to think, feel, and imagine for themselves? (Marcuse 1964, 50)

People are accordingly driven to anti-reflexivity. Thinking is unwarranted. Expanded commoditization and the expansionist nature of consumer capitalism have thus invaded the inner space of privacy and eliminated the possibility for the individual to think, question and search. Marcuse wrote this almost sixty years ago. His theory may appear totalizing, but what part of it is untrue?

CONCLUSION

Our socially shared stock of knowledge helps us continue with unsustainable lifestyle patterns. People in welfare societies live in contexts where it is perfectly normal and legitimate to continue with habits that destroy the planet. Despite increasing ecological and climate consciousness, despite the experience of a pandemic that significantly altered many consumer practices (for a while), and despite Russia's invasion of Ukraine, which has resulted in food and energy shortages as well as escalating inflation, it still appears odd and deviant not to continue pursuing unsustainable habits. Shame on you if you don't consume!

Text Box 5.4 is the last invitation to reflect on opportunities for change before the Conclusion of this book. The next and concluding chapter will address the question of whether consumerism really makes us happier and provides quality of life. It will also show what defensive justification strategies people employ to cope with increasing awareness of the unsustainability of mass consumption. The Conclusion will then acknowledge the importance of existing countermovements and suggest things that can be done.

Text Box 5.4: Invitation to Reflect on Opportunities for Change

How can culture offer an alternative to the current situation of normalized excess consumption? How can society, politics and policy facilitate critical thinking and transformative learning? How can society make visible/understandable everything that has become unseen/neglected behind the global complexity of supply chains, the unprecedented specialization and division of labor, and the long-term consequences of present-day actions? How can society educate the public to deal with problems in other ways than by purchasing goods and services? As with the other drivers discussed in the book, no quick fix is in sight, but we ought to begin discussing the problems in the public sphere, in the Habermasian sense, to facilitate open-minded, creative and critical discussion. This would involve all institutions—formal education, civil society education, all kinds of media including social media, cultural institutions (art, museums, theater, film, and music), deliberative political forums with the ability to nurture transformative learning (see next chapter) and associated practices such as revealing the dark side of consumerism, envisioning alternatives, and developing skills—in other words, new frames of reference. This could counteract drivers related to normalization, ignorance, and defensive justification strategies. What is needed is pretty far from the current state of narrow, anti-reflexive, neoliberal, shortsighted thinking (or perverted into neo-conservative, far-right populism/denialism), in other words, one-dimensional thinking. What is needed is nothing less than a public sphere devoid of the flawed promises of consumerism, in which questions of social norms and the quality of life can be addressed, confronted, and reframed. Where can we find a window of opportunity for change?

NOTES

1. I am grateful to Monika Berg and Carolin Zorell for constructive comments on an earlier version of this chapter, as well as to an anonymous reviewer.

2. This focus on knowledge should not be conflated with the concept of "truth." Those who believe in false conspiracy theories also know, even if it is false knowledge.

3. Wilk (2002, 11) uses the term submersive naturalization to refer to a situation where you cannot even express your desire, much less act on it, or where there seems to be no name for what you want.

4. See Rinkinen et al. (2021) for similar arguments, based on social practice theory, related to the concept of demand. They argue that in policy, economic doctrines and common thinking, demand is seen as something that just exists. It is not made (by society) but only met. Therefore, opportunities for demand reduction in areas of energy and transport fail to enter the public debate.

5. On framed activities, see Miller (2010).

6. An interesting recent article explores broad factors explaining why climate change continues despite several decades of climate awareness (Stoddard et al. 2021). One of the nine factors concerns the currently poor conditions for "social imaginaries," and the authors discuss the "epistemological monoculture" of our time. Future visions of today are dominated by constrained social imaginaries. Transformative change appears to be impossible. They argue that "the psychological, social, and emotional capacity of individuals and groups to understand, explore, and create different social imaginaries has been steadily weakened" (675). Hence, conceiving social imaginaries involves profound cognitive and emotional challenges in our societies. This appears similar to what the classical sociologist C. Wright Mills (2000 [1959]) would argue with his notion of "social imagination": being able to see that things could be different, that we are part of creating history.

7. See also Stuart et al. (2020) on the role of the ideology of overconsumption, and how it conceals the contradictions of capitalism.

8. There is a similar distinction between the actual and the potential, as well as between the immanent and the transcendent.

9. This should not be confused with the negative knowledge referred to earlier in the chapter.

Conclusion

A Collective Detox from Consumerism

In the book I have elaborated on the macro-institutional and infrastructural drivers of mass consumption: capitalism, industrial/technological revolutions, social stratification, global supply chains, pro-growth politics, and consumer culture.[1] I have focused on how interaction rituals in social life feed consumerism through the positive emotional energies and social solidarity that rituals give rise to in relationships and groups, as well as through the normative pressures to conform with such rituals. I have shown how consumerism connects with our human tendency to make social comparisons—through identity formation, status consumption, and the experience of relative poverty—within socially stratified and increasingly unequal societies. I have explored ways that the (fast) socio-temporal rhythms in (hurried) social life spur consumerism—through demands for timesaving goods and services, commoditized leisure (retreat, reward, and compensation for sacrificed time), consumption for anticipated abundant leisure time in the future—and how, by celebrating novelty, consumer culture drives consumerism through a general sense of insatiability (cycles of desire, fashion anxieties, and rapid obsolescence). The book has demonstrated that drivers of consumerism connect to different sites of consumption. One is the "happy home," in which both conspicuous consumption (wealth, success, and the happy personal/family life objectified in the social display of the home) and inconspicuous consumption (comfort, convenience, cleanliness, connectedness, and coherence), interact, often in path-dependent ways, and which is a core setting when new generations are socialized into consumer culture. Another comprises shopping centers, malls, city centers, amusement parks and similar places, which have linked consumerism with the spheres of entertainment and social interaction. Yet another is the internet, which has expanded the buyosphere into an omnipresent 24/7 phenomenon as well as a sphere of peer interactivity and social judgment. I have discussed what we as consumers know about our consumption, often as taken-for-granted, practical, tacit, and symbolic knowledge, and do not know, its wider socio-ecological circumstances, and have found that processes of normalization, ignorance, and anti-reflexivity play powerful roles in reproducing unsustainable mass consumption. It has been demonstrated in all the chapters that we consume because we are social. Consumption is involved when we care for each other, when we compare, and when we imitate. It is involved when we boast and when we are envious, when we identify with others, when we communicate, share living spaces, spend time, and socialize. It is involved when we separate ourselves from others, as well as when we synchronize with them, coordinate, belong, and respect group norms.

Three issues remain to be dealt with in this book. The first has to do with justification strategies. Even if we become aware of the socio-ecological problems connected to consumerism, many of our reactions are defensive rather than progressive. We employ a range of justification strategies to defend unsustainable ways of living. I discuss nine such strategies in the first section. The next section and second issue deals with a tragic and ironic problem connected to a general flaw with consumerism. Consumerism is not just a socio-ecologically destructive force; it cannot even deliver on its promises. Quality of life does not seem to require consumerism. In fact, consumerism can even reduce it. People can become aware of this, however, and of other flaws in consumerism, and this provides an opportunity for change, for a collective detox. I use this phrase in the title of this chapter and as the heading of the last section of the book, because I see the task ahead as largely being a matter of weaning ourselves off the social and ecological narcotic of consumerism and approaching a sense of sufficiency. And this must be a collective affair. I present a figure of how I understand the possible process of transformative change, which I discuss in terms of transformative learning, social influence, and reorganizing societies. This concluding chapter mainly focuses on the micro/meso-level dynamics of social life, although it will also address links to macro-institutional and infrastructural factors.

JUSTIFICATION STRATEGIES FOR CONTINUED CONSUMERISM

I began this book by addressing something akin to a paradox: citizens in wealthy societies are increasingly becoming aware of and worried about aspects of the global crisis, including our overconsuming lifestyles, yet somehow things go on as usual. There is a gap between knowledge and action.[2] Why do people retain socio-ecologically destructive habits despite their knowledge and worries? The answer arrived at in this section is that growing awareness may trigger defensive rather than progressive responses, both among individual and collective actors.

Indeed, defensiveness is to be expected in any situation where radical change is called for. The observation that broad segments of the population of a given society defend and legitimize the existing institutional order—including the "symbolic universe"—is a classic topic of sociological theory (see, e.g., Berger and Luckmann 1991 [1966]; Boltanski and Thévenot 2006). Because of people's inclination to defend existing norms and practices in a given society, we should not expect sudden, widespread enthusiasm for change, despite there being good reasons for it. Moreover, in the context of the problems discussed in this book, an important reason for the defensive responses, and one that is consistent with many of the arguments in this book, is that people feel powerless and find themselves socially, culturally, and materially locked into practices of excess consumption. It is no wonder that people attribute responsibility to "structures." Defenses are typically connected to existing "orders of worth" (Boltanski and Thévenot 2006) other than "greenness" as such; and hence they are linked to other values related to, for instance, the market, industry, civil society or the domestic context (jobs, freedom, sovereignty, solidarity, equality, etc.).

However, even if a sense of powerlessness surrounding the ecological/climate case certainly reflects actual conditions (Gunderson 2022), there is a gray zone regarding the extent to which consumption is actually "locked in," and it is important to recognize that defensive actions help to reproduce consumerism and block the envisioning of alternatives. I should remind the reader that my intention is not to blame consumers, but to encourage reflection on defensive actions so we can better understand how arguments justifying the status quo might be revealed and questioned. Such reflection could provide openings for seeking alternative arguments in favor of activities and actions that are less reliant on excessive consumption. More will be said about this later in the chapter. In this section, based on earlier findings in the book as well as on readings of various parts of the literature,[3] I discuss the problem in terms of nine general justification strategies or defensive arguments that people employ to defend their right to live and behave as before. I do not claim that the list is necessarily exhaustive. These strategies can be combined and expressed in many different ways, and they may also be used by collective actors, for instance as part of "corporate social responsibility" schemes and greenwashing or integrated in political ideologies and arguments.

The first justification strategy is the "small agent" argument. Even someone who recognizes the existence of human-induced climate change might use the small agent argument to defend inaction. This defensive attitude is assisted by a perceived inability or unwillingness to change a lifestyle reliant on high levels of consumption, in other words, by an ideology of "impossibilism" (Jackson 2017). The person may externalize responsibility to larger institutions and infrastructures, such as those discussed in the Introduction.

Immediate practical circumstances are viewed as unchangeable. Society is considered to be too complex, and the structures too coercive. Such impossibilism also includes the micro-setting, one's domestic home environment (chapter 4), which one perceives as given, thereby locking oneself into path-dependent habits.

A second justification strategy—linking in particular to themes developed in chapter 1—is the "caring" argument. Goal- and value-conflicts play an important role here. For instance, one may feel that it is more compelling to nurture one's social relationships—and respect the consumption-laden interaction rituals—than to give much thought to the bigger picture. Accordingly, one can feel locked into various consumerist patterns simply out of care for one's social relationships. Seen on a more global, abstract level, this kind of argument may be linked to caring for other cultures. Thus, international air travel may be defended as a way of cultivating a human-centered and cosmopolitan worldview, which includes facilitating encounters with foreign cultures (see Cocolas et al. 2021). If several of the other justification strategies discussed here lean toward individualistic value framings, this caring argument has more of a communitarian quality. However, it is a present-oriented (see chapter 3) and delimited sort of caring that does not consider the needs of future generations (as Greta Thunberg 2019 reminds us) or the nonhuman living world.

A third justification strategy is the "social comparison" argument, which reflects findings from chapter 2. The idea here is that someone else is always to blame, such as the superrich, the upper social classes, or at least those who own or consume much more than oneself. Hence, they bear more responsibility for the problems and should take the lead in reducing consumption. "Why should I sacrifice my prosperity and consume less if others don't?" Such attitudes may flourish in a context of relative poverty combined with rather unattainable (but firmly socialized) ideals. Social comparison is also implied in the drivers related to imitation discussed in chapter 5: "Everyone else does it, so therefore it is legitimate."

A fourth justification strategy has to do with time, or rather the felt lack of time to search for slower alternatives. This is the "I can change later" argument. It postpones action to some abstract and idealized time-rich future. For example, the path dependencies combined with the hurriedness of social life can be felt to be external sources that one can do little to counteract. As shown in chapter 3, perception of time pressure is the driver behind much consumption.

A fifth justification strategy, linked to themes in several chapters, is the "entitlement" argument, which relates to the idea of ownership (of a home, position, identity, etc.). Consumers may reason that they somehow have the right to consume in accordance with an inherited/achieved position—their "extended selves"—that they occupy in society and/or in agreement with current standards. Drivers related to normalization are important here. Phrases such as "standard of living" implicitly legitimize the notion that one is entitled to what one owns (or more). Just the fact that something exists and is legally available in the marketplace provides sufficient legitimacy (see chapter 5): "Why shouldn't I have the right to buy it?" This is particularly the case when there is a (perceived) lack of alternatives. Entitlement arguments can be associated with notions related to inheritance and ownership. It is also an important component of ideologies, discourses, and systems of welfare provision, and is associated with the right to be compensated and rewarded. Some compensation for time sacrificed at work could be seen as part of the contract between the welfare society and its citizens, and it follows the structural separation between time for work and time for leisure (chapter 3). Consider retirement, for example: "I deserve this because of all the hard work I've done in my life."

A sixth justification is the "just-in-case" argument. This refers to the perceived need on the household level to possess and accumulate a buffer of goods that are never, or only infrequently, used. Southerton and Warde aptly argue that just-in-case thinking "provides a rationale for the accumulation of material goods in anticipation of 'peak loads' of social activities" (2023, 346). They list a range of scenarios which trigger such justification: emergencies (being self-sufficient in problematic situations, such as an electrical blackout), occasional needs (for example, possessing tools for repairing the house, equipment for occasional outdoor activities, or an SUV for infrequent journeys in the countryside and to carry extra luggage), unexpected events (for example, extra capacity, such as a spare room to accommodate guests; see chapter 4), anticipated boredom (items for entertainment), anticipated future practices (see chapter 3 on consumption for future leisure), revisiting past practices (possessing objects that recall nostalgic memories; see chapter 1). Another example is excessive cleaning, just in case someone comes by to say hello (Jack 2017). Southerton and Warde argue that this is an area where sharing economies and collaborative consumption provide viable alternatives, though they are rarely considered. Private possessions are the norm and practice.

A seventh justification strategy links to the cognitive dimension and ignorance of the issues discussed in chapter 5. This is the "no or only minor harm" argument, which can be seen as a soft denial of the negative effects of consumerism. I say "soft denial" (Carroll et al. 2018) because only a minority of people today categorically deny that climate change and ecological destruction are happening and are caused by human practices. However, soft denial can be as effective of a discursive tool as full denial for keeping things going as usual. It implies that people deny the magnitude of the risks, the scale of the effects on the environment, or some of the root causes. One's own consumption is simply not a significant part of the problem. Hence, many people still deny that mass consumption and lifestyle matters play a significant role in socio-ecological destruction. Sticking one's head in the sand, that is, remaining ignorant and uninformed (or only partially informed) about the negative consequences of, say, meat consumption, can be a deliberate strategy if one is tempted to continue eating meat and wishes to avoid feeling guilty about it.[4]

An eight type is the "I do my bit" argument, which is fairly similar to the previous category but should be treated separately. Instead of denying individual responsibility using the small-agent argument (type 1 above), this strategy rests on a notion of exaggerated individualism. The response is not inaction, but superficial action. Psychological research speaks of cognitive dissonance, confirmation bias, inner goal conflicts, moral accounting, and similar mechanisms. It has been found that people engage in compensatory behavior if they do something that causes worry and build up a set of arguments to defend their unsustainable habits. Such behaviors have deep roots in the human mind. They rely on "cognitive heuristics," that is, recurring thought patterns that people use to restore their inner balance (Sörqvist and Langeborg 2019). People can exercise a range of external devices such as climate-compensation schemes and "green" labels. Selective exposure and processing of knowledge/information/news is another theme, which includes how selectivity is mediated by ideologies and other cultural frames (Newman et al. 2018; Klintman 2019). There is a very dominant ideology and cultural frame surrounding "green" consumerism (and green growth, eco-modernism) that can boost this type of justification strategy. People may think in terms of a balance between "environmentally friendly" and harmful behaviors. The misconception is to believe that "green" choices can compensate for unsustainable ones, like flying to one's vacation destination after habitually bicycling to work. Goods labeled "environmentally friendly" may even fool people into thinking they are doing something good for the environment by buying them. When people think in terms of balancing, they fail to see the whole. People are doing their bit, but lack the concepts or measures that would enable them to consider the rebound effects (see Introduction).

The last type is the "we're doomed anyway" argument. "After all, it's too late, so I might as well continue as before." Last-chance tourism is an illustrative case: "Maybe I should hurry up and visit this rain forest, because soon it will be gone."

All such arguments are easier to apply if they are already being used and legitimized, both within public discourse and by peers in one's social network (see Klintman 2019). There are abundant possibilities to find an argument to continue as before and claim "I know about the problem, but I need this thing."

But do you really need it?

THE FLAWS OF CONSUMERISM

On the most general level, the great flaw of our culture of consumerism is that it cannot deliver on its implicit and explicit promises. The sad irony of our mass consumption society is that it destroys the conditions for life on Earth and is based on huge global inequalities (see Introduction), while at the same time it fails to deliver quality of life for us humans. I use the plural form "flaws" in the section heading, because there is some variety in the ways that consumerism fails to deliver.

Before I develop these arguments, the above statement needs to be qualified and nuanced. I am not suggesting that there are no positive values, experiences, sensations, or feelings associated with the purchase and use of commoditized goods and services. For example, in chapter 1, I described how consumption is associated with positive emotional energies and helps people to socialize and to form and maintain relationships. Markets can be the site of many forms of pleasure, excitement, and entertainment. As shown in chapter 4, we decorate our lovely homes with commodities and consume culture in the home. As emphasized in chapter 3, much of people's leisure time is spent on enjoying the goods and services that others have made and sold to us. Consumption of goods and services is obviously a necessary condition for living a healthy, convenient, and decent life in our modern societies. Moreover, people are not simply passive dupes of macro-level forces that supposedly manipulate our needs/wishes/desires. Yes, we are strongly shaped by powerful external circumstances and are fooled by advertisements and endless expectations, but we can also resist and counteract these forces (more about this later in the chapter). The Marxist concept of "false needs" is problematic, to say the least, and it is not necessary to assume that people cannot feel actual happiness through commoditized experience.

That said, the gains of consumer culture in terms of well-being, life satisfaction, happiness, and quality of life are grossly exaggerated. I hope this book has shown that a sociological analysis can shed important light on this issue, not least by considering all the anxiety and frustration that are involved in social life dynamics. In this section I summarize and develop this argument a bit further and refer back to previous chapters.

Can Higher Volumes of Consumption Bring Greater Quality of Life?

For decades, plenty of research has questioned whether Western levels of consumption in the global North really bring quality of life, well-being, life-satisfaction, happiness, or the good life.[5] Much of this research has focused on income rather than consumption, but the former is assumed to be an indicator of the latter.[6] A typical finding regarding wealthy societies is that happiness or well-being increase significantly with income only up to a modest threshold level (e.g., Easterlin et al. 2010; Kahneman and Deaton 2010; Brülde 2015; Hylland Ericsen 2015; Jackson 2017; Kallis et al. 2018).[7] The ironic and sad fact is that the dramatic increase in material welfare in wealthy countries since the 1950s does not appear to correspond with any significant increase in human happiness or subjective well-being. Recall that the 1950s is often portrayed as the embryonic period of the acceleration of mass consumption, and climate emissions have increased by a factor of seven since then. A factor of seven for what?

It seems that there are other values than material and consumerist ones that are important for quality of life. A consistent finding in much research is that people who are more oriented toward materialist values experience lower quality of life. The studies by ecopsychologist Tim Kasser (2009, 2017) are well known. He consistently found, in his own and others' research, that people with a preference for intrinsic values such as personal growth, affiliation, and connection with community, rather than extrinsic ones such as financial reward and status, are generally happier and healthier.[8]

Why is it so difficult to use consumption to increase quality of life (happiness, well-being, life-satisfaction) above a certain point? To be sure, excessive consumerism can result in all sorts of individual and collective problems, such as heavily indebted consumers, personal bankruptcy, destroyed relationships, compulsive buying and shopaholics, obesity and other public health problems, mental illness, social conflicts, and criminality.[9] In what follows, and based on themes discussed in earlier chapters, I do not discuss such problems directly, although they are important and relevant, as they tend to draw attention to phenomena that are considered deviant and atypical (even if they are very common). Instead, I see the following problems as internal aspects of a culture of consumerism affecting everyone: (1) consumerism as a zero/negative-sum game; (2) the restlessness and insatiability of consumerism, which also diverts attention and ambitions away from more meaningful activities; and (3) cluttered experience (a sense of too muchness).

Consumerism as a Zero/Negative-Sum Game

The first general flaw has to do with a zero-sum or even negative-sum game associated with consumerism and reflects key findings from chapter 2 on social comparison. Consumerism drives and reproduces a status hunt among many groups and strata in society. It feeds anxiety about social judgment as well as the perception of relative poverty.

It is relevant to return to the research on happiness and well-being. This research, which is based on long-term time-series data from a variety of international data sources, contains a consistent but puzzling finding. Although higher-income groups in a society generally do report higher levels of life satisfaction, average life satisfaction appears to be remarkably stable over the long term. It seems that it does not significantly change despite drastic increases in real income. This phenomenon is called the "Easterlin paradox," as it is based on a research program led by the economist Richard Easterlin (see Easterlin et al. 2010; Easterlin and Kelsey O'Connor 2022).[10] It is also called the "relative income effect" (Brülde 2015; Jackson 2017). This paradox is generally interpreted as follows. On aggregate level, having more income does not make the nation as a whole happier. However, for an individual, it is better to be among the richer part of the population. This pattern has been explained as primarily due to competition for social position. You are happier if you belong to the rich group; you do not feel "relatively poor." A complementary interpretation is that it reflects hedonic adaptation (Easterlin et al. 2010); as soon as you get used to an increased standard you cease to experience the added value it offers. (I return to this effect in the next subsection.)

Income (and consumption) in a wealthy context therefore appears to be a zero-sum game, or perhaps even worse, because the constant pursuit of higher income and greater consumption opportunities increases social judgment anxiety in society (Wilkinson and Pickett 2010; Jackson 2017, 57). Inequality gets under one's skin, Wilkinson and Pickett (2010) write, because human beings are very sensitive to inequality, and what matters to us is where we stand in relation to others in the same society. They argue that social anxiety and insecurity are the most common sources of stress in modern societies. Social judgments and evaluations are at the core: How do people rate me? "This vulnerability is part of the modern psychological condition and feeds directly into consumerism" (Wilkinson and Pickett 2010, 42–43).

On one hand, being poor or having low income can certainly worsen your life, both in an absolute and a relative sense. An increase in income matters significantly more for those with lower incomes. Yet, above a certain level well-being does not increase with increasing income (Kahneman and Deaton 2010; Brülde 2015; Jackson 2017, 57), at least not in a time frame encompassing several years (Easterlin et al. 2010; Easterlin and Kelsey O'Connor

2022). The same pattern appears if we compare countries. Whereas differences in life satisfaction across nations show that rich economies on the whole report higher levels of life satisfaction than poor economies, the absolute gains associated with an increase in income are much smaller for richer economies than they are for poorer ones (Jackson 2017, 57). On any level of analysis, one finds diminishing marginal utility with increasing income.

There appears to be a back-and-forth interaction between these forces. Relative poverty feeds consumerism, which in turn increases the risk of feeling relatively poor. Perceived peer pressure is a very powerful force in people's social lives, especially in countries with large and increasing inequalities. As humans, we crave positive and fear negative feedback, but more equal societies could dampen this pressure. Unfavorable social comparison and judgment could even be seen as an epidemic of anxiety, with envy and narcissism spreading in society: "The consumption of the rich reduces everyone else's satisfaction with what they have, by showing it up as inferior—as less than the best" (Wilkinson and Pickett 2010, 227). Likewise, in her social-psychological studies, Helga Dittmar finds consistently rigorous evidence that consumerist culture ideals and the search for a perfect body and the materially good life have a negative impact on children, teenagers, and adults (see chapter 2). "Consumer culture is a 'cage within' because its unrealistic ideals lead many people to experience identity deficits and negative emotions, which they then seek to remedy through the futile and damaging pursuit of a better identity through consumption" (Dittmar 2008, 199).

So, within the promises of consumer culture, in their role as sovereign consumers, people are supposedly empowered and liberated through the choice of consumer goods. They are thought to achieve greater uniqueness and self-expression through consumption. They are free individuals. However, such aspirations are better seen as a form of entrapment, and they can even spur feelings of loneliness. Unhappiness is a function of the distance between (unattainable) ideals/standards and reality. This is an experience, and a structural position, for many people on earth today. The problem becomes all the more alarming with the growth of negative social comparisons caused by broadcasting and social media (see, e.g., de Vries and Kühne 2015, and chapters 2 and 4 in this book).

Restless Insatiability

The second major flaw is temporal in kind; it has to do with the insatiability of needs/wishes/desires; an insatiability which is not merely psychological, but is activated by a range of macro-institutional forces and drivers on the level of social life. The above analysis—the status hunt, risk of falling down the social ladder, identity deficit—shows the restless nature of consumerism.

In chapter 3, I discussed how the common experience of time pressure and difficulty achieving work-life balance fuels the consumerist fire. Drawing on concepts such as cycles of desire, I discussed how the incessant search for novelty and hedonistic consumption fails to deliver satisfaction. Even though there may be some pleasure and excitement in this "desire for desire," the restless process is nonetheless characterized by emotions such as frustration (when longing for goods) and a sense of anticlimax (when one finally acquires them).

Hartmut Rosa, who is known for his social acceleration theory, uses the concept of *frenetic standstill* to denote a somewhat paradoxical feature of late-modern experience. While people are experiencing an accelerated pace of life, which results in all sorts of social stressors, at the same time there is a general experience of "aimless drifting." The paradox is that everything appears to be constantly changing while on a more fundamental level of experience nothing ever changes. Stuff, activities, identities, and personal relations are exchanged at a frenetic pace, while the basic structural and cultural forms remain intact. Life is experienced as a constant flow of new content in old bottles. At the same time, the mass consumption context implies an unlimited range of possible choices combined with an absolute impossibility (in terms of time and money) to try out even a small portion of all the opportunities. Unattainable goals and ideals, and constant fear of missing out the latest fashions and novelties contribute to an inner state of unhappiness. So many things, experiences and adventures are *almost* within reach.

Leisure and consumption intensify. A given time frame can be filled by more experiences. However, each experience loses depth, quality and meaning. Mass consumerism becomes a never-ending hunt for fast, superficial experiences and low-quality commodities, which are quickly forgotten in the hunt for new experiences/objects. The late modern consumer has a tremendous number of experiences, in a historical comparison, but has an unhealthy, even pathological, scarcity of deep and genuine experiences. This, according to Rosa, connects with many late-modern symptoms such as stress, a blasé attitude, indifference, paralysis, boredom, and depression.[11]

To be sure, it has often been claimed that late modernity is an era and culture in which the individualized self can, and is expected to, constantly create him or herself. Processes of detraditionalization and individualization seem to be opening up more spaces to freely create one's identity, life projects and ambitions (Beck et al. 1994). The late modern individual in the wealthy part of the world has historically unique cognitive, material, and democratic possibilities to engage in a variety of self-enhancing and enriching projects. It is unquestionable that a series of economic, political, cultural and social developments have provided this historically unprecedented opportunity. But all coins have two sides. There is a risk that the drivers of consumerism in the mass consumption context will undermine these opportunities. Again, linking back to Rosa, contemporary flexible individuals are adapting well to the fast structures, but a consequence of this is that people are losing their ability to creatively formulate long-term ambitions and projects. Consumerism diverts attention away from ambitions that are likely to be felt as more meaningful.

This restless pattern of non-satisfaction is systemic; it is a core element in consumer capitalism. The economy, which itself is an anxious and restless growth-dependent institution (see Introduction) depends on consumer frustration. Satisfied consumers are the biggest threat to consumer capitalism, and therefore the society of consumers must be kept unsatisfied. Zygmunt Bauman argues:

> The yawning gap between promise and delivery is neither a sign of malfunction, nor a side-effect of neglect or the outcome of a mistaken calculation. *The realm of hypocrisy stretching between popular beliefs and the realities of consumers' lives is a necessary condition of a properly functioning society of consumers.* (Bauman 2007, 47)

Or in the words of Tim Jackson: "Consumer culture perpetuates itself precisely because it succeeds so well at failure!" (2017, 116).

Cluttered Experience: Too Muchness

I believe the above picture should be supplemented by a more place-based understanding of flaws. I therefore suggest that one key flaw is best described in terms of a materially oversized and overcrowded place, which causes a somewhat cluttered experience. This might be seen as contradicting the notion of insatiability discussed above, because "cluttered experience" seems to suggest that the individual feels one has too much of something, not too little (and hence feels unsatisfied). However, these experiences can and do coexist. One's wardrobe can be absurdly oversized, yet one is still unable to find anything to wear.

Even if any single object might appear reasonable to possess at the point of purchase, the total sum of them does not. Everything that a consumer owns can cause stress and anxiety. The more one has, the more one has to take care of. The more one has, the more time, energy, and money has to be spent on cleaning, maintaining, discarding, protecting, and insuring things. The demand for locks, alarm systems, and insurance plans is growing. Things that one owns are things to worry about. The more space one has, the more one has to fill. The purchase of any particular item may make sense, may appear rational. But it is notoriously difficult to make a rational assessment of the indirect effects that a purchase may cause. On one level, there is all time and energy needed to learn to use and handle the item, clean it, fix it, and dispose of it. On another level, there are indirect consequences related to how it becomes entangled with all the other stuff in the material landscape, and how it actually fits spatially/temporally with the various social practices and the overall material landscape that the person is situated in. The resources needed to take care of the particular item are underestimated because the consumer has forgotten about all the other stuff that he is using and needs to take care of: "the cost of each convenience adds up" (Schor 1998, 19).

This is the experience of clutter. One is overwhelmed by the abundance within which one is situated. The larger the material landscape surrounding the individual becomes, the less possible it is to assimilate. "What we cannot assimilate oppresses us," argues material culture anthropologist Daniel Miller (2010, 62). The opposite, having fewer objects, facilitates a more genuine relationship with the objects, even a "true materialism" in the words of Schor and Thompson (2014), because each single item gets more time, attention, and care.

Perhaps the flat, distorted happiness of Herbert Marcuse's "one-dimensional man" that I discussed in chapter 5 is an apt image of the sum of these three general flaws. In any case, the concept points to how consumerism undermines the creative and critical attitude. Such a homogenization of thought, value and understanding, sometimes labeled "McDonaldization" or "epistemological monoculture," includes the loss of social imagination (see Stoddard et al. 2021). There is no counternarrative for a better future.

I will not end the book on this note, which would be unnecessarily pessimistic, but I will end this section with a quote from Eriksen, who argues that what is missing in contemporary life is hope: "The serpent in this earthly paradise may be called hopelessness. It is tautologically true that you lose hope in the end if you are hopelessly poor, but you may also lose it if you are hopelessly rich" (Hylland Eriksen 2015, 248).

A COLLECTIVE DETOX

How can we get rid of consumerism? How can we achieve a sense of sufficiency, of being satisfied with sustainable levels of consumption? How can we, and all the circumstances that structure our overconsuming social lives be changed? There are no easy answers to such questions. And there is no obvious and easy pathway toward reducing unsustainable volumes of consumption. The mass-consumption society we inhabit today is a result of centuries of sedimented processes that have accelerated since World War II, propelled by the interplay of macro-institutions and infrastructures described in the Introduction, and the dynamics of social life explored in the rest of the book's chapters. The mass consumption society we have inherited locks us into a multitude of path dependencies.

It is extraordinarily difficult to make a qualified assessment of how society and social life can be changed, and what is the best political strategy going forward: incremental, reformist, re-configurative, radical, or revolutionary. The difficulties stem from our society's extremely high level of complexity, that the issue involves human agency and multiple competing interests, power structures, and resistance, and that any proposed changes will generally have both intended and unintended consequences.[12] In this final section, I address what I consider to be key elements for the necessary change.

I suggest that what is needed, as the beginning of a long-term process, is for society to go through a kind of global, collective detox from the addiction of consumerism. The goal, to be sure, is both diffuse and overwhelming, but the current state of our planet offers no other alternative than to undertake this endeavor. The task is also difficult because, given the existing macro-institutions and infrastructures, we obviously must continue to consume within presently existing patterns in order to survive (see also Introduction, on the difference between consumerism and consumption). The collective task of reducing consumption must be performed within a societal and social context that consistently resists and opposes this task. It is diffuse because where exactly is the point where we reach sufficiency? This collective task must recognize the ambivalence involved in defining limits, sufficiency, and the distinction between unsustainable consumerism and essential consumption.

> Sociological analysis of consumption cannot resolve, but must stay attuned to the ambivalence of consumption. It is not a matter of celebration or critique per se, but is always to be analysed and debated in full awareness of ambivalent personal, social, cultural, political and environmental effects. (Rief 2008, 571)

This process must be collective. It must occur on all levels, in all spheres of society, everywhere. It must begin at once, and there are already many promising grassroots experiments and movements. However, even if the task is urgent, a very important cautionary note is in order: it will simply not be possible to change the mass consumption society overnight. If it took five hundred years or more to establish (cf. Trentmann 2016), it will surely require some years to transform into a new sustainable form. Imperatives such as "overhaul the system now" may lead to very unappealing, undemocratic results. The process must be somehow fast and slow at the same time. The transformation may evolve through catastrophes or by design (such as through "degrowth" policies or similar), or more likely something in between. This final section of this book relies on the normative assumption that we had better stick with—and bolster—one existing institution: democracy (albeit taking many forms and always improvable). This should be done in combination with other existing (but very improvable) institutions such as states, international organizations, science, education, independent mass media, cultural institutions, and a variety of more sustainable ways of running companies and economic practices.

A collective detox from consumerism can only be achieved through transformative change, which involves a reorganization of society. I see transformative change as a dialectical process involving structure and social agency,[13] or in more popular language, an interplay between top-down and bottom-up processes.[14] This is illustrated by the vertical two-way arrow in Figure C.1.

An essential part of this reorganization of society is transformative learning, which is both an individual and a collective enterprise. I will discuss a variety of processes connected with it: developing consciousness, revealing the harmful side of consumerism, and envisioning and practicing alternatives.

Another central process of transformative change is social influence. In the figure, I distinguish between frontrunning (practices of living well with less and counteracting consumerism), adapting (ability and willingness to adapt to changing circumstances), and resisting (defensive action, e.g. by

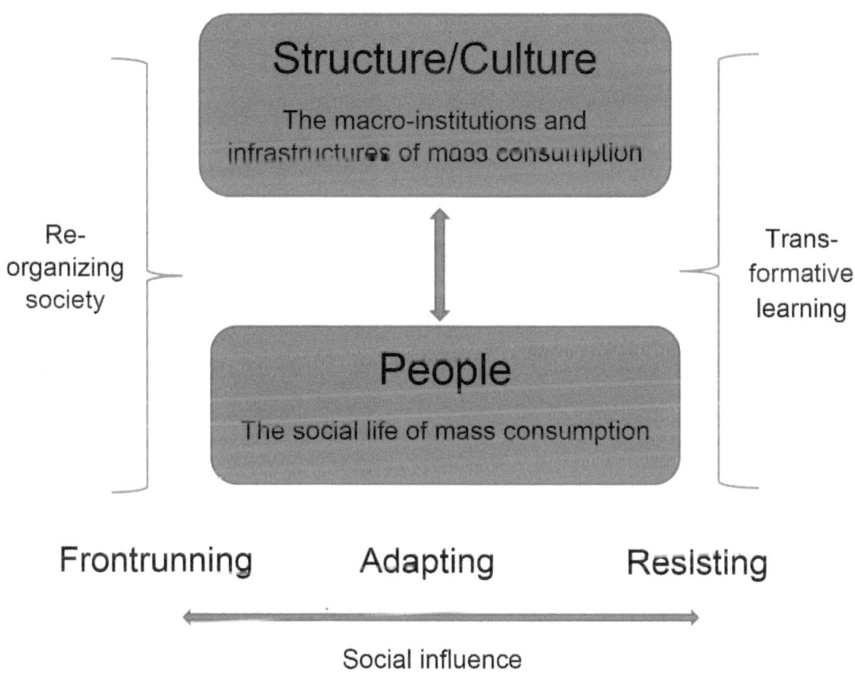

Figure C.1. Collective Detox from Consumerism. ***Source:*** **Author**

using justification strategies). Social influence is illustrated by the horizontal two-way arrow in the figure, which suggests that people can influence each other in either direction through social networks. The category in between, adapting, suggests a propensity to be influenced by either side. All the different modes—frontrunning, adapting, and resisting—can exist in one individual (or collective actor such as a group or organization) in different areas of consumption or social situations, although a particular actor may generally incline more toward one of them.

The rest of the book has three subsections. I first discuss transformative learning, then social influence, and finally reorganizing society.

Transformative Learning

In this book, I have emphasized that consumption is considered the default tool for solving a huge variety of problems, satisfying needs/wants/desires, and searching for happiness and well-being. There is a need to confront the socialized and habitualized tacit knowledge of the consumerist default mode, in order to challenge cycles of desire and feelings of incessant insatiability, and gradually integrate *not buying* into tacit knowledge. In contrast, a more sustainable mode would be to consume commodities (goods, services) only after a wide range of other ways of satisfying needs/wants/desires or solving a problem have been seriously considered. At the level of social life, I argue that people, groups, and communities will have to engage in a process of deep change characterized by *transformative learning*.

Transformative learning theory emphasizes the kind of learning that occurs in situations where actors (self-)critically recognize and reassess the basic assumptions and expectations that steer their thinking, feeling, and acting (Boström et al. 2018; Boström 2022). The theory has evolved from critical social theory's assumption that existing societal structures are reproduced and made to appear normal, natural, and inevitable through dominant ideologies and beliefs (Cranton and Taylor 2012; Brookfield 2012). "Transformative learning is defined as the process by which we transform problematic frames of reference (mindsets, habits of mind, meaning perspectives)" (Mezirow 2009, 92). A frame of reference can be seen as a structure of meaning that encompasses moral, conative, aesthetic, affective, and cognitive aspects, among others (Kovan and Dirkx 2003; Wals 2010; Lotz-Sisitka et al. 2015; Ojala 2016).

The concept of transformative learning is suitable for envisioning both personal and societal transformation, and such learning can take place among both individual and collective (or communities of) actors. Actors need frames of reference to navigate and make sense of the surrounding world. These frames of reference are supplied by past socialization, learning and experiences within the context of social life, communities, and overall culture. Dominant frames of reference are not challenged until one encounters a genuinely problematic situation, a "disorienting dilemma" (Mezirow 2009). Such a disorienting situation—for instance, one may have suddenly or gradually become concerned about the socio-ecological problems and flaws of consumerism—can via (self-)reflexivity set off a transformative learning process.

Transformative learning cultivates the ability to see through the empty promises of consumer culture. A starting point for any individual or collective actor could be to honestly reflect on the justification strategies that one is using. Hence, self-reflexivity is important. In relation to the topics discussed in this book, such reflexivity concerns scrutinizing the person one has become (and wants to be), which reference groups, ideals, and sense of belonging that one is oriented toward and finds important for comparison and inspiration (and whether this needs to change), how one engages with one's social relationships (and whether this needs to change), what kinds of rituals these social relations (should) maintain, whether one can be proud about something else than status consumption (cultural capital), how one can deal with time constraints, how one can expose the role played by inconspicuous sources of excessive demand that are built into buildings, technologies and household practices, and finally how one's needs/wants/desires are shaped by contemporary understandings of "normal," "natural," and "necessary" consumption. Such self-reflexivity can furthermore be jointly undertaken within groups and communities. Transformative learning involves coming to understand how needs/wants/desires have been shaped by the institutions, infrastructures, and social dynamics of consumerism.

As transformative learning involves altering the frames of reference that guide one's actions, thoughts and feelings, such a learning process goes hand in hand with envisioning, testing, and practicing alternatives. The actions and experiences of frontrunners who voluntarily engage in reduced consumption and try to achieve a sense of sufficiency far below current average levels of consumption in wealthy societies are crucial. Well-known examples of practices include engaging in more making, growing, sewing, maintaining, repairing and sharing of things, more gardening, walking, bicycling, and slow traveling, more interacting with each other in ways that assume fewer commoditized goods and services, and reconsidering what sorts of things are luxuries. Some people experiment with buy-nothing periods and similar actions (Isenhour 2010; Callmer 2019). Practitioners are called downsizers, downshifters, voluntary simplifiers, anti-consumers, minimalists, and so on, and there are movements promoting conviviality and transition towns.[15]

The experiences of frontrunners can provide important clues for our reflections on possibilities for radical transformative change. Even if their efforts occupy a small niche within the mass consumption context, they point to challenges and possible ways forward. In an interview study of people engaging in reduced consumption, I explored the challenges, possibilities, and transformative learning experiences that these frontrunners encountered (Boström 2021c, 2022).[16] Their experiences are mixed. Even among the most committed downsizers, many of the drivers explored in the various chapters of this book are strongly felt (see Boström 2021c).[17] Fully escaping from normalized mass consumption patterns is impossible. It would not only be impractical, but might even impair one's ability to express love, care, and friendship (see chapter 1), or cause one to appear like a disreputable person in the eyes of society (see chapter 2, 5). Hence, this study revealed that changing lifestyles is a complex enterprise that involves much questioning of society's structures, routines, values, and norms around consumption. The experiences of people involved in radical lifestyle change tell us that this is a gradual, time-consuming, demanding, and disruptive process of transformative learning, which involves both forgetting old habits and frames of reference and inventing new ones.

In a study (Boström 2022), I characterized their lifestyle change in terms of transformative learning and emphasized five components of learning. First, there was an element of factual and theoretical learning, which are needed, among other reasons, in order to defend one's new positions against others' criticism and justification strategies. Second, participants developed practical, corporal, and tacit learning, which included learning the craft of practicing alternatives. As an example, things that previously were considered impossible or inconvenient, for example walking or cycling to work, can after some practice be experienced as joyful, healthy, and refreshing. Third, they developed personal and emotional learning, which includes reflecting on and learning about what actually fosters true quality of life, as well as recognizing and dealing constructively with ambivalence, inconsistencies (e.g. value-action gaps), and emotional dissonance—in other words, dealing with one's justification strategies. Fourth, they engaged in social relational learning, including insights into how consumerism is embedded in social relations, comparisons, norms, and discourses of "happy family life," insights which are often gained in concrete interactions, and sometimes conflicts, with people in one's social surroundings. Finally, they nurtured their critical learning, which involves imagining that life could be otherwise, for example, by envisioning, testing, and practicing alternatives. The last component involves an increasingly sharp critique of how society boosts consumerism and blocks the ambition to reduce one's consumption, and may set off more externally directed social and political engagement, including a politicization of consumption (Boström et al. 2019; Forno 2019).

Another key insight from frontrunners is that transforming lifestyles toward less consumption can go hand in hand with maintained or even increased quality of life (Boström 2021c, 2022). One could say that, through practice, they have revealed the flaws, the empty promises, of consumerism. Tim Jackson (2017) uses the word "prosperity," and argues that it must be sought in a sphere beyond material pleasures. Prosperity cannot rely on a default assumption about relentless growth of material consumption. Prosperity has to do with living well, while consuming less:

> From at least the time of Aristotle, it has been clear that something more than material security is needed for human beings to flourish. Prosperity has vital social and psychological dimensions. To do well is in part about the ability to give and receive love, to enjoy the respect of your peers, to contribute useful work, and to have a sense of belonging and trust in the community. (Jackson 2017, 48)

Prosperity involves participating actively in society, expressing concern for others, experiencing freedom and a sense of autonomy, and feeling a sense of meaning and purpose in life, as well as being engaged in something and feeling the enjoyment of creativity.[18] Once again Hartmut Rosa's critique of social acceleration is relevant to bring up. In contrast with the frenetic standstill and aimless drifting that characterize consumerism, people can experience well-being, happiness, and good health by independently formulating goals, plans, projects, visions, and ambitions and then realizing them.

Positive experiences of reducing consumption may not appear only deliberately and through voluntary efforts. Several studies, including one of my own (Boström et al. 2022), document such positive experiences even when caused by the involuntary disruption of many (consumer) practices during the COVID-19 pandemic. Although the pandemic caused tragedies, trauma, anxiety, boredom, isolation, loneliness, and other suffering, we should not neglect the positive effects that were experienced, at least in some segments of society. This includes appreciation of a slower pace of life, which created possibilities to try out new practices (e.g. slower food practices, gardening, new leisure activities), greater prioritization of social relationships over consumerism and materialism, the discovery of new activities that can be done at home and the local outdoors, an appreciation of what one has (dampening cycles of desire), and recognition of the importance of good health, savings, and mindful consumption (see, e.g., Echegaray et al. 2021; Boström 2021a, 2021b; Boström et al. 2022; Greene et al. 2022; Moynat et al. 2022). These experiences and insights may not qualify as transformative learning, as they do not question basic frames of reference and habits of mind, but they are important in their own right and can be stored in people's collective memory for later use, as a bank of experiences able to legitimize and inspire transformative change. Indeed, the COVID-19 experience showed that the public was generally able to *adapt* to quite different conditions and situations (although very much depending on social position; again, inequalities matter). The ability to adapt thus seems to be a key issue. Using the concept of "hedonic adaptation," Brülde suggests that we could fairly quickly adapt to substantially lower standards and levels of consumption. "Hedonic adaptation is a rather common phenomenon. When we experience positive or negative events, our happiness can be strongly affected in the short run, but for most events we tend to return to our former levels [of happiness] relatively soon" (Brülde 2015, 89).

Social Influence

Extremely powerful structures and interest groups with entrenched privileges in the current framework of macro-institutions seek to maintain the existing order. Given this fact, it is difficult to imagine a theory of change that does not take into account the actions and counterpower of people coordinating themselves in change-driven processes. Collective action is thus needed. At the same time, collective change must take root and make sense all the way down to the inner lives of the individual person (within the context of social life). A change agent could be a single person, like Greta Thunberg sitting in front of the Swedish parliament building, or an international organization like the EU. Indeed, consumerism can be resisted and counteracted on all levels: households, partners, teams, groups, workplaces, schools, organizations, communities, cities, regions, nations, and international organizations.

It is important to view processes of change as social events. If mass/excess consumption is social in nature, counteracting it is equally so. The change process is about developing social empowerment and mobilizing social capital (Kennedy 2011; Schor and Thompson 2014; Boström 2021c). When a person enters into a process of lifestyle change, the first layer of support is one's immediate interpersonal relations and broader social network, including family, friends, relatives, and colleagues (Boström 2021c). Collaboration and support are of a practical, cognitive, moral, and emotional nature, and are generally required to achieve transformative lifestyle change. My empirical studies of practitioners of reduced consumption, both within families and in the larger social sphere beyond the household, show that people support, discuss, debate, negotiate, compromise, question purchases, help resist each other's impulsive buying, assess purchases made, and try out and critique activities together (Boström 2021c). Within the family and among neighbors and colleagues there is generally a need to come to agreement about a variety of matters, because you share a home and household economy with your family, an office or shared workspace with colleagues, and local facilities with neighbors.

People engaged in voluntary downsizing tend to be involved in different collaboration-oriented social networks, online or in real life, for example in the form of civil society associations (Boström 2021c). Social capital can be converted into other resources: material/practical (sharing goods and services), cognitive (tips, ideas and skills), and symbolic (legitimacy and positive role models). Developing social ties and bridges on the community level is a necessary step toward effecting transformative change on larger scale. However, it should never be forgotten that these groups of people generally tend to be well positioned in the class structure of society, and thus may not feel the burden of relative poverty to the same extent as many other groups (see, e.g., Schor 1998; Carfagna et al. 2014).

Engagement can be channeled in civil society groups, such as adult education classes, conventional environmental organizations, and transition town movements (Bay 2013; Barr and Pollard 2017; Feola and Nunes 2014). Many such groups succeed in addressing (internally) a social dimension of the lifestyle transformation challenge, that is, in providing social support within a collaborative environment, while they often fail (externally) to generalize their struggle to wider society (or rather, society fails to recognize them and listen to their voices). Macro change will require success on both points. What is still lacking is a broader social movement around these issues.

However, as regards the scaling up of action, the concept of *social tipping points* is of interest. Borrowed from natural science, the idea of "earth system tipping points" refers to critical thresholds that, if transgressed, result in irreversible harmful consequences, potentially leading to a "hothouse Earth" state. A change in one element of the grand system, such as a collapse of the Amazon rain forest, could have irreversible impacts on other systems, and consequently the entire Earth. Scholarship has begun to ask if a similar type of dynamics regarding the social/societal could prevent this from happening? Could social tipping points prevent the activation of earth system tipping points?

To be sure, social and natural dynamics are not the same.[19] Nevertheless, it might be possible to understand several historical changes at least partly in terms of social tipping points. Otto et al. (2020) discuss the spread of Protestantism, the abolition of slavery, and the growth of labor unions in this way. Many countries have experienced radical shifts of norms around sexuality, smoking, and recycling. We can view processes like these as "contagious" processes of diffusion of social norms, ideas, ideologies, opinions, knowledge, and habits. These elements can spread via *social relations* within and across social networks, through both unconscious processes of imitation and conscious processes of opinion-formation and norm-breaking. Each person, group, organization, and community could have its own "critical threshold" for conditions under which they are *adaptive* and likely to change (habits, viewpoints, etc.). Such dynamics can be set in motion by positive role models (Otto et al. 2020; Zorell 2020; Zorell and Denk 2021), for instance trendsetters, intellectual leaders, writers, journalists, famous people such as Greta Thunberg and David Attenborough, and social media "influencers."

To be sure, the extremely complex, penetrating, multifaceted, elusive and overwhelming nature of consumerism makes it especially problematic. It is not just a simple norm that is to be changed, but rather a way of life that cannot be transformed from one day to another, or transmitted between people like a virus. Consumerism detox is not like quitting smoking. It is about everything we do in society. Moreover, individual detox is to a considerable extent outside of a person's control because of the influence of existing institutions, infrastructures, power structures, and vested interests. Established institutions are by nature inert and have stabilizing mechanisms that oppose change (Otto et al. 2020). They promote individualized responsibility while resisting real change. For instance, the until now dominant policy approach in the area of "sustainable consumption," which only relies on information, encouragement (e.g. through eco-labeling), nudging and incentivizing "green choice" is not just very insufficient (for a review, see Soneryd and Uggla 2015), but it diverts attention away from the more fundamental processes of consumerism, supports the ideology of overconsumption (Stuart et al. 2020) or imperial mode of living (Brand and Wissen 2021), neglects the institutional and social drivers at play, neglects the critical role of collective opinion-formation (Maniates 2001), and brings arguments for the justification strategies described earlier in the chapter. "It is clear that the required reductions in consumption-related emissions cannot be achieved through the politically palatable options of focusing on marginal lifestyle changes and technical efficiencies." (Welch and Southerton 2019, 32)

Thus, we should not expect social tipping dynamics alone to induce transformative lifestyle change.

Reorganizing Society

Universal schemes for basic income/services, general working hours reduction, economic democracy, regulation of advertising, banning/restricting cars in cities, integrating community gardens and other blue and green infrastructures into cities, progressive taxes, prohibition, divestment, rationing, provision of infrastructure for slow mobility and alternative types of retailing, infrastructure for repairing products, facilitating new models of running companies, transition towns, farmers' markets, local supply chains, and so on—there is no lack of policy ideas and concrete proposals for ways to combat consumerism and reduce consumption with new institutions and infrastructures. But there is a lack of implementation, a lack of political will, and a hegemonic ideology that firmly insists on increasing rather than reducing consumption (see Introduction).

Unfortunately, many consumption-oriented approaches in current politics and policy are fairly useless, because they do not address the root problem of consumption volumes. Even worse, they legitimize business as usual. Many policies are based on either improving things to become more material/energy efficient (like fuel-efficient cars) or shifting to new technologies (like electric cars and eco-labeling). Such policies are not necessarily wrong, but they neglect the rebound effect. Measures related to efficiency and shifting to new technologies have their place if they are based on an overarching policy of reduction/relinquishment, guided by the sufficiency principle (Princen 2005).

The main obstacle at the macro-institutional and infrastructural level is the vested interests of capitalist industrial structures in the economic geographies of mass production, distribution, and consumption, which are expressed in pro-growth dogmas, overconsumption ideologies, welfare policies that depend on high levels consumption, and a dominant consumer culture that equates happiness with consumption (see Introduction). These are no small matters. Getting rid of the root causes of consumerism would require completely new societies, a new social organization of production and consumption (Welch and Southerton 2019; Brand and Wissen 2021). The COVID-19 pandemic offered glimpses of what the disruption of some consumer practices could lead to on a policy level: massive promotional efforts, from both business and politics, to get us back to the "normality" of high consumption and energy-intensive lifestyles. The sphere of politics, suddenly rejecting neoliberal doctrines, showed that states actually could play highly interventionist roles using progressive financial policies. However, this progressive role was only employed to boost economic growth and business and consumerism as usual. The inflation and energy crisis following the 2022 Russian invasion of Ukraine indeed reveals the prospects of reducing energy consumption: suddenly measures like saving, restricting, and rationing have become not only conceivable but even practiced. Time will tell if this is a short-lived phenomenon, or if temporary thriftiness in this area can encourage long-term transformative learning and change.

There is no lack of promising theories and visions of a more sustainable future framed in terms of macro-institutions. I consider the concepts/theories of degrowth (Kallis et al. 2018; Diesendorf 2020), post-growth (Jackson 2017, 2021), sufficiency (Princen 2005; Jungell-Michelsson and Heikkurinen 2022), the well-being economy (Coscieme et al. 2019), doughnut economics (Raworth 2012), economies of plenitude (Schor and Thompson 2014), economic democracy (Wilkinson and Pickett 2010, 2019), solidary mode of living (Brand and Wissen 2021) and others as all very important and promising approaches suggesting radical new ways of organizing society and offering a fundamental critique of consumerism.

But the question remains of how to set off the change process. As argued above, in my view change can only take place in a complex interplay between bottom-up processes (transformative learning, social influence like empowerment and mobilization, and social tipping points) and top-down radical reform based upon an overall democratic foundation. Radical macro-institutional and infrastructural change will probably not happen until a much larger share of the population—who knows how large?—is taking part in the mobilization. This may happen in response to even more serious/evident/alarming/large-scale environmental hazards: famines, starvation, migration flows, violence, and war. Growing social criticism constitutes a political, monetary, and cultural threat to existing power elites. It provides public legitimacy for tougher, structural, rule-altering, and radical policies.

At the same time, powerful yet responsible actors and regimes could provide legitimacy, space, and capacity for bottom-up public critique and promising niche activities to grow (Karimzadeh and Boström 2022). And they could accept that they potentially possess constructive transformative power rather than defending the existing order. Indeed, the COVID-19 pandemic demonstrated broad public acceptance of hard intervention and a strong role of the state. The risk was considered immediate and serious (though transitory). A key policy lesson is to take advantage of this collective experience and "real-time experiment to downsize the consumer economy" (Cohen 2020, 1). People displayed an ability to adapt to new circumstances (Kirk and Rifkin 2020) and were able to assume personal responsibility for the sake of a collective goal (Perkins et al. 2021). The public also become sensitized to how health, environment, and (in)equality are interrelated, thus exposing the unsustainability of current society (Stegeman et al. 2020).

Traditional consumption-oriented politics and policy using carrots and sticks will certainly continue to be important. However, a core sociological insight which I hope this book has conveyed is that consumption as such is often a symptom of something else. The key sociological insight is that there are social root causes of consumerism. Politics and policy ought to address these causes and not just the symptoms.

How can a culture that is less permeated by consumerism be nurtured? Each chapter has ended with a text box inviting readers to reflect on opportunities for change and suggesting some critical questions to ask. You might wish to return to these and reflect on what needs to be done to accomplish the task of reorganizing societies and communities. How can societies/communities counteract consumerism and bring about change in everyday and public life? What digital or physical infrastructures need to be put in place in cities, workplaces, schools, and buildings? How can societies/communities combat rising inequalities, oppose the "polluter elite" (Kenner 2019), facilitate a collaborative rather than competitive atmosphere, and deal with the common experiences of hurriedness in contemporary social life? How can societies/communities work to broadly support alternative practices like sharing, repairing, and running alternative nonprofit economies? What is needed to facilitate critical thinking and transformative learning? As regards the latter, institutions like formal education, civil society education, all kinds of media including social media, cultural institutions (art, museums and music), and deliberative political forums can potentially nurture transformative learning and associated practices, for instance by revealing the dark side of consumerism, envisioning alternatives, and developing skills. In other words, they can provide new frames of reference. Indeed, there is an urgent need to move away from the current condition of narrow, one-dimensional, anti-reflexive, neoliberal, shortsighted thinking, as well as far-right populist and denialist thinking. We need a public sphere devoid of the flawed promises of consumerism, one in which questions about social norms and the quality of life can be addressed, confronted, and reframed.

Democratic planning, decision-making, and deliberation are at the bottom of it all. Particularly important is the fostering of a critical sphere characterized by reflexivity and deliberative democracy. Deliberative democracy is a precondition for sustainability transformation, because only democratic engagement can foster a collective rethinking of taken-for-granted views (Fischer 2018; Hammond 2020). Open public debate is needed to widen the range of alternative views. In the first place, it is only democratic institutions that invite public participation and dialogue. Only a vitalized democracy can enable transformative learning on a wider scale. Democracy and deliberation are necessary, though not sufficient, for sustainability transformation. A society that is not deliberative cannot be sustainable, while a society that is deliberative has the potential be sustainable, as Marit Hammond (2020) argues. The existing conditions for deliberative democracy are poor, however. Hammond uses the metaphor of a "glass ceiling" that powerfully shapes the actions and feeling of people, narrows the horizon of imagination, and blocks societal transformation. The glass ceiling within environmental politics relies on fixation with the idea of green growth, technology, and consumerism being the path to prosperity.

At the end of the day, the possibility of a more radical growth/consumerist critique perspective taking root in societies, not least on the political level and as part of the democratic debate, is only likely to be realized if dominant public discourses genuinely accept that we live in a time of societal crisis, perhaps a "cultural trauma."

> Cultural trauma is a social process that involves the systematic disruption of the cultural basis of a social order. The individual routines, institutional behaviors, ideological beliefs, and overall regime of practice become subject to questioning and uncertainty, resulting in profound challenges to routine ways of interacting, which are normally taken for granted. (Brulle and Norgaard 2019, 9)

Such a cultural trauma would entail a major disenchantment with consumer culture, "a growing disquiet over the negative legacy of the consumerist lifestyle itself" (Soper 2015, 43)—and provide an opening for imagining something very different, the possibility to see that what exists could be radically transformed (Mills 2000 [1959]), that there is potential for a paradigm shift.

Even if massive amount of goods will still be necessary in a sustainable society that is able to meet the needs of 8–10 billion people, we can envision that this is possible without the kind of consumerism described in this book, without the excessiveness that we see around us. In the long run this will probably require completely new ways of organizing societies, economies, and social relationships. A complex interplay between bottom-up and top-down initiatives may show the way. Or it may not. Failure, on a huge scale, has become a horribly real prospect. The current expansionist/accelerationist institutions of late modern societies cannot be sustained if we human beings and millions of other species will have a chance to survive and live well on this one and only lovely planet.

NOTES

1. I am grateful to Linda Soneryd and Kjell Vowles for constructive comments on an earlier version of this chapter, as well as to an anonymous reviewer.

2. Consumer research speaks of the "attitude-behavior gap," "knowledge-behavior gap," or "value-action gap" when addressing the often eclectic or inconsistent approach to both alternative consumption and more radical anti-consumerism (Holt 2002; Sassatelli 2007; Boström and Klintman 2019ab).

3. In order to distinguish between these categories, I found inspiration in a number of rather heterogeneous sources like Keller 2005; Princen 2005; Jackson 2017; Carroll et al. 2018; Lasarov et al. 2019; Sörqvist and Langeborg 2019; Klintman 2019; Aro 2020; Cocolas et al. 2021; and Southerton and Warde 2023.

4. See Klintman (2019) for a sociological analysis of knowledge resistance.

5. See, e.g., Lykke Syse and Mueller (2015) on overlapping concepts such as "well-being," "life-satisfaction," "happiness," and "the good life."

6. Income is of course not the same as consumption (income can be saved, for instance), but a measure of the relation between income and happiness still gives a fairly good indication of how closely consumption and happiness (or similar terms) are linked (on this topic, see, e.g., Brülde 2015).

7. To be sure, there are difficulties involved in measuring and comparing happiness between generations, cultures and eras. According to Bauman, it is very hard to compare the happiness of contemporary consumers with that of historical consumers, one reason for this being that "the assessors remain limited to their own preferences from their own context" (Bauman 2007, 43).

8. For similar results, see Dittmar 2008; Hellevik 2015; Kahneman and Deaton 2010; Brülde 2015; and Solér 2018.

9. Many of these negative effects are well documented in the studies by Wilkinson and Pickett (2010, 2019).

10. A recent article by Richard Easterlin and Kelsey O'Connor (2022) confirmed the result that economic growth does not increase life satisfaction, but also showed that a set of welfare policy arrangements (more generous unemployment insurance, pensions, and sickness insurance) was positively related to life-satisfaction. They used time-series data from the European Values Studies from 1981/1982 to 2017/2018 in ten Northern, Western, and Southern European countries.

11. There is a classic sociological insight connected with this. At the beginning of the previous century Georg Simmel commented on the blasé attitude of the modern urban consumer. See also Schor 1998; Bauman 2007; Miller 2010, 62.

12. For an analysis of transformative change including both the concept itself and historical examples, see Linnér and Wibeck 2019.

13. For example, see Rief 2008 and Warde 2022 on socially embedded agency.

14. There are a number of dead ends in the debate about (un)sustainable consumption and processes of change. First, there is a debate about whether consumption (demand) drives production (supply) or vice versa, or if agent/micro change leads to structure/macro change or vice versa. Such "chicken or egg" debates tends to be fruitless and pointless. The argument in this book has been that production/consumption, supply/demand, structure/agency, macro/micro are always interrelated. Indeed, even if consumption is only viewed as a dependent factor, my argument in the following paragraphs is still relevant. If current lifestyles are fundamentally unsustainable, they will by definition have to be transformed, either by the forces of nature or by human purpose (or both). To the extent that people can foresee a major undermining of consumerism and adjust their way of life, they may be better equipped to adapt to changing conditions.

15. For the literature on these examples, see, e.g., Schor 1998; Callmer 2019; Uggla 2019; Lee et al. 2020; Osikominu and Bocken 2020; Rebouças and Soares 2020; and Boström 2021c, 2022.

16. See also studies by Kerton and Sinclair (2010) and Moyer and Sinclair (2020), who applied the concept to lifestyle change.

17. For further studies documenting similar results, see Isenhour 2010; Cherrier et al. 2012; Walther and Sandlin 2013; Armstrong et al. 2016; Lorenzen 2017; and Callmer 2019.

18. There is a rich and heterogeneous interdisciplinary research field on this topic, see, e.g., Jackson 2005, 2017; Kasser 2009, 2017; Schor and Thompson 2014; and Lykke Syse and Lee Mueller 2015.

19. There are several arguments for why social tipping points cannot be treated precisely like natural tipping points (Bentley et al. 2014 and Otto et al. 2020). Social tipping points may be even more difficult or impossible to predict than natural dynamics, due to the very heterogeneous and unpredictable—indeed human—responses to various risks among social groups.

Afterword

Excess consumption has both fascinated me and been a source of frustration for almost all my adult life. Although my lifestyle involves overconsuming in a wealthy society, and I have my own repertoire of defensive justifications for this, my frustration has increased over the years as I have studied and learned more about the topic. Particularly troubling is the sad irony described in the last chapter: by incessantly consuming more, we are destroying the environment and the living conditions for both existing and future generations, yet without even enhancing quality of life in the present. I find myself in an ambivalent and ongoing struggle about how to consume less stuff and more wisely, and oftentimes feel very much locked into existing structures. Changing this situation is truly a both personal and collective enterprise. The promising side of it is that quality of life is not likely to worsen during the struggle, rather the opposite.

Although I have thought about these matters from time to time since at least the mid-1990s when I began my academic career, and although my research projects have often touched on the relationship between the environment and consumption, it wasn't until some years ago that I saw the opportunity—due to my privileged position as a university professor—to focus more systematically on the topic of this book. So, I decided to read extensively, write a book about mass/excess consumption, and undertake empirical studies of people who voluntarily or involuntarily reduce their consumption. This is the resulting book, and my research program continues. Many people around me have helped to shape my thinking, both in my private life and in research environments. In recent years, the most important research environment has been the sociology department at Örebro University, and especially the environmental sociology team. Many other people have been extremely helpful as well. I am grateful to everyone who has taken my work with this book seriously, has given me constructive comments, or has engaged in conversations about it in academic or nonacademic settings. By now there have been quite a few seminars and discussions, and it would be impossible to list the names of everyone whose valuable help I have received. However, some people who have given especially pertinent feedback on specific chapters are mentioned in the endnotes.

The topic I am writing about is a difficult one. The destructive force of consumerism is a source of worry and frustration, to say the least. I feel deep reverence for nature and for all life that exists and has existed: trees, the oceans, mountains, elephants, people. I also grieve over destroyed natural environments, extinct species, and lost people. Grief can be a way forward, a motivator. Deep personal grief afflicted me during the writing of this book. I lost a person very dear to me, and this loss sharpened my motivation to complete the book. I dedicate it to my dear son Ivar, who, I am sure, had many happy years here. His happiness, good spirits, and warm laughter came from somewhere else than consumerism. Why he couldn't continue living I don't know, but I hope and believe that we can create a much better society for coming generations.

Magnus Boström
Strängnäs, May 26, 2023

References

Akenji, Lewis. 2014. "Consumer Scapegoatism and Limits to Green Consumerism." *Journal of Cleaner Production* 63: 13–23.

Akenji, Lewis, Magnus Bengtsson, Viivi Toivio, et al. 2021. *1.5-Degree Lifestyles: Towards A Fair Consumption Space for All.* Hot or Cool Institute, Berlin.

Alsarve, Jenny. 2017. "Working It Out: Strategies to Reconcile Work and Family among Swedish Lone Mothers." *Families, Relationships, and Societies* 6(3): 325–40.

Armstrong, Cosette M. Joyner, Kim Y. Hiller Connell, Chunmin Lang, Mary Ruppert-Stroescu, and Melody L.A. LeHew. 2016. "Educating for Sustainable Fashion: Using Clothing Acquisition Abstinence to Explore Sustainable Consumption and Life Beyond Growth." *Journal of Consumer Policy* 39(4): 417–39.

Aro, Riikka. 2020. "'A Bigger Living Room Required a Bigger TV': Doing and Negotiating Necessity in Well-to-do Households." *Journal of Consumer Culture* 20(4): 498–520.

Banerjee, Robin, and Helga Dittmar. 2008. "Individual Differences in Children's Materialism: The Role of Peer Relations," *Personality and Social Psychology Bulletin,* 34(1): 17–31.

Bardhi, Fleura, and Eric J. Arnould. 2004. "Thrift Shopping: Combining Utilitarian Thrift and Hedonic Treat Benefits." *Journal of Consumer Behaviour* 4(4): 223–33.

Barr, Stewart, Gareth Shaw, and Tim Coles. 2011. "Times for (Un)sustainability? Challenges and Opportunities for Developing Behaviour Change Policy. A Case-study of Consumers at Home and Away." *Global Environmental Change* 21: 1234–44.

Barr, Stewart, Gareth Shaw, Tim Coles, and Jan Prillwitz. 2010. "'A Holiday is a Holiday': Practicing Sustainability Home and Away." *Journal of Transport Geography* 18(3): 474–81.

Barr, Stewart, and Justin Pollard. 2017. "Geographies of Transition: Narrating Environmental Activism in an Age of Climate Change and 'Peak Oil.'" *Environ. Plan. A* 49(1): 47–64.

Bauer, Katherine W, Mary O. Hearst, Kamisha Escoto, Jerica M. Berge, and Dianne Neumark-Sztainer. 2012. "Parental Employment and Work-family Stress:

Associations with Family Food Environments." *Social Science & Medicine* 75(3): 496–504.

Bauman, Zygmunt. 2007. *Consuming Life*. Cambridge: Polity Press.

Bay, Uschi. 2013. "Transition Town Initiatives Promoting Transformational Community Change in Tackling Peak Oil and Climate Change Challenges." *Australian Social Work*, 66(2): 171–86. DOI: 10.1080/0312407X.2013.781201.

Beck, Ulrich, Anthony Giddens, and Scott Lash. 1994. *Reflexive Modernization: Politics, Tradition, and Aesthetics in the Modern Social Order.* London: Blackwell.

Becker, Howard S. 2018 (1963) *Outsiders: Studies in the Sociology of Deviance.* New York: Free Press.

Belk, Russell W. 1988. "Possessions and the Extended Self." *Journal of Consumer Research* 15(2): 139–68.

Belk, Russell W., Güliz Ger, and Søren Askegaard. 2003. "The Fire of Desire: A Multisited Inquiry into Consumer Passion." *Journal of Consumer Research* 30(3): 326–51.

Bentley, R. A., Eleanor J. Maddison, P. H. Ranner, et al. 2014. "Social Tipping Points and Earth Systems Dynamics." *Frontiers in Environmental Science.* http://www.frontiersin.org/Environmental_Science/editorialboard.

Berger, Jonah, and Morgan Ward. 2010. "Subtle Signals of Inconspicuous Consumption." *Journal of Consumer Research* 37: 555–69.

Berger, Peter, and Thomas Luckmann. 1991 (1966). *The Social Construction of Reality: A Treatise in the Sociology of Knowledge.* London: Penguin Books.

Black, Iain, and Hélène Cherrier. 2010. "Anti-consumption as Part of Living a Sustainable Lifestyle: Daily Practices, Contextual Motivations and Subjective Values." *Journal of Consumer Behaviour* 9: 437–53.

Blumer, Herbert. 1986 (1969). *Symbolic Interactionsim: Perspective and Method.* University of California Press.

Boltanski, Luc, and Laurent Thévenot. 2006. *On Justification: Economies of Worth.* Princeton, NJ: Princeton University Press.

Boström, Magnus. 2019. "Rejecting and Embracing Brands in Political Consumerism." In *Oxford Handbook of Political Consumerism*, edited by Magnus Boström, Michele Micheletti, and Peter Oosterveer. Oxford: Oxford University Press.

———. 2020. "The Social Life of Mass and Excess Consumption." *Environmental Sociology* 6(3): 268–78.

———. 2021a. "Social Relations and Everyday Consumption Rituals: Barriers or Prerequisites for Sustainability Transformation?" *Frontiers in Sociology.* doi.org/10.3389/fsoc.2021.723464.

———. 2021b. "Take the Opportunity Afforded by the COVID-19 experiences: Progressive Non-growth Policies for Sustainable Lifestyles." *Frontiers in Sustainability.* doi.org/10.3389/frsus.2021.726320.

———. 2021c. "Social Relations and Challenges to Consuming Less In a Mass Consumption Society. *Sociologisk Forskning,* 58(4) 383–406. doi.org/10.37062/sf.58.22818.

———. 2022. "Lifestyle Transformation and Reduced Consumption: a Transformative Learning Process. *Sozialpolitik.ch* Vol 1/2022, Article 1.2. DOI: doi.org/10.18753/2297-8224-186.

Boström Magnus, Erik Andersson, Monika Berg, Karin M. Gustafsson, Eva Gustavsson, Erik Hysing, Rolf Lidskog, Erik Löfmarck, Maria Ojala, Jan Olsson, Benjamin E. Singleton, Sebastian Svenberg, Ylva Uggla, and Johan Öhman. 2018. "Conditions for Transformative Learning for Sustainable Development: a Theoretical Review and Approach." *Sustainability* 10(12), 4479. doi.org/10.3390/su10124479.

Boström, Magnus, and Debra Davidson (eds.). 2018. *Environment and Society: Concepts and Challenges*. London: Palgrave Macmillan.

Boström, Magnus, and Mikael Klintman. 2008. *Eco-standards, Product Labelling, and Green Consumerism* London: Palgrave Macmillan.

———. 2019a. "Can We Rely on 'Climate Friendly' Consumption?" *Journal of Consumer Culture* 19(3): 359–78.

———. 2019b. "Mass-consumption and Political Consumerism." In *The Oxford Handbook of Political Consumerism,* edited by Magnus Boström, Michele Micheletti, and Peter Oosterveer. Oxford: Oxford University Press.

Boström, Magnus, Michele Micheletti, and Peter Oosterveer (eds.). 2019. The *Oxford Handbook of Political Consumerism.* Oxford: Oxford University Press.

Boström, Magnus, Helena Römmelmann, and Lina Sandström. 2022. "Could Practices of Reduced Consumption during the Covid-19 Pandemic Facilitate Transformative Change for Sustainability? Experiences from Sweden and Ireland." *Frontiers in Sustainability.* doi.org/10.3389/frsus.2022.994108.

Bourdieu, Pierre. 1984. *Distinction: A Social Critique of the Judgement of Taste*. (R. Nice, tran.). Cambridge, MA: Harvard University Press.

———. 1990. *The Logic of Practice*. Cambridge, UK: Polity Press.

Brand, Ulrich, and Markus Wissen. 2021. *The Imperial Mode of Living: Everyday Life and the Ecological Crisis of Capitalism.* London: Verso.

Briceno, Tania, and Sigrid Stagl. 2006. "The Role of Social Process for Sustainable Consumption." *Journal of Cleaner Production* 14: 1541–51.

Brook, Paul, Gertraud Koch, and Andreas Wittel. 2013. "Thirty Years after Hochschild's 'Managed Heart': Exploring the Commodity Frontier." *Culture and Organization*, 19(4): 275–87. DOI: 10.1080/14759551.2013.827419.

Brookfield, Stephen D. 2012. "Critical Theory and Transformative Learning." In *The Handbook of Transformative Learning: Theory, Research and Practice*, edited by Edward W. Taylor and Patricia Cranton, 131–46. Hoboken, NJ: Wiley & Sons.

Brülde, Bengt. 2015. "Well-being and Environmental Responsibility." In *Sustainable Consumption and the Good Life: Interdisciplinary Perspectives,* edited by Karin Lykke Syse and Martin Lee Mueller, 80–110. London: Earthscan.

Brulle, Robert J., and Kari Marie Norgaard. 2019. "Avoiding Cultural Trauma: Climate Change and Social Inertia." *Environmental Politics* 28(5): 886–908.

Cachero-Martínez, Silvia, and Rodolfo Vázquez-Caselles. 2021. "Building Consumer Loyalty through E-shopping Experiences: The Mediating Role of Emotions." *Journal of Retailing and Consumer Services* 60: 102481.

Callmer, Åsa. 2019. "Making Sense of Sufficiency. Entries, Practices and Politics." PhD diss., School of Achitecture and the Built Environment, KTH Royal Institute of Technology, Stockholm.

Camargo, Lucas R., and Susana C. F. Pereira. 2020. "Fast and Ultra-fast Fashion Supply Chain Management: An Exploratory Research" *International Journal of Retail & Distribution Management.*

Campbell, Colin. 2018 (1987). *The Romantic Ethic and the Spirit of Modern Consumerism. New Extended Edition.* London: Palgrave Macmillan.

Carfagna, Lindsey B., Emilie A. Dubois, Connor Fitzmaurice, Michelle Y. Ouimette, Juliet B. Schor, Margaret Willis, and Thomas Laidley. 2014. "An Emerging Eco-habitus: The Reconfiguration of High Cultural Capital Practices among Ethical Consumers." *Journal of Consumer Culture* 14(2): 158–78.

Carroll, William, Nicolas Graham, Michael Kl. Lang, Zoe Yunker, and Kevin McCartney. 2018. "The Corporate Elite and the Architecture of Climate Change Denial: A Network Analysis of Carbon Capital's Reach into Civil Society." *Canadian Review of Sociology* 55(3): 425–50.

Chan, Kara, and Gerard Prendergast. 2007. "Materialism and Social Comparison among Adolescents." *Social Behavior and Personality* 35(2): 213–28.

Chancel, Lucas, and Thomas Piketty. 2015. "Carbon and Inequality: From Kyoto to Paris. Trends in the Global Inequality of Carbon Emissions (1998–2013) and Prospects for An Equitable Adaptation Fund." Paris: Paris School of Economics. http://piketty.pse.ens.fr/files/ChancelPiketty2015.pdf.

Chebat, Jean-Charles, Narjes Haj-Salem, and Sandra Oliviera. 2014. "Why Shopping Pals Make Malls Different." *Journal of Retailing and Consumer Services* 21: 77–85.

Cherrier, Hélène, Mathilde Szuba, and Nil Özçağlar-Toulouse. 2012. "Barriers to Downward Carbon Emission: Exploring Sustainable Consumption in the Face of the Glass Floor." *Journal of Marketing Management* 28(3–4): 397–419.

Chipp, Kerry, Nicola Kleyn, and Thando Manzi. 2011. "Catch Up and Keep Up: Relative Deprivation and Conspicuous Consumption in an Emerging Market." *Journal of International Consumer Marketing* 23(2): 117–34.

Christen, Markus, and Ruskin M. Morgan. 2005. "Keeping up with the Joneses: Analysing the Effect of Income Inequality on Consumer Borrowing." *Quantitative Marketing and Economics* 3(2): 145–73.

Cialdini, Robert B., and Noah J. Goldstein. 2004. "Social Influence: Compliance and Conformity." *Annual Review of Psychology* 55: 591–621.

Cocolas, Nicole, Gabrielle Walters, Lisa Ruhanen, and James Higham. 2021. "Consumer Attitudes towards Flying amidst Growing Climate Concern." *Journal of Sustainable Tourism* 29(6): 944–63. DOI: 10.1080/09669582.2020.1849234.

Cohen, Mauri J. 2020. "Does the COVID-19 Outbreak Mark the Onset of a Sustainable Consumption Transition?" *Sustainability: Science, Practice, and Policy* 16(1): 1–3.

Collins, Randall. 2005. *Interaction Ritual Chains.* Princeton, NJ: Princeton University Press.

Cook, Nicole, Susan J. Smith, and Beverley A. Searle. 2013. "Debted Objects: Homemaking in an Era of Mortgage-Enabled Consumption." *Housing, Theory and Society* 30(3): 293–311.

Coroamă, Vlad C., and Friedemann Mattern. 2019. "Digital Rebound—Why Digitalization Will Not Redeem Us Our Environmental Sins." Proceedings, 6th International Conference on ICT for Sustainability. Lappeenranta. http://ceur-ws .org. Vol. 2382. 2019.

Coscieme, Luca, Paul Sutton, Lars F. Mortensen, et al. 2019. "Overcoming the Myths of Mainstream Economics to Enable a New Wellbeing Economy" *Sustainability* 11(16): 4374.

Cranton, Patricia, and Edward W. Taylor. 2012. "Transformative Learning Theory: Seeking a More Unified Theory." In *The Handbook of Transformative Learning: Theory, Research and Practice*, edited by Patricia Cranton and Edward W. Taylor, 3–20. San Francisco: Wiley.

Denegri-Knott, Janice. 2011. "Have It Now: eBay and the Acceleration of Consumer Desire." *European Advances of Consumer Research* 9(1): 373–79.

Devetter, François-Xavier, and Sandrine Rousseau. 2011. "Working Hours and Sustainable Development." *Review of Social economy* 69(3): 333–55

Devine, Carol M., Margaret Jastran, Jennifer Jabs, Elaine Wethington, Tracy J. Farell, and Carole A. Bisogni. 2006. "'A Lot of Sacrifices': Work-Family Spillover and the Food Choice Coping Strategies of Low-Wage Employed Parents." *Social Science & Medicine* 63: 2591–2603.

de Vries, Dian A., and Rinaldo Kühne. 2015. "Facebook and Self-perception: Individual Susceptibility to Negative Social Comparison." *Personality and Individual Differences* 86(Nov): 217–21. doi:10.1016/j.paid.2015.05.029.

Diesendorf, Mark. 2020. "COVID-19 and Economic Recovery in Compliance with Climate Targets." *Global Sustainability* 3: e36. 1–9.

Dittmar, Helga. 2008. *Consumer Culture, Identity and Well-Being. The Search for the 'Good Life' and the 'Body Perfect.'* New York: Psychology Press.

Doling, John, and Rowan Arundel. 2020. "The Home as Workplace: A Challenge for Housing Research." *Housing, Theory and Society* 39(1): 1–20. DOI: 10.1080/14036096.2020.1846611.

Dowling, Robyn, and Emma Power. 2012. "Sizing Home, Doing Family in Sydney, Australia." *Housing Studies* 27(5): 605–19

Dubois, David, and Nailya Ordabayeva. 2015. "Social Hierarchy, Social Status and Status Consumption," in *Cambridge Handbook of Consumer Psychology*, edited by Michael I. Norton, Derek D. Rucker, and Cait Lamberton, 332–67. New York: Cambridge University Press.

Dubois, David, Derek D. Rucker, and Adam D. Galinsky. 2012. "Super Size Me: Product Size as a Signal of Status." *Journal of Consumer Research* 38: 1047–62.

Dubois, Ghislain et al. 2019. "It Starts at Home? Climate Policies Targeting Household Consumption and Behavioral Decisions are Key to Low-carbon Futures." *Energy Research and Social Science* 52: 144–58.

Duffy, Brooke Erin, and Emily Hund. 2015. "'Having it all' on Social Media: Entrepreneurial Femininity and Self-branding among Fashion Bloggers." *Social media + Society.* DOI: 10.1177/2056305115604337.

Dunn, Elizabeth W., Lara Aknin, and Michael I. Norton. 2008. "Spending Money on Others Promotes Happiness." *Science* 319: 1687–88.

Easterlin Richard A., Laura Angelescu McVey, Malgorzata Switek, Onnicha Sawangfa, and Jaqueline Smith Zweig. 2010. "The Happiness-Income Paradox Revisited." *PNAS* 107(52): 22463–68.

Easterlin, Richard A., and Kelsey J. O'Connor. 2022. "Explaining Happiness Trends in Europe." *PNAS* 119 (37). doi.org/10.1073/pnas.2210639119.

Easthope, Hazel. 2004. "A Place Called Home." *Housing, Theory and Society* 21(3): 128–38.

Echegaray, Fabián. 2021. "What POST-COVID-19 Lifestyles May Look like? Identifying Scenarios and Their Implications for Sustainability." *Sustainable Production and Consumption* 27(July): 567–74. doi:10.1016/j.spc.2021.01.025.

Echegaray, Fabián., V. Brachya, P. J. Vergragt, and L. Zhang. 2021. *Sustainable Lifestyles After COVID-19.* London: Routledge.

Eldén, Sara, and Terese Anving. 2019. *Nanny Families. Practices of Care by Nannies, Au Pairs, Parents and Children in Sweden.* Bristol: Bristol University Press.

Elliot, Rebecca. 2013. "The Taste for Green: The Possibilities and Dynamics of Status Differentiation through 'Green' Consumption." *Poetics* 41: 294–322.

Ellsworth-Krebs, Katherine, Louise Reid, and Colin J. Hunter. 2021. "Home Comfort and 'Peak Household': Implications for Energy Demand." *Housing, Theory and Society* 38(1): 1–20. DOI: 10.1080/14036096.2019.1694579.

Evans, David. 2011. "Blaming the Consumer—Once Again: The Social and Material Contexts of Everyday Food Waste Practices in some English Households." *Critical Public Health* 21(4): 429–40.

Feola, Giuseppe, and Richard Nunes. 2014. "Success and Failure of Grassroots Innovations for Addressing Climate Change: The Case of the Transition Movement." *Global Environmental Change* 24(Jan.): 232–50.

Festinger, Leon. 1954. "A Theory of Social Comparison Processes." *Human Relations* 7(2): 117–40.

Firat, Aytekin, Kemal Y. Kutucuoglu, Isil Arikan Saltik, and Özgur Tuncel. 2013. "Consumption, Consumer Culture and Consumer Society." *Journal of Community Positive Practices* 13(1): 182–203.

Fischer, Frank. 2018. "Environmental Democracy: Participation, Deliberation and Citizenship," in *Environment and Society: Concepts and Challenges*, edited by Magnus Boström and Debra J. Davidson, 257–80. Basingstoke: Palgrave Macmillan.

Fitzmaurice, Julie, and Charles Comegys. 2006. "Materialism and Social Consumption." *Journal of Marketing Theory and Practice* 14(4): 287–99.

Fletcher, Kate. 2012. "Durability, Fashion, Sustainability: The Processes and Practices of Use." *Fashion Practice* 4(2): 221–38.

Forno, Francesca. 2019. "Protest, Social Movements, and Spaces for Politically Oriented Consumerist Actions—Nationally, Transnationally, and Locally." In The

Oxford Handbook of Political Consumerism, edited by M. Boström, M. Micheletti, and P. Oosterveer, 69–88. Oxford: Oxford University Press.

Fromm, Erich. 1976. *To Have or To Be.* New York: Harper & Row.

García de Frutos, Nieves, José M. Ortega Egea, and Javier Martínez del Río. 2018. "Anti-consumption for Environmental Sustainability: Conceptualization, Review, and Multilevel Research Directions." *Journal of Business Ethics* 148(2): 411–35.

Giddens, Anthony. 1984. *The Constitution of Society.* Cambridge, UK: Polity Press.

———. 1991. *The Consequences of Modernity.* Cambridge, UK: Polity Press.

Goffman, Erving. 1990 (1963). *Stigma: Notes on the Management of Spoiled Identity.* New York: Penguin.

Gojard, Séverine, and Bérangère Véron. 2018. "Shifts in Provisioning Routines: Do Holidays Favour more Local and Seasonal Food Purchases?" *Environmental Sociology* 5(3): 283–93.

Goldman, Robert, and Stephen Papson. 2006. "Capital's Brandscapes." *Journal of Consumer Culture* 6(3): 327–53.

Gössling, Stefan, and Andreas Humpe. 2020. "The Global Scale, Distribution and Growth of Aviation: Implications for Climate Change." *Glob. Environ. Change-Human Policy Dimen* 65: 102194.

Gram-Hanssen, Kirsten. 2009. "Standby Consumption in Households Analyzed with a Practice Theory Approach." *Journal of Industrial Ecology* 14(1): 150–65.

Gram-Hanssen, Kirsten, and Claus Bech-Danielsen. 2004. "House, Home and Identity from a Consumption Perspective." *Housing, Theory and Society* 21(1): 17–26.

Grauerholz, Liz, and Anne Bubriski-McKenzie. 2012. "Teaching about Consumption: The 'Not Buying It' Project." *Teaching Sociology* 40(4): 332–48.

Greene, Mary, Arve Hansen, Claire Hoolohan, Elisabeth Süßbauer, and Lorenzo Domaneschi. 2022. "Consumption and Shifting Temporalities of Daily Life in Times of Disruption: Undoing and Reassembling Household Practices during the COVID-19 pandemic." *Sustainability: Science, Practice, and Policy* 18(1): 215–30.

Griskevicius, Vladas, Joshua M. Tybur, and Bram van den Bergh. 2010. "Going Green to be Seen." *Journal of Personality and Social Psychology* 98(3): 392–404.

Grönlund, Anna. 2007. "More Control, Less Conflict? Job Demand-Control, Gender and Work-Family Conflict." *Gender, Work, and Organization* 14(5): 476–97.

Gross, Matthias. 2010. *Ignorance and Surprise: Science, Society, and Ecological Design.* Cambridge, MA: The MIT Press.

Guillen-Royo, Mònica. 2008. "Consumption and Subjective Well-being: Exploring Basic Needs, Social Comparison, Social Integration and Hedonism in Peru." *Soc Indic Res* 89: 535–55.

Gunderson, Ryan. 2022. "Powerless, Stupefied, and Repressed Actors Cannot Challenge Climate Change: Real Helplessness as Barrier between Environmental Concern and Action." *Journal for the Theory of Social Behaviour.* DOI: 10.1111/jtsb.12366.

Guthman, Julie. 2009. "Unveiling the Unveiling: Commodity Chains, Commodity Fetishism and the 'Value' of Voluntary, Ethical Food Labels." In *Frontiers of*

Commodity Chain Research, edited by J. Bair. Stanford, CA: Stanford University Press, 190–206.

Hagbert, Pernilla, and Karin Bradley. 2017. "Transitions on the Home Front: A Story of Sustainable Living beyond Ecoefficiency." *Energy Research & Social Science* 31: 240–48.

Hamlin, David. 2003. "The Structures of Toy Consumption: Bourgeois Domesticity and Demand for Toys in Nineteenth Century Germany." *Journal of Social History* 36(4): 857–69.

Hammond, Marit. 2020. "Sustainability as A Cultural Transformation: The Role of Deliberative Democracy." *Environmental Politics* 29(1): 173–93.

Han, Young Jee, Joseph C. Nunes, and Xavier Drèze. 2010. "Signaling Status with Luxury Goods: The Role of Brand Prominence," *Journal of Marketing* 74(4): 15–30.

Hand, Martin, Elizabeth Shove, and Dale Southerton. 2007. "Home Extensions in the United Kingdom: Space, Time and Practice." *Environment and Planning D* 25(4): 668–81.

Hellevik, Ottar. 2015. "Is the Good Life Sustainable? A Three-decade Study of Values, Happiness and Sustainability in Norway." In *Sustainable Consumption and the Good Life. Interdisciplinary Perspectives*, edited by Karen Lykke Syse and Martin Lee Mueller, 55–79. London: Earthscan.

Hickel, Jason. 2019. "Degrowth: A Theory of Radical Abundance." *Real World Economics Review* 87(March): 54–68.

Hiller Connell, Kim Y. 2018. "Utilizing Political Consumerism to Challenge the 21st century Fast Fashion Industry." In *The Oxford Handbook of Political Consumerism,* edited by Magnus Boström, Michele Micheletti, and Peter Oosterveer, 293–312. Oxford: Oxford University Press.

Hine, Thomas. 2002. *I Want That! How We All Became Shoppers.* New York: HarperCollins.

Hochschild, Arlie. 2003. *The Commercialization of Intimate Life: Notes From Home and Work.* Berkeley: University of California Press.

———. 2011. "Emotional Life on the Market Frontier." *Annual Review of Sociology* 37: 21–33.

Holmberg, Ulrika (ed). 2022. *Konsumtionsrapporten 2021.* Gothenburg: Centrum för konsumtionsforskning, Centre for Retailing, Handelshögskolan vid Göteborgs Universitet. https://www.gu.se/sites/default/files/2021-12/TE_konsumtionsrapporten%202021_korr.pdf.

———. 2023. "Hushållens konsumtion" In *Konsumtionsrapporten* 2022, edited by Johan Hagberg, Lena Hansson, Ulrika Holmberg, and Niklas Sörum, 7–25. Gothenburg: Centrum för konsumtionsforskning, Centre for Retailing, Handelshögskolan vid Göteborgs Universitet.

Holt, Douglas B. 2002. "Why do brands cause trouble? A dialectical theory of consumer culture and branding. *Journal of Consumer Research*, 29(1), 70–90.

Hruska, Jan, and Petra Maresova. 2020. "Use of Social Media Platforms among Adults in the United States—Behavior on Social Media," *Societies* 10: 27. doi:10.3390/soc10010027.

Hu, Xi, Xiayu Chen, and Robert M. Davison. 2019. "Social Support, Source Credibility, Social Influence, and Impulsive Purchase Behavior in Social Commerce." *International Journal of Electronic Commerce* 23(3): 297–327.

Hylland Eriksen, Thomas. 2015. "Afterword. Beyond the Paradox of the Big, Bad Wolf." In *Sustainable Consumption and the Good Life. Interdisciplinary Perspectives*, edited by Karen Lykke Syse and Martin Lee Mueller, 244–56. London: Earthscan.

Isaksen, Katja Jezkova, and Stuart Roper. 2008. "The Impact of Branding on Low Income Adolescents: A Vicious Cycle." *Psychology & Marketing* 25(11): 1063–87.

Isenhour, Cindy. 2010. "On Conflicted Swedish Consumers, the Effort to Stop Shopping and Neoliberal Environmental Governance." *Journal of Consumer Behaviour* 9(Nov–Dec): 454–69.

Jabs, Jennifer, and Carol M. Devine. 2006. "Time Scarcity and Food Choices: An Overview." *Appetite* 47: 196–204.

Jack, Tullia. 2017. "Cleanliness and Consumption: Exploring Material and Social Structuring of Domestic Cleaning Practices." *International Journal of Consumer Studies* 41: 70–78.

———. 2020. "Representations—A Critical Look at Media's Role in Cleanliness Practices and Inconspicuous Consumption." *Journal of Consumer Culture* 20(3): 324–46. doi.org/10.1177/1469540518806958.

———. 2022. "Sovereign Dupes? Representations, Conventions, and (Un)sustainable Consumption." *Journal of Consumer Culture* 22(2): 331–58.

Jack, Tullia, Manisha Ananatharam, and Alison L. Browne. 2022. "'Without Cleanliness We Can't Lead the Life, No?' Cleanliness Practices, (In)accessible Infrastructures, Social (Im)mobility and (Un)sustainable Consumption in Mysore, India." *Social and Cultural Geography* 23(6): 814–35.

Jackson, Tim. 2017. *Prosperity without Growth. Foundations for the Economy of Tomorrow.* (2nd ed) London: Routledge.

———. 2021. *Post Growth. Life After Capitalism.* Cambridge, UK: Polity Press.

Jacobs, Keith, and Jeff Malpas. 2013. "Material Objects, Identity and the Home: Towards a Relational Housing Research Agenda." *Housing, Theory and Society* 30(3): 281–92.

Japutra, Arnold, Yuksel Ekinci, and Lyndon Simkin. 2022. "Discovering the Dark Side of Brand Attachment: Impulsive Buying, Obsessive-Compulsive Buying and Trash Talking." *Journal of Business Research* 145: 442–53.

Jenkins, Rebecca, Elizabeth Nixon, and Mike Molesworth. 2011. "'Just Normal and Homely': The Presence, Absence and Othering of Consumer Culture in Everyday Imagining." *Journal of Consumer Culture* 11(2): 261–81.

Jiang, Peng, Yee van Fan, and Jirí Jaromír Klemes. 2021. "Impacts of COVID-19 on Energy Demand and Consumption: Challenges, Lessons and Emerging Opportunities." *Applied Energy* 285: 116441.

Jorgenson; Andrew K., Shirley Fiske, Klaus Hubacek, Jia Li, Tom McGovern, Torben Rick, Juliet B. Schor, William Solecki; Richard York, and Ariela Zycherman. 2019. "Social Science Perspectives on Drivers of and Responses to Global Climate Change." *WIREs Clim Change* 10(2019): e554. doi.org/10.1002/wcc.554.

Jungell-Michelsson, Jessica, and Pasi Heikkurinen. 2022. "Sufficiency: A Systematic Literature Review." *Ecological Economics* 195(2022): 107380.

Kahneman, Daniel, and Angus Deaton. 2010. "High Income Improves Life but Not Emotional Well-being." *Psychological and Cognitive Sciences.* 107(38): 16489–93.

Kallis, Giorgos, Vasilis Kostakis, Steffen Lange, Barbara Muraca, Susan Paulson, and Matthias Schmelzer. 2018. "Research on Degrowth." *Annual Review of Environment and Resources* 43: 291–316.

Kanwal, Maria, Umar Burki, Raza Ali, Robert Dahlstrom. 2021. "Systematic Review of Gender Differences in Online Consumers' Shopping Behavior." *Journal of Consumer Marketing* 39(1): 29–43.

Karimzadeh, Sara, and Magnus Boström. 2022. "Ethical Consumption: Why Should we Understand It as A Social Practice within a Multilevel Framework?" *Open Res Europe* 2(2022): 109. doi.org/10.12688/openreseurope.15069.2.

Kartha, Sivan, Eric Kemp-Benedict, Emily Ghosh, Anisha Nazareth, Tim Gore. 2020. *The Carbon Inequality Era: An Assessment of the Global Distribution of Consumption Emissions among Individuals from 1990 to 2015 and Beyond.* Oxfam & Stockholm Environment Institute. oxfamilibrary.openrepository.com/bitstream/handle/10546/621049/rr-carbon-inequality-era-210920-en.pdf.

Kasser, Tim. 2009. "Psychological Need Satisfaction, Personal Well-being, and Ecological Sustainability. *Ecopsychology* 1(4): 175–80.

———. 2017. "Living Both Well and Sustainably: A Review of the Literature, with Some Reflections on Future Research, Interventions and Policy." *Phil. Trans. R. Soc. A* 375: 20160369. doi.org/10.1098/rsta.2016.0369.

Keller, Margit. 2005. "Needs, Desires, and the Experience of Scarcity: Representations of Recreational Shopping in Post-Soviet Estonia." *Journal of Consumer Culture.* 5(1): 65–85.

Kennedy, Emily Huddart. 2011. "Rethinking Ecological Citizenship: The Role of Neighbourhood Networks in Cultural Change," *Environmental Politics*, 20(6): 843–60.

Kennedy, Emily Huddart, and Christine Horne. 2019. "Do Green Behaviours Earn Social Status?" *Socius: Sociological Research for a Dynamic World* 5: 1–9.

Kenner, Dario. 2019. *Carbon Inequality: The Role of the Richest in Climate Change.* London: Earthscan.

Kerton, Sarah, and John Sinclair. 2010. "Buying Local Organic Food: A Pathway to Transformative Learning." *Agriculture and Human Values* 27: 401–13.

Kim, Hyunji, Mitchell J. Callan, Ana I. Gheorghiu, and Willian J. Matthews. 2017. "Social Comparison, Personal Relative Deprivation, and Materialism." *British Journal of Social Psychology* 56: 373–92.

Kim, Jeehye Christine, Brian Park, and David Dubois. 2018. "How Consumers' Political Ideology and Status-Maintenance Goals Interact to Shape Their Desire for Luxury Goods." *Journal of Marketing* 82(6): 132–49. doi.org/10.1177/0022242918799699.

Kirk, Colleen P., and Laura S. Rifkin. 2020. "I'll Trade You Diamonds for Toilet Paper: Consumer Reacting, Coping and Adapting Behaviors in the COVID-19 Pandemic." *Journal of Business Research* 117(Sep.): 124–31. doi:10.1016/j.jbusres.2020.05.028.

Kišjuhas, Aleksej. 2023. "What Holds Society Together? Emotions, Social Ties, and Group Solidarity in Leisure Interaction Rituals." *Leisure Studies*. DOI: 10.1080/02614367.2023.2183979.

Klintman, Mikael. 2019. *Knowledge Resistance. How We Avoid Insights from Others.* Manchester: Manchester University Press.

Klocker, Natascha, Chris Gibson, and Erin Borger. 2012. "Living Together but Apart: Material Geographies of Everyday Sustainability in Extended Family Households." *Environment and Planning A* 44(9): 2240–59. doi:10.1068/a44594.

Knight, Kyle W., Eugene A. Rosa, and Juliet B. Schor. 2013. "Could Working Less Reduce Pressures on the Environment? A Cross-national Panel Analysis of OECD countries, 1970–2007." *Global Environmental Change* 23(4): 691–700.

Kovan, Jessica T., and John M. Dirkx. 2003. "'Being Called Awake' The Role of Transformative Learning in the Lives of Environmental Activists." *Adult Education Quarterly* 53(2): 99–118.

Lamers, Machiel, Jeroen Nawijn, and Eke Eijgelaar. 2019. "Political Consumerism for Sustainable Tourism: A Review." In *The Oxford Handbook of Political Consumerism,* edited by Magnus Boström, Michele Micheletti, and Peter Oosterveer, 349–66. Oxford: Oxford University Press.

Lamont, Michele, Annette Lareau. 1988. "Cultural Capital: Allusions, Gaps and Glissandos in Recent Theoretical Developments." *Sociological Theory* 6(2):153–68.

Laroche, Michel, Mohammad Reza Habibi, Marie-Odile Richard, and Ramesh Sankaranarayanan. 2013. "The Effect of Social Media Based Brand Communities on Brand Community Markers, Value Creation Practices, Brand Trust and Brand Loyalty. *Computers in Human Behavior* 28: 1755–67.

Lasarov, Wassili, Robert Mai, et al. 2019. "Counter-arguing as Barriers to Environmentally Motivated Consumption Reduction: A Multi-country Study." *International Journal of Research in Marketing* 36(2): 281–305.

Lee, Michael S. W., J. M. Ortega Egea, and N. García de Frutos. 2020. "Anti-consumption Beyond Boundaries: From Niche Topic to Global Phenomena." *Psychology and Marketing* 37(2): 171–76.

Lee, Jaehoon, and L. J. Shrum. 2012. "Conspicuous Consumption versus Charitable Behavior in Response to Social Exclusion: A Differential Needs Explanation." *Journal of Consumer Research* 39: 530–44.

Linnér, Björn-Ola, and Victoria Wibeck. 2019. *Sustainability Transformations: Agents and Drivers across Societies.* Cambridge, UK: Cambridge University Press.

Lo, Hui-Yi, and Nigel Harvey. 2010. "Shopping without Pain: Compulsive Buying and the Effects of Credit Card Availability in Europe and the Far East." *Journal of Economic Psychology* 32: 79–92.

Lockie, Stewart, and Catherine Wong. 2018. "Conflicting Temporalities of Social and Environmental Change?" In *Environment and Society: Concepts and Challenges,* edited by Magnus Boström and Debra Davidson, 327–50. Basingstoke: Palgrave Macmillan.

Lorenzen, Janet. 2017. "Social Network Challenges to Reducing Consumption: The Problem of Gift Giving." *Symbolic Interaction* 41(2): 247–66.

Lotz-Sisitka, Heila, Arjen Wals, David Kronlid, and Dylan McGarry. 2015. "Transformative, Transgressive Social Learning: Rethinking Higher Education Pedagogy in Times of Systemic Global Dysfunction." *Current Opinion in Environmental Sustainability* 16: 73–80.

Loukianov, Anastasia, Kate Burningham, and Tim Jackson. 2019. "Living the Good Life on Instagram" An Exploration of Lay Understandings of What It Means to Live Well." *Journal of Consumer Ethics.*

Loveland, Katherine E., Dirk Smeesters, and Naomi Mandel. 2010. "Still Preoccupied with 1995: The Need to Belong and Preference for Nostalgic Products," *Journal of Consumer Research* 37(Oct.): 393–408.

Lykke Syse, Karen, and Martin Lee Mueller. 2015. "Introduction." In *Sustainable Consumption and the Good Life: Interdisciplinary Perspectives*, edited by Karin Lykke Syse and Martin Lee Mueller, 1–6. London: Earthscan.

———. (eds.) 2015. *Sustainable Consumption and the Good Life: Interdisciplinary Perspectives.* London: Earthscan.

Löfgren, Orvar. 2013. "Changing Emotional Economies: The Case of Sweden 1970–2010." *Culture and Organization* 19(4): 283–96. DOI: 10.1080/14759551.2013.827420.

Madsen, Line Valdorff. 2018. "The Comfortable Home and Energy Consumption." *Housing, Theory and Society* 35(3): 329–52. DOI: 10.1080/14036096.2017.1348390.

Mandel, Naomi, Petia K. Petrova, and Robert B. Cialdini. 2006. "Images of Success and Preference for Luxury Brands." *Journal of Consumer Psychology* 16(1): 57–69.

Mangleburg, Tamara F., Patricia M. Doney, and Terry Bristol. 2004. "Shopping with Friends and Teens' Susceptibility to Peer Influence." *Journal of Retailing* 80: 101–16.

Maniates, Michael F. 2001. "Individualization: Plant a Tree, Buy a Bike, Save the World?" *Global Environmental Politics* 1(3): 31–52.

Marcuse, Herbert. 1964. *One-dimensional Man.* Boston: Boston Press.

Mauss, Marcel. 1990 (1954). *The Gift. The Form and Reason for Exchange in Archaic Societies.* London: Routledge.

Max-Neef, Manfred 2010. "Development and Human Needs." In *Development Ethics,* edited by Des Gasper, Asuncion Lera St. Clair. London: Routledge.

May, Frank, and Caglar Irmak. 2014. "Licensing Indulgence in the Present by Distorting Memories of Past Behavior." *Journal of Consumer Research* 41: 624–641

McCright, Aaron M. 2016. "Anti-reflexivity and Climate Change Skepticism in the US General Public." *Human Ecology Review* 22(2): 77–108.

McCright, Aaron M., and Riley E. Dunlap. 2010. "Anti-reflexivity: The American Conservative Movement's Success in Undermining Climate Science and Policy." *Theory, Culture & Society* 27: 100–33. doi.org/10.1177/0263276409356001.

Mead, George Herbert. 1962 (1934). *Mind, Self & Society from the Standpoint of a Social Behaviorist.* Chicago: University of Chicago Press.

Mead, Nicole L., Roy F. Baumeister, Tyler F. Stillman, Catherine D. Rawn, and Kathleen D. Vohs. 2011. "Social Exclusion Causes People to Spend and Consume

Strategically in the Service of Affiliation," *Journal of Consumer Research* 37(Feb.): 902–19.

Merton, Robert. 1938. "Social Structure and Anomie." *American Sociological Review* 3(5): 672–82.

Mezirow, Jack. 2009. "An Overview on Transformative Learning." In *Contemporary Theories of Learning: Learning Theorists—in their Own Words*, edited by Knud Illeris, 90–105. London: Routledge.

Mick, David G., and Michelle DeMoss. 1990. "Self-Gifts: Phenomenological Insights from Four Contexts." *Journal of Consumer Research* 17(3): 322–32.

Miller, Daniel. 1998. *A Theory of Shopping.* Cambridge, UK: Polity Press.

———. 2001. "The poverty of morality." *Journal of Consumer Culture.* 1(2): 225–43.

———. 2010. *Stuff.* Cambridge: Polity Press.

Mills, C. Wright. 1959 (2000). *The Sociological Imagination.* New York: Oxford University Press.

Moore, Jennie. 2015. "Ecological Footprints and Lifestyle Archetypes: Exploring Dimensions of Consumption and the Transformation Needed to Achieve Urban Sustainability." *Sustainability* 7: 4747–63.

Morgan, David H. J. 2020. "Family Practices in Time and Space." *Gender, Place & Culture* 27(5): 733–74.

Moss, Mark. 2007. *Shopping as An Entertainment Experience.* Lanham, MD: Rowman & Littlefield.

Moyer, Joanne M., and A. John Sinclair. 2020. "Learning for Sustainability. Considering Pathways to Transformation." *Adult Education Quarterly* 70(4): 340–59.

Moynat Orlane, Johannes Volden, and Marlyne Sahakian. 2022. "How do COVID-19 Lockdown Practices Relate to Sustainable Well-being? Lessons from Oslo and Geneva." *Sustainability: Science, Practice, and Policy* 18(1): 309–24

Muller, Astrid, Maithilee Joshi, and Tobias A. Thomas. 2022. "Excessive Shopping on the Internet: Recent Trends in Compulsive Buying-Shopping Disorder." *Current Opinion in Behavioral Sciences* 44: 101106.

Muniz, Albert M. Jr., and Thomas C. O'Guinn. 2001. "Brand Community." *Journal of Consumer Research* 27: 412–32.

Nethercote, Megan. 2019. "Immaterial Inheritance: The Socialization of Cultures of Housing Consumption." *Housing, Theory and Society* 36(3). 359–75. DOI: 10.1080/14036096.2018.1471002.

Newman, Todd P, Erik C. Nisbet, and Matthew C. Nisbet. 2018. "Climate Change, Cultural Cognition, and Media Effects: Worldviews Drive News Selectivity, Biased Processing, and Polarized Attitudes." *Public Understanding of Science* 27(8): 985–1002.

Nistor, Laura. 2022. "'There's More to It than Buying Cheap Clothes' A Qualitative Study of Second-hand Clothes Shopping in the Szekerland Region (Transylvania, Romania)" *Corvinus Journal of Sociology and Social Policy* 13(1): 73–93.

O'Cass, Aron, and Hmily McEwen. 2004. "Exploring Consumer Status and Conspicuous Consumption." *Journal of Consumer Behaviour* 4(1): 25–39.

O'Guinn, Thomas, and Ronald J. Faber. 1989. "Compulsive Buying: A Phenomenological Explanation." *Journal of Consumer Research* 16(2): 147–57.

Ojala, Maria. 2016. "Facing Anxiety in Climate Change Education: From Therapeutic Practice to Hopeful Transgressive Learning." *Canadian Journal of Environmental Education* 21: 41–56.

———. 2023. "Hope and Climate Change Engagement from a Psychological Perspective." *Current Opinion in Psychology* 49: 101514.

Ojala, Maria, Ashlee Cunsolo, Charles A. Ogunbode, and Jaqueline Middleton. 2021. "Anxiety, Worry, and Grief in a Time of Environmental and Climate Crisis: A Narrative Review." *Annual Review of Environmental Resources* 46: 35–58.

Ordabayeva, Nailya, and Pierre Chandon. 2011. "Getting Ahead of the Joneses: When Equality Increases Conspicuous Consumption among Bottom-tier Consumers." *Journal of Consumer Research* 38: 27–41.

Osikominu, Jessica, and Nancy Bocken. 2020. "A Voluntary Simplicity Lifestyle: Values, Adoption, Practices and Effects." *Sustainability* 12(5):1903.

Otto, Ilona M., Jonathan F. Donges, Roger Cremades, et al. 2020. "Social Tipping Dynamics for Stabilizing Earth's Climate by 2050." *PNAS* 117(5): 2354–65.

Oxfam. 2020. Confronting Carbon Inequality. Oxfam media briefing.

Ozen, Hilal, and Nil Engizek. 2014. "Shopping Online without Thinking: Being Emotional or Rational? *Asian Pacific Journal of Marketing and Logistics* 26(1): 78–93.

Packard, Vance. 1988 (1960). *The Waste Makers.* New York: Ig Publishing.

Parguel, Béatrice, Renaud Lunardo, and Florence Benoit-Moreau. 2017. "Sustainability of the Sharing Economy in Question: When Second-hand Peer-to-peer Platforms Stimulate Indulgent Consumption." *Technological Forecasting and Social Change,* 125(Dec.): 48–57.

Park, Eun Joo, Eun Young Kim, Vanessa Martin Funches, and William Foxx. 2012. "Apparel Product Attributes, Web Browsing, and E-impulse Buying on Shopping Websites." *Journal of Business Research* 65: 1583–89.

Peattie, Ken. 2010. "Green Consumption: Behavior and Norms." *Annual Review of Environmental Resources* 35: 195–228.

Perkins, Krystal M., Nora Munguia, Michael Ellenbecker, Rafael Moure-Eraso, and Luis Velazquez. 2021. "COVID-19 Pandemic Lessons to Facilitate Future Engagement in the Global Climate Crisis." *Journal of Cleaner Production* 290: 125178.

Persson, Ola, Jörgen Larsson, and Jonas Nässén. 2022. "Working Less by Choice: What are the Benefits and Hardships?" *Sustainability: Science, Practice and Policy* 18(1): 81–96.

Piacentini, Maria, and Greig Mailer. 2004. "Symbolic Consumption in Teenagers' Clothing Choices." *Journal of Consumer Behaviour* 3(3): 251–63.

Powell, Helen. 2009. "Time, Television, and the Decline of DIY." *Home Cultures* 6(1): 89–107.

Princen, Thomas. 2005. *The Logic of Sufficiency.* Cambridge, MA: The MIT Press.

Ramanathan, Suresh, and Ann L. McGill. 2007. "Consuming with Others: Social Influences on Moment-to-Moment and Retrospective Evaluations of an Experience." *Journal of Consumer Research* 34(4): 506–24.

Rauschmayer, Felix, and Ines Omann. 2015. "Well-being in Sustainability Transitions. Making Use of Needs." In *Sustainable Consumption and the Good Life. Interdisciplinary Perspectives*, edited by Karin Lykke Syse and Martin Lee Mueller, 111–25. London: Earthscan.

Raworth, Kate. 2012. *A Safe and Just Space for Humanity: Can We Live Within the Doughnut?* Oxfam Discussion Paper.

Rebouças Raquel, and Ana Maria Soares. 2020. "Voluntary Simplicity: A Literature Review and Research Agenda." *International Journal of Consumer Studies* 45(3): 303–319.

Richins, Marsha L. 1994. "Valuing Things: The Public and Private Meanings of Possessions," *Journal of Consumer Research* 21(3): 504–21.

Rief, Silvia. 2008. "Outlines of a Critical Sociology of Consumption: Beyond Moralism and Celebration." *Sociology Compass* 2(2): 560–76.

Rinkinen, Jenny, Elizabeth Shove, and Greg Marsden. 2021. *Conceptualizing Demand: A Distinctive Approach to Consumption and Practice.* London: Routledge.

Ritchie, Hannah, and Max Roser. 2017. "Obesity." Published online at OurWorldInData.org. Retrieved from: ourworldindata.org/obesity 2022-11-22.

Rook, Dennis. 1985. "The Ritual Dimension of Consumer Behavior." *Journal of Consumer Research* 12(Dec.): 251–64.

———. 1987. "The Buying Impulse." *Journal of Consumer Research* 14(Sep.): 189–99.

Rosa, Hartmut. 2013. *Social Acceleration: A New Theory of Modernity*. New York: Columbia University Press.

Rostow, W. W. 1959. "The Stages of Economic Growth." *The Economic History Review, New Series* 12(1): 1–16.

Ruppel Shell, Ellen. 2009. *Cheap: The High Cost of Discount Culture*. New York: Penguin.

Sahakian, Marlyne. 2017. "Constructing Normality through Material and Social Lock-on: the Dynamics of Energy Consumption among Geneva's More Affluent Households," in *Demanding Energy: Space, Time, and Change*, edited by A. Hui, R. Day, and G. Walker, 51–71. Basingstoke: Palgrave Macmillan. doi: 10.1007/978-3-319-61991-0_3.

———. 2022. "'More, Bigger, Better' Household Appliances: Contesting Normativity in Practices through Emotions." *Journal of Consumer Culture* 22(1): 21–39.

Sassatelli, Roberta. 2007. *Consumer Culture. History, Theory and Politics.* London: Sage.

Sayer, Andrew. 2002. *Method in Social Science: A Realist Approach*. London: Routledge.

———. 2016. *Why We Can't Afford the Rich.* Cambridge, UK: The Polity Press.

Schoonmaker, Sara. 2006. "Piece of Cake: Children's Birthday Celebrations and Alternatives to Consumer Culture." *Sociological Focus* 39(3): 217–34.

Schor, Juliet B. 1992. *The Overworked American: The Unexpected Decline of Leisure.* New York: Basic Books.

———. 1998. *The Overspent American: Why We Want What We Don't Need.* New York: Harper.

———. 2004. *Born To Buy.* New York: Scribner.

———. 2005. "Sustainable consumption and worktime reduction." *Journal of Industrial Ecology* 9(1–2): 37–50.

Schor, Juliet, and Craig Thompson (eds.). 2014. *Sustainable Lifestyles and the Quest for Plenitude: Case Studies of the New Economy.* New Haven, CT: Yale University Press.

Sharma, Sarah. 2014. *In the Meantime: Temporality and Cultural Politics.* Durham, NC: Duke University Press.

Sheth, Jagdish. 2020. "Impact of Covid-19 on Consumer Behavior: Will the Old Habits Return or Die?" *Journal of Business Research.* 117(Sep.): 280–83. doi:10.1016/j.jbusres.2020.05.059.

Shove, Elizabeth. 2003. *Comfort, Cleanliness + Convenience. The Social Organization of Normality.* Oxford, UK: Berg.

———. 2010. "Beyond the ABC: Climate Change Policy and Theories of Social Change." *Environment and Planning A* 42(6): 1273–85.

Shove, Elizabeth, and Alan Warde. 2002. "Inconspicuous Consumption: The Sociology of Consumption, Lifestyles and the Environment." In *Sociological Theory and the Environment. Classical Foundations, Contemporary Insights*, edited by R. Murphy, F. H. Buttel, P. Dickens, and A. Gijswijt, 230–51. Lanham, MD: Rowman & Littlefield.

Shove, Elizabeth, Mika Pantzar, and Matt Watson. 2012. *The Dynamics of Social Practice*. London: Sage.

Shukla, Paurav. 2008. "Conspicuous Consumption among Middle Age Consumers: Psychological and Brand Antecedents." *Journal of Product and Brand Management* 17(1): 25–36.

Simmel, Georg. 1957 (1904). "Fashion." *American Journal of Sociology* 62(6): 541–58.

———. 1971 (1903). "The Metropolis and Mental Life," in *Georg Simmel: On Individuality and Social Forms* (ed. Donald N. Levine), 324–39. Chicago: University of Chicago Press.

Smith, Philip B., and Manfred A. Max Neef. 2011. *Economics Unmasked: From Power and Greed to Compassion and Common Good.* Cambridge, UK: Green Books.

Solér, Cecilia. 2018. *Stress, Affluence, and Sustainable Consumption.* New York: Routledge.

Soneryd, Linda, and Ylva Uggla. 2015. "Green Governmentality and Responsibilization: New Forms of Governance and Responses to 'Consumer Responsibility.'" *Environmental Politics* 24(6): 913–31.

Soper, Kate. 2015. "Towards a Sustainable Flourishing. Democracy, Hedonism and the Politics of Prosperity," in *Sustainable Consumption and the Good Life.*

Interdisciplinary Perspectives, edited by Karin Lykke Syse and Martin Lee Mueller, 43–54. London: Earthscan.

Sörqvist, Patrik, and Linda Langeborg. 2019. "Why People Harm the Environment although They Try to Treat it Well: An Evolutionary-cognitive Perspective on Climate Compensation." *Frontiers in Psychology*: 10:348 doi.org/10.3389/fpsyg.2019.00348.

Southerton, Dale. 2020. *Time, Consumption and the Coordination of Everyday Life.* London: Palgrave Macmillan.

Southerton, Dale, and Alan Warde. 2023. "Towards Sustainable Consumption: Reflections on the Concepts of Social Loading, Excess and Idle Capacity," in *Consumption, Sustainability and Everyday Life,* edited by Arve Hansen, and Kenneth Bo Nielsen, 339–61. London: Palgrave Macmillan.

Spaargaren, Gert. 2011. "Theories of Practices: Agency, Technology, and Culture: Exploring the Relevance of Practice Theories for the Governance of Sustainable Consumption Practices in the New World-order." *Global Environmental Change*, Symposium on Social Theory and the Environment in the New World (dis)Order, 21(3): 813–22.

Stegeman, Ingrid, Alba Godfrey, and Maria Romeo-Velilla et al. 2020. "Encouraging and Enabling Lifestyles and Behaviours to Simultaneously Promote Environmental Sustainability, Health and Equity: Key Policy Messages from INHERIT. *International Journal of Environmental Research and Public Health* 17: 1–22.

Stoddard, Isak, Kevin Anderson, and Stuart Capstick et al. 2021. "Three Decades of Climate Mitigation: Why Haven't We Bent the Global Emission Curve?" *Annual Review of Environment and Resources* 46: 653–89.

Stolle, Dietlind, and Micheletti, Michele. 2013. *Political Consumerism. Global Responsibility in Action.* Cambridge University Press.

Stuart, Diana, Ryan Gunderson, and Brian Petersen. 2020. "Overconsumption as Ideology. Implications for Addressing Global Climate Change." *Nature and Culture* 15(2): 199–223.

Sullivan, Oriel. 2008. "Busyness, Status Distinction and Consumption Strategies of the Income Rich, Time Poor." *Time & Society* 12(1): 5–26.

Sullivan, Oriel, and Jonathan Gershuny. 2004. "Inconspicuous Consumption: Work-rich, Time-poor in the Liberal Market Economy." *Journal of Consumer Culture* 4(1): 79–100.

Swedberg, Richard. 2003. *Principles of Economic Sociology*. Princeton, NJ: Princeton University Press.

Szabo, Michelle. 2011. "The Challenges of 'Re-engaging with Food': Connecting Employment, Household Patterns and Gender Relations to Convenience Food Consumption in North America." *Food, Culture & Society* 14(4): 547–66.

Thompson, Craig J., and Zeynep Arsel. 2004. "The Starbucks Brandscape and Consumers' (Anticorporate) Experiences of Glocalization." *Journal of Consumer Research* 31(3): 631–42.

Thorkild, ÆRØ. 2006. "Residential Choice from a Lifestyle Perspective." *Housing, Theory & Society* 23(2): 109–130.

Thunberg, Greta. 2019. *No One Is Too Small to Make a Difference.* New York: Penguin.

Trentmann, Frank. 2016. *Empire of Things: How We Became a World of Consumers, from the Fifteenth Century to the Twenty-First.* London: Allen Lane.

Uggla, Ylva. 2019. "Taking Back Control: Minimalism as a Reaction to High Speed and Overload in Contemporary Society." *Sociologisk Forskning* 56(3–4): 233–52.

Uggla, Ylva, and Ulrika Olausson. 2012. "The Enrollment of Nature in Tourist Information: Framing Urban Nature as the 'Other.'" *Environmental Communication* 7(1): 97–112.

Urry, John. 2010. "Consuming the Planet to Excess." *Theory, Culture and Society* 27(2–3): 191–212.

Van Loon, Patricia, Lieven Deketele, Jost Dewaele, Alan McKinnon, and Christine Rutherford. 2015. "A Comparative Analysis of Carbon Emissions from Online Retailing of Fast Moving Consumer Goods." *Journal of Cleaner Production* 106: 478–86.

Veblen, Thorstein. 1994 (1899). *The Theory of the Leisure Class: An Economic Study of Institutions.* New York: Funk & Wagnalls.

Wallerstein, Immanuel M. 2004. *World-systems Analysis: An Introduction.* Durham, NC: Duke University Press.

Wals, Arjen E. J. 2010. "Mirroring, Gestaltswitching and Transformative Social Learning. Stepping Stones for Developing Sustainability Competence." *International Journal of Sustainability in Higher Education* 11(4): 380–90.

Walters, Trudie, and Neil Carr. 2019. "Changing Patterns of Conspicuous Consumption: Media Representations of Luxury in Second Homes." *Journal of Consumer Culture* 19(3): 295–315.

Walther, Carol S., and Jennifer A. Sandlin. 2013. "Green Capital and Social Reproduction within Families Practising Voluntary Simplicity in the US." *International Journal of Consumer Studies* 37(1): 36–45.

Wang, Xueqin, Yiik Diew Wong, and Kum Fai Yuen. 2021. "Rise of 'Lonely' Consumers in the Post-Covid-19 Era: A Synthesised Review on Psychological Commercial and Social Implications." *International Journal of Environmental Research and Public Health* 18: 404.

Warde, Alan. 1999. "Convenience Food: Space and Timing." *British Food Journal* 101(7): 518–27.

———. 2005. "Consumption and theories of practice." *Journal of Consumer Culture* 5(2): 131–53.

———. 2022. "Society and Consumption." *Consumption and Society* 1(1): 11–30.

Welch, Daniel, and Dale Southerton. 2019: "After Paris: Transitions for Sustainable Consumption." *Sustainability: Science, Practice and Policy* 15(1): 31–44, DOI: 10.1080/15487733.2018.1560861.

White, Katherine, and Darren Dahl. 2006. "To Be or Not Be? The Influence of Dissociative Reference Groups on Consumer Preferences." *Journal of Consumer Psychology* 16(4): 404–14.

Wiedmann, Thomas, Manfred Lenzen, Lorenz T. Keyßer, and Julia K. Steinberger. 2020. "Scientists' Warning on Affluence." *Nature Communications* 11: 3107.

Wiesel, Ilan, Simon Pinnegar, and Robert Freestone. 2013. "Supersized Australian Dream: Investment, Lifestyle and Neighbourhood Perceptions among 'Knockdown-rebuild' Owners in Sydney." *Housing, Theory and Society* 30(3): 312–29.

Wilk, Richard. 2002. "Consumption, Human Needs, and Global Environmental Change." *Global Environmental Change* 12: 5–13.

Wilkinson, Richard, and Kate Pickett. 2010. *The Spirit Level: Why Greater Equality Makes Societies Stronger.* London: Bloomsbury.

———. 2019. *The Inner Level: How More Equal Societies Reduce Stress, Restore Sanity and Improve Everyone's Well-being*. London: Allen Lane.

Xi, Nannan, and Juho Hamari. 2021. "Shopping in Virtual Reality: A Literature Review and Future Agenda." *Journal of Business Research* 134: 37–58.

Zhou, Lianxi, and Amy Wong. 2008. "Exploring the Influence of Product Conspicuousness and Social Compliance on Purchasing Motives of Young Chinese Consumers for Foreign Brands." *Journal of Consumer Behaviour* 7(6): 470–83.

Zorell, Carolin V. 2021. "Nudges, Norms, or Just Contagion? A Theory on Influences on the Practice of (Non-)Sustainable Behavior." *Sustainability* 12(24).

Zorell, Carolin V., and Thomas Denk. 2021. "Political Consumerism and Interpersonal Discussion Patterns." *Scandinavian Political Studies* 44(4): 392–415.

Index

Page references for figures (f) and textboxes (b) are italicized.

abundance, xiii, xviii, 65, 113–17; of choice opportunities, 80, *81f*, 84, 89, 125n13, 163
accessibility, xxii, 32, 65, 87–88, 111, 114; by credit money, 122, *123b*, and legitimation of consumerism, 134, 155, and luxury and status consumption, 31–32, 44, 53
acquisition, xxxiii–xxxiv, *47b*, 77–78, 85, 119
advertisement, 32, 52, 85, 115, *123b*, 172; and consumer culture, xxiii, 135, 145, 157, industry, xvi, 10, 33–35, 56, 88, 120
agency, xix, xxiv–xxvi, xxxn6, 16, 27, 164–65, 177n13, 177n14
Akenji, Lewis, xii, xiv, xix

the Anthropocene, xi, xx, xxii, xxiv, xxxn2

anti-consumption, xxiv, 12, *14b*, 46, 115, 167, 176n2. *See also* downsizing; voluntary, reduction of consumption
anti-reflexivity, xxix, 142–43, 147–48, *149b*, 152, 175
anxiety: of appearance, xxvii, 39, and cleanliness, 104, of climate change and environmental destruction, xv, xxxn6, and fashion, xxviii, 84–86, 89–90, and social comparison and judgment, 8, 45, 51–52, 159–60, and social relationships, 10, 23, 75, 141
Aro, Riikka, 124n5, 131–32, 136, 176n3
artificial intelligence, 20, 69
Asia, 129
Australia, xii, 12, 107, 124n10
Austria, xii
availability. *See* accessibility
aviation, xii

Barr, Stewart, *66*, 171
Bauman, Zygmunt, xvii, xxiii, 37, 59n10, 76, 80, *86b*, 121, 136, 139, 143, 145, 162, 177n7, 177n11
Beck, Ulrich, 161
Becker, Howard, 138
Belk, Russell, xvi, xxv, 6, 8, 22, 34–35, 37–38, *46b*, 58n6, 77–81, *79f*, *81f*, 84, *100b*, 101, 136
Berger, Peter, xxv, xxxin12, 127, 153
biodiversity loss, xi–xiii

birthday party, xxvii, 1, 5, 11–13, 16–17, 52, 70
Black Friday, 23
borrowing, 23, 52, 60n19, 87, 109–11, 121, *123b*, 133
Boström, Magnus, xv, xix, xxv, xxxin13, 15–17, 27n6n7, 32, *47b*, 83, 92n2n3n10, 135, 139, 142–43, 145, *146b*, 166–70, 174, 176n2, 177n15
Bourdieu, Pierre, 41, 43–44, 47, 59n14, 85, 104, 127, 134
brands, 31–3, 36–9, 44–45, *46b*, 53–54, 111, 115, 121, 136; case study of, 31–33, and communities, 19–20, 32–33, 144, and consumer culture, xxiii, 32, and rituals, 4–6, 8, 23–24, 19, 21. *See also* fashion
Brülde, Bengt, 158–59, 170, 176n6, 177n8
Brulle, Robert, 128, 176
buyosphere, 112, 116–17, 122, 151

Callmer, Åsa, xviii, 15, 17, 167, 177n15n17
Campbell, Colin, xvi, xxiii, 9, 30–31, 43, 58n2, 76–77, 81, 84, 92–93n11
Canada, 125n11
capitalism: definition, xx, as/and institution and infrastructure, xx–xxiii, 63, 80, 83, 91, 142, 145, 147–48, 162, and consumer culture, ideology, x, xxiii, 11, 31–32, 58n2, 83, 93n11, 147–48, 150n7, 162
car: and climate footprint, xii, and cycles of desire, 79, and identity, symbol of status, 32, 45, *46b*, *48b*, 52–53, 37, 40, 44, 53, 69, 144, and infrastructure, xxii, xxiv, 121, *123b*, 172–73, and rituals, 5–9, 16, 18, 22, and time-saving, 70
carbon emissions, xi, 47–48
carbon footprint, and high/low carbon intensive consumption, xii–xiv, xix, 45, *48b*, 68, 70, 106, 139
care-taking: for others, xxv, 1, 8–10, *26b*, 28n9, *47b*, 52, 96, 99, 121, 152, 154, 168, of goods, 89, 143–44, 162–63
celebrities, 33–34, 85, 120
cheap, xxii, 23–24, 65, 70, 83, 134, 144; vs. expensive, status goods, 42, 44, 45
Cherrier, Hélène, 7, 139, 177n17
children: and family life, 10, 15–17, 27, *47b*, 52, 64, 75, 99, 106, 124n9, 134, and peer influence, 38–39, *47b*, 160, and socialization, xxvi, 32–33, 35–37, 43, 99, 121, 129
China, xiv, 39, 53
Christmas, 16–17, *18b*, 114
cleanliness, 69, 70, 102–5, 130–31, 133, 135, *140b*, 151, 155, 162
clothing, shoes, textiles, xii, 5, 8, 18, 39, 42, *46b*, 54, 68, 84, 138, *140b*. *See also* fashion
clutter, 20, 89, 105, 115, 158, 162–63
cognitive dimension, xv, xviii, xxiii, 127–28, 145, 147, 150n6, 155–56, 161, 166, 170–71
coherence of home environment, 103, 108, 121, 131, 151
collecting, rituals of, 22–23, *25b*
collective dilemmas, 50, *51b*, 56
Collins, Randall, xxvii, 1–7, *4f*, *7f*, 10, 20, 24, 27n4, 138
comfort, 98–99, 102–6, 129–31, 136, 151
commercialization. *See* commoditization.
commoditization, xvii–xviii, xxi, 10–14, *14b*, 32, *46b*, 56, 59n10, 120, 143–44, 148; vs. commodification, xxxn9, and de-commoditization, 105
compensation-seeking behavior, 19–20, 50, *55f*, 56, 64, 72, 151, 155
compulsive buying, 23, 90, 114, 117, *130b*, 158
connectivity, 105, 129, 134

consciousness: collective, 3, ecological, green, climate, 66, 148, 165, false, 145, 147–48, happy, 147, practical, 127, 134–35
conspicuous consumption, 41–45, *46–47b*, *48b*, 52–53, 55–57, *57–58b*, 59n13, 69, 76, 82, 92n9, 96, 120; and home, 101–3, 106, 110, 121, *122b*, 151. *See also* inconspicuous consumption
consumer: capitalism, xvi, 76, 80, 83, 145, 147–48, 162, rights and sovereignty, xxxiii–xiv, 37, 127, 134, 160, society, xvi, *25b*, 32, 80, 136, 139, symbol, 6, *7f*, 26, 36, *47b*. *See also* green consumer/consumption; modern consumer; responsibility
consumer culture: critique of, xvi, xxiii, 35, 40, 160, 162, 167, 176, and entertainment, ideals and (unmet) promises, 65, 72, 89, 119, 138, 145, 151, 157, 162, history of, xiii, 31–32, 58n2, 64–65, 129, and identity, 35–36, 145, as institution, xxiii–xxiv, 173, and social stratification, 29, 32. *See also* fashion; novelty
consumerism: definition of, xvii, detox from, 163–76, *165f*, flaws of, 157–63
consumption: definition of, xvi–xvii
convenience, xxvi, 65, 68–70, 102, 105, 117, 129, 130, 151, 163
corporate social responsibility, xxiii, 153
cosmetics, 23, 39, 111, 133
Covid-19, xii, 5, 15, 19–20, 69, *92b*, 92n3n10, 95, 96, 105, 108, 117, *123b*, 124n7, 125n15, 169–70, 173, 174
credit. *See* borrowing
cultural: capital, xxi, *18b*, *25b*, 40, 43–45, 56, *57b*, 66, 101–2, 144, 167, consumption, *99b*, 100, 115, factors, xiv, 63, *73b*, *86b*, *91–92b*, 128–29, 161, frames, xiii, 31, 56, 63, 134, 156, ideals, meanings, and values, 15, 93n11, 95, 97, 98, 124n9n11, institutions, *149b*, 165, 175, norms, xxvi, xxvii, 24, 130, *140b*, sociology, 1, trauma, 175–76. *See also* consumer culture; framing, pre-framed activities; ideals, unattainable
cycle of desire, 77–81, *79f*, *81f*, 89–90, 119–120, 122. *See also* desire
Czechia, xii

debt. *See* borrowing
degrowth, *91b*, 164, 173
demand: escalation of, 102–3, 124n3, 130–31, 150n4, insatiable, 77, for space and stuff, 75, 106–8, *109f*, *122b*, 124n9n11, 125n11, vs. supply, 177n14
democracy, xxiii, *57b*, 161, 165, 172–75
denial: and climate change, *48b*, of negative effects of consumerism, *146b*, *148b*, 155–56
desire, definition of, xvi–xvii. *See also* cycle of desire
digital: infrastructure, *26b*, *57b*, 63, 88, 95, 96, 100, 111, 117–18, 122, *122–23b*, 174, platform, 20, 71, 120, rebound, 125n14
discount, 23–25, 88. *See also* cheap
dissatisfaction, and vicious circle of spending, 34, 41–42, 50, 78, *81f*, 84–85
distinction, *18b*, 29, 43–44, 56, 83
Dittmar, Helga, xxiii, 23, 32–40, *36f*, 59n8, 65, *100b*, 116, 117–18, 160
downsizing, 14–16, 27n8, 135, 167–68, 171
drivers, definition of, xix
durability of products, 31, 77, 83, *86–87b*, 89, 144
Durkheim, Émile, 2–3

Earth Overshoot Day, xii
Easterlin, Richard, 158–59, 177n10
eating/meals, 2, 5, 7, 8, 15, 42, 69, 70, 74, 77, 102, 107–8, 115, 132, 143, 156

eBay, 119–20
Echegaray, Fabián, 5, 27n7, 106, 124n11, 169
eco-labeling, *146b*, 156, 172, 173
Ecuador, xii
electronics, appliances, xii, 21, 52, *73b*, 75, 83, 86, 88, 111, 116, 124n6
elite, xiii, 59n12; the polluter, *48–49b*, 175. *See also* the rich
emotional: bonds, *18b*, dimension, xiv–xv, xviii, 98, 150n6, 170, energy, 2–8, *4f*, *7f*, 12, 17, 20, 21–22, 24, *26b*, 26–27, 38, 84, 86, 157, labor, 11, 112–13, learning, 168, and place attachment, 101, and shopping, 111, 116, support 33
emotions, xxv, 3, 5, 8, 11, 23, 27n5, *57b*, 77, 84, 118, 140, 160–61. *See also* anxiety; dissatisfaction; emotional energy; envy; pride; shame
energy consumption, xii, 68, *97b*, 100, 102–3, 106, 109, 121, 124n9, 124n15, 130–31, 133, 140b, 150n4, 173
environmental consciousness. *See* consciousness
environmental sociology, xv
envy, 50, 81, 84, 160
Estonia, 114, 125n12
Europe, xiv, 11, *18b*, 103, 129, 177n10
excess, definition of, xviii
extended self, 34–38, 49, 56, *58b*, 76, 95, *100b*, 106, 155

family: and happy home, 96–97, 98–101, 111, 120, 121, 168, rituals, 1, 7–13, 15–17, *18b*, 21, fashion, xxiii, 40, 81–87, 101, 104, 111, fear of missing out, *81f*, 161
Festinger, Leon, 38
fetishism, 144–5, 148; ethical/green, *146b*, 148
Fletcher, Kate, *86–87b*
food: consumption of, xii, 6, 31, 54, 66, 68–70, fast, 61, 69, 106, 129, 134, practices, 92n10, 95, 169. *See also* eating/meals
footprint, climate/ecological, xiii, xviii, xix, *26b*, 45, *57b*, 68, 70, 86, 106, 121, 129, 140, *146b*
frames of reference, *57b*, *149b*, 166–69, 175
framing, pre-framed activities, 65, 121–22, 137, 148, 150n5. *See also* cultural frames
France, 44, 113, 119
free choice, xxiv, 135
friendship, xvii, 6, 139, 168; and peer influence, 28n10, 39, *47b*, 55, 79, 136, 170, and rituals, 7, 9, 11, 15–16, 21, 33, 74, 112
Fromm, Erich, 37, 79
future: generations, 91, 154, 179, leisure, 75–76, 90, 155, vs. present, 72, 77, 79, 81, 89–91, *91b*, 143, visions, constrained, 150n6, 163, 173

gender dimension, 29, 40, 65, *72b*, 86, 118, *140b*, 143. *See also* identity, masculine
Germany, xii
Giddens, Anthony, 87, 127, 128
gift-giving, 12, 16–18, *26b*, 77. *See also* birthday party; Christmas
Goffman, Erving, 2, 27n4, 104, 138
Gössling, Stefan, xii, 48
Gram Hansen, Kirsten, 99, *100b*, 101, 105, 124n6
green consumer/consumption, 45, 59n15, 142–43, 145, *146b*. *See also* eco-labelling
Gross, Mathias, 141
group solidarity, 1–3, *4f*, 6, 7, *7f*, 17, 20, *26b*, 151
growth: critique of, 50, 173, 175, 177n10, dogma, xxii–xxiii, 56, 63, 173, economic, xi, xiii, xx–xxii, xxxin15, 67, 129, 162, 173, green, xxii, 156

habit, 14–15, 42, *51b*, 59n10, 66, 74, 127, 137, 141, 147–48; disruption of, 85, 108, 127–28, 166, 168, 171–72, and embodied knowledge, 134–35, justification of, 152, 154, 156, and socialization, xxvi, 121, and tacit knowledge, 144
habitus, 43, 59n14, 134
happiness, xviii, xxiii, 13, 16, *18b*, 28n9, 50, 53, 148, 157–59, 163, 166, 169–70, 176n5n6, 177n7
health, xi, 50, 59n17, 68, 104, 158, 169, 174
hedonism, xxv, 9, *25b*, 30, 76, 84, 161. *See also* indulgence; pleasure
Hine, Thomas, xxv, 11, 17, 32, 44, 84, 111–12, 117
Hochschild, Arlie, 11–12, 70, 121
holiday, 5, 6, 8, 22, *26b*, 43–44, 64–66, 68, 75, 77, *86b*, 88, 110, 114–15, 120–21, 156
home: entertainment facilities, 15, 20–22, 106–7, extension of, xii, 106–9, 124n10, and identity, 37, 98, *100b*, 101–2, 121, and inconspicuous consumption, 102–6, *140b*, and mortgage financed products, 109–11, and path-dependent consumption, *97b*, and social status, 101–2, as stage for consumption, 6, various meanings of, 96–97, 98–101, *122–23b*, 151
homeliness, 6, 95, 99, 101
homemaking practices, 99, *100b*, 110
household appliances, 68, *73b*, 105–6
housing, xii, xxi, 43, *46b*, 60n19, 68, 69, 95, 99, 109
hurriedness, xii, 61, 62, *91b*, 129, 154, 175. *See also* social acceleration; speed

Iceland, xii
ideals, unattainable, 34–6, *36f*, 42, 49, 55, 56, *57b*, 154, 160, 161
identity, xvii, 18, 22, 25, 30, 31, 34–40, 56, 59n9n10, 75–76, 154; deficit, *36f*, 50, 53, *57b*, 156, 160–61, group, 4, masculine, xix, 6, 69, as need, xxxn8, and normalization, 129, and obsolescence, *86b*, overload, 125n13, and social status, 42, 53, 132. *See also* extended self; home, and identity
ignorance, 127–28, 139, 141–48, *149b*, 152, 155–56; concept of, 141–42
imitation, 83, 135–37, 154, 171
impulse buying, xxvi, 61, 87–88, 90, 114, 117–19, 170
income: gap, 47, 50–52, 54–55, 59n17, and leisure time, 64, 75, 76, and quality of life, 158–60, 176n6, and time scarcity, 64, 67–68, 70, 89–90, *91b*, 92n8. *See also* inequality; social stratification
inconspicuous consumption, xxvi, 43, 96, 102–6, *112b*, 130, *140b*, 151, 167
India, *140b*
individualization, 76, 81, 132, 161
individualized: goals and solutions, 9–10, 70, identity, 40, 161, practices, *51b*, *99b*, 107, 108, responsibility, xv, 145, 172, social lives and societies, 19, 58n6, *73b*, value framings, 40, 154, 156
indulgence, xiii, 9, *25b*, 72, 118–19. *See also* hedonism; pleasure
industrialization, xiii, xxii–xxiii, xxxin10, 31, 96, 111, 129, 141
inequality, 47–56, *47b*, *55f*, *58b*, *72b*, *91b*; and collective dilemmas, *51b*, and the polluter elite, *48–49b*, and quality of life, 159. *See also* income gap; relative poverty
inexpensive goods and services. *See* cheap
influencers, 33–34, 37, 56, 58n4, 85, 88, 120, 122, 172
infrastructure: choice, xxiv, 137, and mass consumption, xvii, xix–xx,

xxiv–xxv, 163–65, *165f*, 167, 172–73, physical, xxii–xxiii, *26b*, *57b*, 61, 67, *71–72b*, 95, 103, 112, 121, *122–23b*, 129–31, *140b*, 172, social, xxii–xxiii, *26b*, *57b*. *See also* digital infrastructure; locked-in
insatiability, xviii, 77, *92b*, 151, 158, 160–62, 166
instant: consumption, 100, offers, 117, reward, 72–74, 76, 87–88, 90
institution, xviii, xx, xiv–xxv, *149b*, 163–65, *165f*, 170, 172, 173–76; concept of, xx, xxin12
interaction ritual chain, 3–8, *4f*, *7f*

the internet, xx, xxii, 20, 80, 87–88, *99b*, 116–121, 122, 124n6, 125n14, 151. *See also* digital; shopping, online

intimate relationship, 8–11, *18b*, 27, 120
Italy, xii

Jack, Tullia, 103, 131, 133, *140b*, 155
Jackson, Tim, xxiii, xxxin16, 76, 153, 158, 159–60, 162, 169, 173, 176n3
Japan, xii
Jenkins, Rebecca, 6–9, 11
justification of consumerism, 128, *149b*, 152–57, 165–67, 168, 172

Kallis, Georgos, xxii, *91b*, *123b*, 158, 173
Kasser, Tim, xv, 158, 177n18
Keller, Margit, 53, 114, 125n12, 176n3
Kennedy, Emily Huddart, 59n15, 170
Kenner, Dario, *48–49b*, 175
Klintman, Mikael, xix, 83, 142, 143, 145, *146b*, 156, 176n2n3n4
knowledge: and action gap, 152, 176n2, embodied, 127, 134–35, false, 150n2, lay, 144, resistance, 156, 176n4, social stock of, xxxin12, 127, 148, symbolic, 43, 144–45, tacit, xxvii, 43, 85, 127, 144, 166, taken-for-granted, 127. *See also* consciousness, practical; ignorance; learning

Lamont, Michele, 40, 43–44, 59n14
learning. *See* transformative learning
leisure: alternative, 169, buying for future, 75–76, 88, 90, 155, 157, class, 41–42, 59n12, and climate intensive activities, 68, 74, 76, 80, 89, 161, conspicuous, 41, 43, and shopping, 21, *25b*, 112–15. *See also* holiday; work, and leisure time, separation of
lifestyle: change of, xxix, 153, 168–72, 177n14n16, and ignorance, 133, 141, magazines, 44, and normalization, 129, and overconsumption, xii–xiii, xvi, *48–49b*, *71b*, 107, 129, 152, 156, 173, 176, project, 15
loans. *See* borrowing
locked-in, xxii, xxvii, 62, 97, 131, 153, 154
logo. *See* brands
loneliness, 5, 19–21, 23, 112, 160, 169
longing, xvi, 5, 8–9, 20, 39, 78, 114, 161
Lorenzen, Janet, 17, 177n17
Lövgren, Orvar, 106, 112–13
Luckmann, Thomas, xxv, xxxin12, 127, 153
Luxembourg, xii
luxury: case study of, 30–31, democratization of, 83, 129, and entertainment, 113, reframing of, *57b*, and social status, 33, 40, 44–45, *48b*, 54

mall, 21, 111–16, 121–22. *See also* shopping center
manzionization, *48b*, 107
Marcuse, Herbert, xvi, xxiii, 145, 147–48
marketing. *See* advertisement industry
Marx, Karl, 58n2, 145

marxist, 145, 157
mass consumption, definition of, xvii–xviii
mass market, xxi–xxii, xxiv, xxxin15, 17, 83
mass media, xxiii, 56, 165
materialism, xvi, 9, 13, 20, 34, 35–36, *36f*, 39, 50, 52–55, *55f*, *57b*, 58n4, 80, 169; definition of, 58–59n8, and quality of life, 158, true, 163
Mauss, Marcel, 16
Max-Neef, Manfred, xviii, xxxn8
Mead, George Herbert, xxvi, 35, 58n7
Merton, Robert, 50

The Middle East, xiv

Miller, Daniel, xxi, xxiv, xxxn5, 6, 7, 9–10, 16, 18, 21, 24–25, *47b*, 52, 59n9, 73–74, 85, 97, 98, 101, 129, 133, 135, 150n5, 163, 177n11
Mills, C. Wright, 150n6, 176
mobility, xxi, *48b*, 69, 70, 95, 96, *122–23b*, 129, 135, 172. *See also* transportation system
modern consumer, *46b*, 77, 93n11, 161, 177n11
moral. *See* standards, of morality
Moss, Mark, 21, 32, 65, 85, 112–13, 115–16
multi-tasking, 63, 66, *73b*

naturalization, 128–29, 138, 150n3. *See also* normalization
necessities, 9, 130–32
needs: concept of, xv–xvii, xxxn8, expansion of, xxi, false, 145, 148, 157, and normalization, 133, 138, 167, and poverty, 50
New Zealand, xii, 44
Norgaard, Kari Marie, 128, 176
normalization, 13, 128–39, 142, *149b*, 155; concept of, 128–30, and prevention of critique, 132–34, 148, and socialization, 99, 129, 133, 139, and social practices, 130–32, and social status, *46b*. *See also* naturalization; norms
norms: descriptive vs. injunctive, 138, and fear of social exclusion, shame, 8, 138–39, and institutional theory, xx, and rituals, 2, 4–7, *4f*, *7f*, 11–12, 17, 22, *26b*, 27, and site of home, 101, 103, 121, and social status, 37, 42, 45, and transformative change, 153, 168, 171, 175. *See also* cultural norms
North America, xiv, *18b*, *72b*
novelty, meaning of, 76–77, 80

obesity, xiv, 60n17, 158
obsolescence, 84, *86–87b*, 90, 151
OECD countries, 67, 92n4
Ojala, Maria, xxxn6, 166
overconsumption. *See* lifestyle, and overconsumption

pace of life, 62–63, 67–68, *71–72b*, 89, *92b*, 135, 161, 169
Packard, Vance, *86b*
pecuniary emulation, 41–42, 49, 50, 82
peer influence, 13, 28n10, 33, 37, 39, 118–19, 136, 151, 160. *See also* social influence
personalization, xviii, 104, 105
Peru, 53
Pickett, Kate, 16, 50–52, *57b*, 159, 160, 173
pleasure, xxiii, xxvi, 9, *18b*, 19, 30, 44, 76, 77, 103–4, 117, 119, 157, 161. *See also* hedonism; indulgence
pollution, xi, xiii, *49b*
possessions, xvii, 30, 34, 37–38, 54, 55, 58n6n8, 98, 103, 132, 155. *See also* extended self
post-Soviet countries, 53, 114
poverty, xiii, xviii, xxiv, 114, *140b*, of time, 67–68, 75, 90, 91, 105, 108. *See also* relative poverty

power: asymmetry, 16, *72b*, and business, xxi, 32, *48–49b*, 164, 174, and institutions, xx–xxi, 164, and rituals, 8, and social status, 31, 54
powerlessness, 52, 54, 153
pride, xxvi, 8, 27n5, *57b*, 139
Princen, Thomas, xviii, xxi, xxiv, xxxin10, 64, 173, 176n3
productivity, xxi, 61, 62–63, 67, 129
prosperity, 169, 175

Qatar, xii
quality: of goods, 22, 30, 32, 84, *86–87b*, 114, 127, 134, 161, of life, 50, 67, 141, *149b*, 152, 157–58, 168–69, 175, of social relations, 59n17

rational choice, xvi, 3, 136, 162
rationality, xxv, 145, 147
Raworth, Kate, 173
rebound effect, 70, 125n14, 143, *146b*, 156, 173; definition of, xix
reciprocity, xvi, 16
recreation, 64–65, 98, 101, 121; and shopping, 111, 114, 119
reference group, 30, 33–34, 39, 40, 42, 50, 82, 84, 167
reflexivity, xxv, 175; self-, 13, 35, 167. *See also* anti-reflexivity
relative poverty, xiii, 24, *47b*, 49–56, *55f*, *58b*, *140b*, 154, 159, 160, 171; definition of, 50
responsibility: avoidance of, 134, 153–54, collective/shared, *51b*, *58b*, 174. *See also* corporate responsibility; individualized responsibility
retreat, 66–67, 104, 107, 151
reward: for achievement, xvii, 18, 64, 72, 76, 89, 112, 118. *See also* instant, reward.

the rich, xiv, 47–50, 52, 56, *71b*, 74, 122, 159, 160, 163
rich countries, xii, 50–51, 59n17, 129, 160
Richins, Marsha, xxvi, 38, 98
Rinkinen, Jenny, xxii, 27n3, 124n3, 131, 150n4
ritual: concept of, 1–3, and concept of culture, xxiii. *See also* interaction ritual chain
Rook, Dennis, 2, 4, 7, 16, 27n4, 87–88
Rosa, Hartmut, 62–63, 67, *73b*, 80, *81f*, *86b*, 89, 129, 161–62, 169
Ruppel Shell, Ellen, 23, 65

Sahakian, Marlyne, *99b*, 124n5, 129, 134
Sassatelli, Roberta, xvii, xxiii–xiv, xxvi, 6, 7, 11, 19, 31–32, 58n2, 64, 76, 81, 83, 98, *99b*, 105, 176n2
saving, *25b*, 52, 68, 72, 173, 169; of energy, 98, 125n15, impression of, 24–25. *See also* thrift
Sayer, Andrew, xiv, xxii, xxxin11, 59n12n16
Schor, Juliet, xxiii, xxvi, 15–6, 32–34, *46–47b*, 57, 67, *91b*, 115, *123b*, 129, 133–34, 163, 170–71, 173, 177n11n15n18

the self, xxvi, 8; ideal, *36f*, 56, *57b*, 125n13, -interest, xxvi, multiple, 35, 56, and ontological security, 128. *See also* extended self; identity; individualized; reflexivity, self

shame, 8, 23, 27n5, 138–39, *140b*, 148
sharing, xvi, *26b*, *123b*, 124n9, 167, 171, 175; economies, 155, platforms, 88, 116, 118–19
Sharma, Sara, 67, 70, *71–72b*, 92n7
shopping: center, xxii, 17, 96, 111–16, 121–2, 151, and entertainment, 64–65, 74, 96, 112–16, 117–18, 121–22, mundane vs entertaining, 9, 74, 125n12, online, 80, 87–88, 116–20, 122, 125n14, with peers,

21–22, 28n10, as ritual, 5, 6, 9–10, 11, 15, 19, 21–25, 28n9, secondhand, 80, 118–20. *See also* mall
shortage, xviii, 114
Shove, Elizabeth, xxii, xxvi–xxvii, 66, 68–69, *73b*, 102–5, 124n4n5, 130–31, 139
Simmel, Georg, 40, 81–83, 143, 177n11
social acceleration, 62–63, 66–67, *73b*, 76, 80, 83, 89–90, 91b, 161, 169
social classes, xii, *18b*, 43–44, 50, 53, 75, 82, 96, 101, 107, 134, 154
social comparison theory, 38
social differentiation, 29, 40, 63, 82, 141, 143. *See also* social stratification
social exclusion, fear of, 19–20, 27, 38–39, *46–47b*, 54, 138–39
social groups, 5–6, 8, 13, 30, 38, 40, 45, *57b*, 63, 178n19
social influence, *165f*, 165–66, 170–72, 174
social interaction, 14–15, 19–20, 22, 23, *26b*, 71, 96, 104, 106, 108, 112, 116, 117, 121, *122–23b*, 151. *See also* interaction ritual chains
socialization, xvii, xxvi, *18b*, 35, 43, *46b*, 56, 59n10n14, 85, 99, 121, 128, 129, 133, 139, 147, 151, 154, 166
socializing, 20, *25b*, 65, 68, 69, *99b*, 111–12, 116, 122, 131–32, 134
social judgment, *46b*, 50–52, *55f*, 56, *57b*, 151, 159
social life; and consumerism, xvii, xix–xx, concept of, xxv–xxix, and institution, xx
social media: and culture, xxiii, case study of, 33–34, 120. *See also* influencers; the internet
social practice theory, xxvi–xxvii, 27n3, 102, 131, 150n4
social psychology, xv, 29, 38, 56
social relations: and change, 171, perspectives of, xxv–xxvii, 1, 26–27, 29. *See also* social interaction; social relationship
social relationship: and justification of consumerism, 154, and object-focused desires, 8–10
symbols of, 3–4, and
transformative change, *26b*, *123b*, 167, 169, 176. *See also* intimate relationship
social status: concept of, 40, and green consumption, 45, 59n15, and inequality, competition, 51, 56. *See also* status; stratification
social stratification, xx, xxii, 29, 43, 56, 63, 151; and cleanliness, *140b*
and ignorance, 143. *See also*
infrastructure, social; social differentation
social tipping points, 171–72, 174, 178n19
sociology of consumption, xv, xvii, xviii, 1, 29, 40, 43, 45
sociology of knowledge, 127
socio-material. *See* infrastructure
Solér, Cecilia, 37, 67, 84, 115, 125n13, 134, 138, 177n8
solidarity. *See* group solidarity
Soper, Kate, 176
South Africa, 53, 56
Southerton, Dale, xviii, xxvii, 64, 66, *73b*, 129, 155, 172, 173, 176n3
Spaargaren, Gert, 7, 27n3
space for privacy and social interaction, *99b*, 104, 106, 112, 116, 121, 131–32
Spain, xii
spatial dimension, xii, xxii, xxvii, 95, 96–97, 106–8, 121, 162–63. *See also* demand, for space and stuff; space for privacy and social interaction
species extinction. *See* biodiversity loss
speed, 61, 63, 66–67, 69, 70, *71b*, *73b*, 89, *91b*, 117, 135; vs. acceleration, 92n2. *See also* social acceleration
standardization, xvii, xxii, 102–3, 130

standard of living, 42, 135–36, 148, 155, 170
standards: of consumption, 10, 27, 170, of morality, 3–4, *4f*, 6, *7f*, 10, 26, 138 of quality, 32, technological, 97, 102–4, 130–31

the state, xvi, *49b*, *51b*, 134, 165, 173, 174

status: consumption, *14b*, 25, 40–47, *48b*, 53–56, *55f*, 59n11n13, 151, 167, as driver, *46–47b*, group, xxii, 6, 29, 41, 44, 66, 131–32, 134, marker/signal/symbol, 29, 32–33, 37, 40, 43, 53–56, 70, 101, 104, *140b*, and quality of life, 158, 159, 160, and symbolic knowledge, 144. *See also* conspicuous consumption; distinction; social status
stigma, 138, *140b*
stress: and abundance, 81, 115, 125n13, 161–62, relief, 66, *91b*, 104, and social anxiety, 51, 159, time, 70, *72b*, 76
Stuart, Diana, xii, xvi, xxiii, 150n7, 172
sufficiency: concept of, xviii, xx, xxxin10, and detox of consumerism, 152, 163–64, 167, 173
Sullivan, Oriel, 44, 66, 70, 75–76, 108
superrich. *See* the rich

the supply, *86b*, 134, 177n14

supply chain, xxii, 87, *123b*, 142, *149b*, 151, 172
Sweden, xii, *14b*, 68, 124n8, *140b*
symbol, and concept of culture and rituals, xxiii, 3–5
symbolic: capital, 43, 171, interactionism, xxvi, 35, meaning of consumption, xvii, xxv, xxxin17, 6, 18, 27n3, 33, 35, 37, 39, 54, 58n6, 59n9, and status, *46b*, universe, 153. *See also* knowledge, symbolic
synchronization, 63, 69, *71–72b*, *73b*, 89, 106

Taiwan, 58n6
taste, 81, 83, 85, *92b*, 134–35
technological: acceleration, 62, *73b*, 80, 89, dependencies, 103, 131, and normalization, 130, rationality, 145, 147, obsolescence, *87b*. *See also* digital; infrastructure; standards, technological
technology, and mass consumption, xx–xxi, 63, 129, 151, 173
temporal: dimension, 5, 61–62, 76, 77, 88, 91, 95, *123b*, and flaws of consumerism, 160–62, infrastructure, *71–72b*, rhythms, 135, 151
thrift, xxxin10, 24, *25b*, 173
Thunberg, Greta, 16, 91, 154, 170, 172
time: average national working time, 67, frame, short-term vs. long-term, 23, 62, *91b*, 161–62, pressure, 68–70, *73b*, 76, 89, *90f*, *91b*, 101, 154, 161, -saving and time-shifting goods and services, 61, 63, 68–71, *73b*, 89–90, *91b*, -space coordination, 61, 63. *See also* work and leisure time, separation; temporal
tourism. *See* holiday
toys, xxvi, 8, 10, 15, 16, *18b*, 74
transformative learning, xv, 128, 135, *149b*, *165f*, 166–70, 173, 174, 175
transportation system, xxii, xxvii, 63, 69, 90, 76, *123b*
the treat, 18, 73–74
Trentmann, Frank, xxiii, 11, 31, 64, 129, 164
Turkey, xii, 79
tv, 34, 43, *99b*, 107, 110, 124n5, 132
The UK, xii, 9, 39, *48b*, 54, 58n6, 66, 75, 102, 107, 110, 113, 119, 124n2

Urry, John, xxi, xxii, xxiii, 22, 49, 64, 96, 114

The USA, xii, xxiv, 18, 23, 38n9, 43, 44, *48b*, 50, 52, 55, 59n15, 78, 84, 113, 124n4n10, 129

vacation. *See* holiday
Veblen, Thorstein, 41–43, *46b*, 47, *48b*, 59n12n14, 82, 85, 92n9, 101
Vietnam, xii
voluntary: reduction of consumption, 85, 135, 169, 171, simplifiers, 15, 17, 27n8, 167. *See also* downsizing.

Wallersten, Immanuel, xx
wants, concept of, xvi–xvii
Warde, Alan, xv, xvi, xxii, xxvi, xxxn7n9, 69, 124n5, 155, 176n3, 177n13
wastefulness, xxv, *14b*, *25b*, 41, 42, *46b*, 49, 56, 82
Weber, Max, 58n2, 92–93n11
Welch, Daniel, 129, 172, 173
welfare, xiii, xviii, 67, 134, 147, 158; policy, 173, 177n10, societies, xxiii, 31, 47, 50, 64, 76, 129, 148, 155
Wiedmann, Thomas, 49, xii, xx
Wilk, Richard, xxv, 138, 150n3
Wilkinson, Richard, 16, 50–52, *57b*, 159, 160, 173
work: from home, 92n10, 102, 105–6, 117, 121, *122b*, 124n7n15, -home division, 96, and leisure time, separation of, 63–64, 76, 89, 155, -life (im)balance, 67–70, *71b*, 76, 89, *91b*, 161, place, *26b*, 170, 171, 175, and spend cycle, 63, weekreduction, 68, 172

Zorell, Carolin, 137, 138, 150

About the Author

Magnus Boström is professor of sociology at Örebro University. He conducts theoretical and empirical research in the fields of environmental sociology and the sociology of consumption. His research interests include politics, representation, lifestyle, and transformative learning in relation to various transnational environmental and sustainability issues. Boström has published several books and articles. He is coeditor of the *Oxford Handbook of Political Consumerism*.

www.ingramcontent.com/pod-product-compliance
Ingram Content Group UK Ltd.
Pitfield, Milton Keynes, MK11 3LW, UK
UKHW041836031026
15587UKWH00002B/797

9 781666 902440